IN THE TIME OF THE NATIONS

IN THE TIME OF THE NATIONS

Emmanuel Levinas

Translated by Michael B. Smith

continuum

Continuum

The Tower Building
11 York Road
London
SE1 7NX

80 Maiden Lane
Suite 704
New York
NY 10038

www.continuumbooks.com

First published in Great Britain in 1994 by The Athlone Press,
1 Park Drive, London NW11 7SG

This edition copyright © 2007 Continuum

British Library Cataloguing in Publication Data
A catalogue record for this book is available from the British library.

Library of Congress Cataloging in Publication Data
A catalog record for this book is available from the Library of Congress.

ISBN-10: 082649904X
ISBN-13: 978 0 8264 9904 2

Typeset by BookEns Ltd, Royston, Herts.
Printed and bound in China by 1010 Printing International Ltd

To Professor Bernhard Casper,
theologian and philosopher,
a friend of great heart and lofty thought

Contents

Translator's Note

As a casual glance at the Table of Contents will suggest, this work moves from Talmudic lessons to 'pure' philosophy. To read these early chapters well, it is important to allow oneself to become enmeshed in the argumentation of the Talmudists, abandoning the impatient illusion that philosophical truth ever exists miraculously disengaged from the specificity of local problematics. Through the *Gemara* we move toward the encounter with the 'nations,' the *goyim* – Greek thought and Christianity. Powerful mediating minds – Maimonides, Moses Mendelssohn and Rosenzweig – bring Judaism face to face with the intellectual and spiritual forces of the West. What remains (and what I believe constitutes the fundamental insights of Levinas's philosophy) is an ethics preceding all else. Ethics as first philosophy – or before philosophy. The book ends, fittingly, with a conversation between Levinas and a contemporary French philosopher, Françoise Armengaud. Their exchange concludes with the concept of *hochmah*, Hebrew for wisdom, which would be a way of reconciling the infinite demand of the other (the uniquely singular) and that of the third party, the other's other, neither I nor thou. Thus, we are left with the problem of reconciling the exigencies of love and justice – plunged into the realities of politics, institutions and the endless effort of mediation toward a Messianic sociality. We are delivered to the 'real' world, though not without the resources and responsibilities of a transcendence Judaism never left.

As for the present translation, it should be noted that the use of 'man,' 'he' and 'his' simply reflects the author's usage, which is that of current French. I feared attempts to conform to 'non-sexist' language would introduce an awkwardness and unclarity the translated text could ill afford.

Biblical references conform to those of the Jewish Bible; they sometimes differ slightly from the Christian one. For the spelling of Hebrew names, I have in most cases followed Rabbi Steinsaltz's *The Talmud: A Reference Guide* (New York: Random House, 1989).

I take pleasure in acknowledging my indebtedness, and extending my thanks to Kathy Gann, Assistant Director of Faculty Research and Sponsored Programs of Berry College, for her expert help in manuscript preparation, to Jenny Overton for her apposite suggestions, and to my wife Helen for her unstinting encouragement.

Glossary of Hebrew Terms

Aggadah (also *Haggadah*). Those portions of Talmudic literature, consisting of parables and apologues, that are philosophical and theological in nature rather than prescriptive or legal (see *Halakhah*). Also used to designate the story of the flight from Egypt, as retold at Passover.

Baraita. 'External' Mishnah, i.e., an opinion or teaching of a *Tannaim* not included in the Mishnah.

Ein-Sof. 'No end.' The Infinite, the aspect of God that is hidden or beyond human understanding.

Gemara. 'Completion.' The commentary on the Mishnah by the *Amoraim,* or sages. The Mishnah together with the Gemara constitute the Talmud.

Goyim (plural of *goy*). Biblical Hebrew term for the 'nations,' the Gentiles or non-Jews, i.e., all the peoples surrounding the land of Israel.

Haggadah. See *Aggadah.*

Halakhah (from *halakh,* 'to walk'). Law or rule of conduct. Refers to that part of the Talmud that concerns laws and ordinances, as opposed to the *Aggadah* portions, which contain ethical teaching, theology, fable and history.

Hallel. 'Praise.' Refers to *Psalms 113–18* and *136*, recited on the new moon and at festivals.

Haskalah. 'Enlightenment' (from *sekhel,* 'intelligence'). A movement begun in the middle of the eighteenth century in Germany to modernize Judaism. Moses Mendelssohn was its leading proponent in Germany.

Hum mash. 'One fifth.' Term used to designate anyone of the five books of Moses; also applied to entire Pentateuch.

Kabbalah. 'Reception, tradition.' Designates the traditions and writings of Jewish mysticism. The most important kabbalistic work is the *Zohar,* which appeared at the close of the thirteenth century.

Mekhilta. (Aramaic, 'measure,' i.e., 'rule'). Name of two *halakhic midrashim* on Exodus, the better known of which is by Rabbi Ishmael ben Elisha (about 90–130 C.E.).

Mezuzah. 'Door-jamb.' A small case, affixed to the doorpost of a Jewish home, containing a parchment scroll bearing the Hebrew text of *Deuteronomy 6:4–9* and *11:13–21.*

Midrash. (From *darash,* 'to seek'). Often translated as 'commentary,' *midrash* is interpretation. A *'midrash'* may refer to just one interpretation, or an entire collection of *midrashim,* such as the Rabbah (*Great Midrash*).

Mishnah. 'Repetition,' i.e., 'learning.' Oral law, with interpretation and application, eventually redacted by Judah Ha-Nasi in 220 C.E. It contains six sections or 'orders.' Together with the commentary on it (the Gemara), it constitutes the Talmud.

Rav. Honorific title for one of the Babylonian *Amoraim.* Used alone, it refers to Rav Abba Ben Ibo (also known as Abba Arikha), an important *amora,* founder of the Sura academy.

Safed. City of Upper Galilee, center of sixteenth-century kabbalist movement (Isaac Luria, Joseph Karo and Moses Cordovera) after Jewish flight from Spanish Inquisition.

Shema. 'Hear.' First word of Jewish declaration of faith, the text of which contains *Deuteronomy 6:4–9.* It is incorporated in the morning and evening services.

Shoah. 'Destruction, disaster, darkness, pit.' The Hebrew term for the Nazi Holocaust.

Talmud. 'Study.' A vast compilation of discussion on the Mishnah, recorded during the early Middle Ages. In the broad sense, the Talmud is the Mishnah and the Gemara; in the narrow sense, the Gemara alone. The Gemara records the discussions of teachers called *Amoraim.* There are two Talmuds: the Palestinian and the Babylonian, or 'Bavli.'

Tannaim. (From Aramaic tena, 'to repeat,' 'teach' or 'study'). Group of Jewish scholars, authorities on the oral Law, whose opinions are recorded in the Mishnah. (They gathered in Palestine from the early years of Herod's rule until the beginning of the third century C.E.)

Tefilin. Hebrew word for phylacteries, or small black leather cubes (containing prescribed Torah passages) strapped onto left arm and forehead with thongs. Worn by Jewish males of thirteen or over during daily morning prayer.

Torah. 'Law, teaching.' In narrow sense, the Pentateuch, revealed to Moses at Mount Sinai. In broader sense, both the written Law (Mosaic code of the Bible) and the oral Law, comprising the Talmudic teachings and later rabbinic literature.

Tzitzit. 'Fringe, tassel.' Refers to the fringes at the four corners of the *Tallit* (prayer shawl), as prescribed by *Numbers 15:37–41*, to remind the faithful of the commandments.

Yeshiva. 'Sitting, dwelling, meeting.' A Talmudical college.

Zohar. The most important source of Kabbalah, central to Jewish mysticism, first published in Spain by Moses de Leon (1250–1305), who attributed it to Simeon ben Yohai of the second century C.E.

Author's Foreword

1 Seventy nations, or seventy languages. This is a metaphor that in the Talmudic manner of speaking, in the oral Torah, designates all mankind surrounding Israel; mankind taken as a whole, in its entirety, although split up by differences that group men into nations. Nations already tabulated in the Bible in lavish or laborious lists of exotic names, baffling to the historian – but nations potentially claimed by Holy History, in which the Torah, a rigorous, divine charter, educates and elevates the *care-for-self* of living beings to the *care-for-the-other* in man. E-ducate: the de-duc-tion of Sublime Reason.

Whether there were exactly seventy of them is of no consequence. A number of nations, neither too great nor too small, permitting either a state of war pitting each against all, or the possibility of dialogue between individual nations. A number great enough to make rare, but not impossible, the man capable of bringing the word to all, or of hearing the voices of all. Capable of perceiving within that medley all the configurations of the word: the threat and agonizing groans of violence, vice's delirium and laughter, the mythology and bloody barbarity of the idols. But also, everywhere, the outcry and tears of suffering, and sometimes the call of genius – of the beautiful and true – and the exploits of ingenious invention.

To understand seventy languages – what a general culture! If we are to believe the Talmudic tradition, this ability was required for one to sit in the Sanhedrin, or at least to help provide, between the members of that high judicial assembly, a collective linguistic competency indispensable to its mission. No less therefore would be required, according to the oral

Torah, to merit the right to be the final judge of one's fellow man. Attention is to be given to all testimony, avoiding the ambiguities of translation. There is a preoccupation with worldly understanding in this mode of thought enamoured of justice and peace, and sounding the secret intentions of the soul. The desire for a peace that is no longer the repose of a self within itself, no longer mere autonomous self-sufficiency. It is not the internal speech of the well-known dialogue of the soul with itself, doors and windows closed. It is an anxious peace, or love of one's fellow man – the watchfulness awakened by the Torah. In the Torah itself, in the Word of the Most High, in which the judges of Israel, eternal students, learn and shape themselves to their task by seeking ceaselessly and ever more deeply within themselves the echoes and traces of its endless meaning – in the Torah itself which remains, for a Jew, more intimate than his or her own inner self, there is a propensity for the outside: a remarkable requirement to enter into relations with all the nations, all the families of humankind. In the 'inner becoming' of the eternal people, there is an incessant reference to the time of the nations, an unfailing presence to their presence and to their present, to the acme of their actuality, to their eventual modernity, their trials and hopes, despite the inextinguishable consciousness of the 'time lag' between the clock of Universal History according to which Israel cannot be late, and the time of Holy History. This consciousness is eschatology itself, the original diachrony of time transcending the simultaneous orders, those wholes that open up onto more comprehensive overviews; that diachrony that Maurice Blanchot calls 'together-and-not-yet.' And despite a mistrust of the seductive chants of Greece, there is a predilection for that country's transparent language, better than any song, into which the Torah can be faultlessly translated. This linguistic privilege was soon recognized. It was the privilege of a form of speech that succeeds in expressing everything that is human in the world, an excellence that does not come from the words – though their roots, as it may sometimes seem, are nourished by the vital essence of that sun-drenched soil of our Mediterranean shores. It is a success doubtless derived from a certain way the words have of fitting together, of ordering themselves into a discourse that questions in affirming, that affirms in denying – a manner that, beneath the various vocables of the nations, was destined, across continents, to become academic, universal discourse. Twists and turns of signs to show, to demonstrate. The beautiful, the good. A suppleness and sobriety not closed to guile, to the much contested technology that nonetheless breaks idols and tyrannies, and that will someday make it possible for bread to be provided to all the men, women and children far and near who hunger.

Hence the extension of Holy History universally, an extension that bad faith will see as a homeless wandering. Its very continuity will be misread as the primitive blindness of a memory closed to the future, and self-centered pride. A universal presence to the lights and shadows of being, including both the shadows cast by the illuminating paraphernalia of this enlightened world and, perhaps, the part of the 'I' attentive to itself that remains unthought. Attention to the reflections of the light of the Torah itself, illuminating the seventy nations through Christianity and Islam. And in the suffering, disdain and blood brought down upon the carrier of the Torah by so many triumphant bursts of its borrowed light, Israel has been able to see the traces of an approach heralding renewed violence – but perhaps also distant possibilities (which the Torah always taught) of a closer relationship than those derived from concepts.

2 Israel, in its soul and conscience, i.e., Israel studying the Torah, is, from its own point of view, already in alliance with the whole universe of nations. A thought awakened, the sobered-up thought of the Talmud, i.e., an inspired thought, cocks its ear to hear, in the revealed word that seems constructed by the rigorous logic of the still impassible world, the premises of the human miracle. Verses 13 and 14 of chapter 29 of *Deuteronomy* relate the Messianic word of Moses addressed to his people: 'Neither with you only do I make this covenant and this oath; but with him that standeth here with us this day before the Lord our God, and also with him that is not here with us this day.' And in the Talmudic tractate *Shevuot 39a* we can already discern the faces of these absentees, inalienably allied to the true humankind that began with that desert pact made with slaves fleeing from Egypt: the descendants of those freed slaves and all who are associated with them but would come from outside. And in another Talmudic passage, *Pesahim 87b*, the voice of Rabbi Eliezer: the Eternal One of Israel dispersed Israel into exile only for the sake of the proselytes that will come in great numbers to join his people. Does not the Eternal One say, in *Hosea* (*2:25*): 'And I will sow her unto Me in the land [of exile]'? And the exegete interprets: Does one not sow a measure to reap a great quantity? And does not Rabbi Yohanan join Rabbi Eliezer (in the same passage of the Talmud) in quoting this verse further on (*Hosea 2:25*): 'I will have compassion upon her that had not obtained compassion. I will say to them that were not

my people: "Thou art my people"; and they shall say: "Thou art my God"?'

These rabbinic interpretations should doubtless be considered in conjunction with the prophetic themes of universalism, in which the diaspora of Israel itself is assigned the mission of monotheism the bearer of justice, in which monotheism takes on meaning in relation to the nations. 'The word of the Lord, of the Eternal who gathereth the dispersed of Israel: there are others whom I shall gather at the same time that his shall be gathered,' says *Isaiah* (*56:8*). 'My house shall be called a house of prayer for all the nations' (*56:7*). 'Neither let the son of the alien who hath joined himself to the Eternal say: "Surely the Lord will separate me from his people"' (*56:3*). To him who 'holds fast' to 'the covenant of the Eternal,' the prophet promises 'a title that will be worth more than sons and daughters.' A bond superior to that of parent.

A diaspora in which, according to the Talmudic tractate *Megillah 29a,* the Eternal One of Israel himself followed his people expelled from their land! Was not the wording of *Deuteronomy 30:3* quite precise on this point? Rather than predicting 'The Eternal, your God, will bring Israel back from exile,' the verse is perfectly clear: 'The Eternal *will return* from exile.' Thus there never was, in these alien lands, any separation of Israel from the God of Israel, nor, because of the sciences and arts of Greece, an extinguishing of the light of the Torah. There was no break in Holy History! The same page 29a of the tractate *Megillah* announces the return of the schools and study centers dispersed in the places of exile back to the Holy Land. So that is the great repatriation! A final recognition (or a daily one) of the terms of the initial covenant. The reverberation of the voice of the Torah in the prolongations of its wisdom, thought in the time of, and in contact with, the peoples of the earth, and with an ear attentive to their Western speech. Marvelous temporality of the eschatological! Behind the chronology of the facts, the events and their logical or fortuitous order in the universal history of nations (including Israel, who always wants to be responsible for everything and who, in its particularity, is a part of the totality and lives in the time of the nations), an intention of eternity is being accomplished and recounted, in accordance with its own logic. It is a discourse that is revealed in the Holy Scriptures, in its literature and even in its literalness, beneath the vigilant, sobered eyes of the disciples of the Law, even though historians continue to decry the disfiguring effect of folklore and legend on the original testimonies, the confusion of cause and effect, and a diachrony riddled with anachronisms.

3 The seventy nations. This significant theme was chosen by the Twenty-Seventh Colloquium of Jewish Intellectuals of the French Language held in Paris in December, 1986. The goal was to reflect upon the meaning for Judaism, conscious of its emergence from Holy History (an emergence the main document of which is the Hebrew Bible), of its presence to universal history, close by the nations or among them, of its openness, so great since the Enlightenment, to their interests and values. *Close by* and *among*: prepositions, but also adverbial determinations of that presence and openness, in harmony with the deepest intentions of Jewish existence, even though their manifestation, in the context of trials and a prolonged diaspora, made those deep promptings look like pure conformism and adaptation to surroundings. Their origin in the beaconing of the Revelation is an ever lively source of reflection, even when the consciousness of that original emanation of modern Judaism from Holy History is diminished to a memory (but an undeniable one) of that consciousness, and whatever name may be assigned to that vestige, even if it was to become the shame of the 'shameful Jew.' A significant theme, involving much thought by Jews reflecting upon themselves, and the meaning of which is not exhausted by the exchanges taking place at a colloquium. That theme has been present since the 1958 opening of the series of meetings between French-speaking Jewish intellectuals with presentations and discussion. It is a theme that had been specifically addressed in the four sessions preceding that of 1986. Their titles were 'The Bible in the Present' in 1981, 'Israel, Judaism and Europe' in 1983, 'Idols' in 1984 and 'Memory and History' in 1985.

In the present volume I publish the 'Talmudic readings' which it was my honour to present during those five sessions, tacitly dominated by the notion of the 'seventy nations' which provided the title for the 1986 colloquium. 'For a Place in the Bible,' 'The Translation of the Scripture,' 'Contempt for the Torah as Idolatry,' 'Beyond Memory' and 'The Nations and the Presence of Israel' – these were the titles of my contributions. As for my way of reading and transposing the brief, often allusive and always multidimensional expression of the Gemara, I refer the reader to my various comments scattered in my introductions to previously published collections: *Quatre lectures talmudiques, Du sacré au saint* and *L'au-delà du verset*. To this I now add the text specially written for the Italian translation of *Au-delà du verset,* entitled 'From Ethics to Exegesis.' In this essay, the rabbinic exegesis of the Word of God, or the Talmudic inspiration, appears as an irreducible design of the spirit in a thought prolonging the dis-inter-estment of the Human, in which being's fundamental *obstinacy* in *being,* the priority of the *conatus essendi,* is put into question in the love of one's neighbor and the stranger. This analysis, while paving the way to an understanding of the teaching of the holiness of the Torah, specifically reminds the modern ethics of the rights of man of its forgotten origins in what Kant, in his 1791 opuscule, *Über das Mißlingen aller philosophischen Versuche der Theodicee,* called, in mid-Enlightenment, 'that old holy book.' Holiness whose conceptual fullness would shed light on the ultimate meaning of the creature and the role devolving upon the humanity of man, the kernel of that condition, adventure or intrigue. In order to bring out that design in Jewish spirituality, I have included in the present volume my study entitled 'Judaism and Kenosis.'

In another context and another frame of discourse I include in this continuation of my 'Talmudic readings' three articles on the same theme, Judaism at the time of the nations, but a Judaism grappling with the immediate problems of integration and distance, the rule and the exception, in our Europe of today, of yesterday or of the fairly recent past, where since the Enlightenment a subtle humanity that is also a difficult humanity, that of Israel, has been formed and has maintained itself. The titles of these three texts are: 'The Bible and the Greeks,' 'Moses Mendelssohn's Thought' (the preface I wrote for Dominique Bourel's translation of Mendelssohn's book *Jerusalem*), 'A Figure and a Period.' The last recalls a characteristic moment in the history of Russian Judaism. Under the political status of exclusion – experienced, in the saintliness of the Torah, as the destiny of election – that moment is an openness, by the end of the nineteenth century, to the enlightened West, in a movement brought about or furthered by the philanthropy of a few elite groups of Jews familiar with the values of the nations, but faithful to the ancient Scriptures, and sensing the ambiguity – or the enigma – of the Universal in the unique.

I add to these studies my preface to the thesis that Professor Stéphane Mosès wrote on the philosophy of Franz Rosenzweig. That philosophy would seem to be in keeping with a new turn in the relations between Jews and Christians that, through frequent personal contact at all levels, is a part of the post-war rapprochement. Franz Rosenzweig, a German Jew who died in 1929, experienced neither the Third Reich nor the Second World War. His work, which reflects full cognizance of Christian anti-Semitism and the theological antagonism that founded or expressed it, renews for philosophy the theme of the doctrinal relation between Judaism and Christian thought, and is therefore invoked in connection with the felicitous present-day rapprochement. His project of general philosophy is authentic reflection and bears no likeness to the pious considerations of a parochial particularism interested only in itself. His speculative daring leads him to an understanding of true knowledge and the manifestation of truth in itself, by means of a mode of thought that advances, in essence, along two paths that are religious: Judaism and Christianity. Two paths of equal rationality – the bifurcation of the Absolute that will only reconverge in God and by God at the end of time. Time, which we are to rethink on the basis of that postponement or that Messianic future in which philosophical thought would return to the original diachrony of meaning: creation-revelation-redemption. Creation-revelation-redemption in its concreteness, which is religious, and the temporal flow of which, moving from the future to the past of the instants of our watches and the days of our calendars, is already but abstraction and formalism. Diachrony or Judaism and Christianity, on this view, would harmonize in their disharmony and in their final union, which would pertain only to God, opening the idea of God no doubt to its ultimate meanings. A divergence without combat, or a peace with neither conquered nor conquerors. That bold thought of Rosenzweig is new to both parties. It revives an earlier concord connected to a common ethical norm, even if the recognition of the other, the neighbour, the stranger and the acts that express it or lead toward it are already saintliness and hence the full approach of the Lord, his coming to mind; even if, for Christians, actions cannot guarantee that approach, and become insignificant next to the Lord incarnate. The question remains an open one, perhaps, as to whether the theology of actions *qua* insignificant is not somewhat responsible for the *Shoah*.

Whatever the case may be, Rosenzweig's work has made Judeo-Christian coexistence, symbiosis and dialogue possible and often a reality, within the society of Western countries, which remain faithful, after the horrors of Hitler, to the nostalgic longing for the Just City and a merciful justice. That is proof positive of a body of thought that ensures that symbiosis by a charity stronger, in its humanity or its weakness, than the age-old violence of power, which ended in the *Shoah*. A charity that could, in the best Christians, show itself during the *Shoah* itself. That is proof positive of peace and holiness, stemming from the Scriptures and dialogues, and that should no more be disturbed by the impatient desire for fusion, in which theology, rhetoric, politics, or ruse would anachronistically try to take the place of what must, according to Rosenzweig, be revealed at the end of time in and through God.

As for the two discussions that end this book, the first is an exchange of ideas and questions between myself and Hans Hermann Hemmerle, the bishop of Aachen, in May, 1986, in the course of a larger public discussion held in a monastery in the Netherlands. Other participants were Hans-Hermann Henrix, the director of the Episcopal Academy of Aachen, Professor Bernhard Casper of the University of Friburg in Breisgan, Professor Hans-Jurgen Görtz of the University of Hanover and Professor Herman J. Heering of the University of Leiden, all eminently well acquainted with Franz Rosenzweig's philosophy. This dialogue, conducted in a broad spirit of understanding in homage to the philosopher the centenary of whose birth was to be celebrated a few months later, has appeared in a publication called *Zeitgewinn*, published by Joseph Knecht in Frankfurt.

The concluding discussion in this book, purely philosophical, that I had with Miss Françoise Armengaud, a professor at the University of Rennes, brings up, beyond any specific problem, several themes of Jewish philosophy that appear at the horizon of the problems of general philosophy.

July, 1988

1

For a Place in the Bible[1]
From the tractate *Megillah, 7a*

1 Rav Shmuel bar Yehudah said: 'Esther sent word to the doctors [the doctors of the law]: ''Set me [set my feast] for the [future] generations.'' The doctors sent word to her: ''You will stir up [in so doing] violent feelings against us among the nations.'' So she sent word to them: ''I am already written [included] in the chronicles of the kings of Persia and Media.'' '

2 Rav, Rav Hanina, Rav Yohanan and Rav Habib – in [the collection of Talmudic texts entitled] Moed [feasts], when the group of these four rabbis appears, there is debate about Rav Yohanan by those who name Rav Yonathan in his stead – [these four rabbis] taught this: 'Esther sent word to the Talmudic doctors [of her day]: ''Write me in for the [future] generations,'' but they sent word to her [the verse of Proverbs 22:20]: *''Is it not for you that I committed important maxims to writing?'' Three times and not four!'*

3 Until they found a text favorable to her [Esther] in the Torah itself. In Exodus 17:14, *'Write this for a remembrance in the Book'; 'Write this' must mean 'that which is written here,' i.e., in* Exodus 17: 8–16 *and* Deuteronomy 25:17–19; *'for a remembrance' must mean 'that which is written in the Prophets' [*I Samuel 15]; *'in the Book' must mean 'in the Scroll of Esther.'*

4 Which is in agreement with the discussion among the Tannaim. *'Write that,' that which is written here [in* Exodus 17:8–16]; *'for a remembrance,' that which is written in* Deuteronomy 25:17–19; *and 'in the Book,' that which is written in the Prophets [*I Samuel 15]. *Such was the opinion of Rabbi Yehoshua.*

1

Whereas Rabbi Elazar Hamodai said: 'Write that,' that which is written in Exodus 17 *and* Deuteronomy 25; *'for a remembrance,' that which is written in* I Samuel 15; *'in the Book,' that which is written in the Scroll of Esther.*

5 *Rav Yehudah has said in the name of Shmuel: '[The Scroll of] Esther does not make the hands impure.' Would that mean that, in Shmuel's opinion, the Scroll of Esther does not come from the Holy Spirit, whereas [elsewhere] Shmuel does say that the Scroll comes from the Holy Spirit? The Holy Spirit must have recommended that it be read, and not have consecrated its writing.*

6 *There were objections. Rabbi Meir said that Qohelet* [Ecclesiastes] *'does not make the hands impure' and that there is debate as to* The Song of Songs. *Rav Yossi said: '*The Song of Songs *makes the hands impure and there is debate as to Qohelet.' Rav Shimon said: 'Qohelet benefits from the indulgence of the school of Shammai and the severity of the school of Hillel, whereas* Ruth, The Song of Songs *and* Esther *make the hands impure.' [Response* to *the objection]: Shmuel thinks as Yehoshua does.*

7 *We have a baraita. 'Rav Shimon ben Manassa said: "*Qohelet *does not make the hands impure, for it is only the wisdom of Solomon.'' Someone answered: ''Is he not also the author of another wisdom? Is it not written [I* Kings 4:32]: *'He composed three thousand parables, one thousand and five poems'?'' Furthermore, it is said* [Proverbs 30:6]: *''Do not allow yourself any addition. . . .'' What is the purpose of this ''Furthermore''? [Answer]: '*It *might have been possible* to *think that he wrote more of them, but that he would write down some, and not write down others. [Hence] the ''Furthermore'' means: ''Come and listen.* Do *not allow yourself to add anything.'' '*

8 *We have a baraita. 'Rabbi Eliezer used* to *say: ''The Scroll of Esther is the work of the Holy Spirit, for it is written therein: 'Now Haman said in his heart . . .'' '* [Esther 6:6]. *Rabbi Akiva said: 'The Scroll of Esther is the work of the Holy Spirit, for it is written therein: ''And Esther found favor in the sight of all who looked upon her''' [*Esther 2:15]. *Rabbi Meir said: 'The Scroll of Esther is the work of the Holy Spirit, for it is written therein: ''Mordecai learned of the plot'' ' [*Esther 2:22]. *Rabbi Yossi ben Durmaskit said: ''The Scroll of Esther is the work of the Holy Spirit, for it is written therein: 'But on the spoil they laid not their hand' '' [*Esther 9:15].'

9 *Shmuel said: 'If* I *had been there,* I *would have said a stronger word than all those: it is written therein [9:27]: ''The Jews fulfilled and accepted. . . .'' It was recognized on high what the Jews had accepted down below.'*

10 *Rabba has said: 'In the remark of each one there is difficulty, except in the*

remark of Shmuel. As for Rabbi Eliezer, it is only a conclusion. Since no one had with the king the favor Haman did, nor was any more honored, one can conclude that he applied to himself [the king's word]. As for Rabbi Akiva, [the text he cites] can be explained, according to Rabbi Elazar: Esther appeared to each as belonging to his nation [cf. treatise Megillah *13a]. As for Rabbi Meir, the text to which he appeals can be explained by what Rav Hiya bar Abba says: ''Bigthana and Teresh must have been from Tarsus.'' As for Rabbi Yossi ben Durmaskit, perhaps the messengers were delegates [in the places where the events took place]. As for Shmuel's position, there is no difficulty with it [it is irrefutable].' Rabba has said: 'That is what the proverb says: ''A speck of pepper is better than a basket full of squash.''* '

11 Rabbi Yosef deduces [the inspired nature of Esther*] from this: 'These days of Purim will never disappear from among the Jews.' Rav Nachman deduces it from this: 'Their memory will not disappear from among their descendants.'*

In order to reflect upon 'the Bible today,' I have chosen, from among numerous possibilities, a passage from the tractate *Megillah 7a* in which the acceptance of the Book (or Scroll) of Esther into the biblical canon is discussed.

1 Anachronisms

I hope to bring out a few traits that would attest, according to the Talmudic doctors, to the prophetic inspiration of this text. Naturally, the point is, through the reasons that have a particular bearing on the Book of Esther, to seek general reasons – or some of the general reasons – that would authorize our finding the dignity of the Word of God in the Bible today, whatever terms might have to be substituted for that venerable word or that theological notion, God. Let us realize, however, that in our world, the parts of which are more interdependent than they once were, and in which transcendence can no longer be conceived of, with a clear conscience, as another world hidden behind the appearance of this one, and in which there is great suspicion directed against any thinking not devoted to technical or political calculations, substitution is not easy. It might also be asked whether the old Talmudic text, which employs a vocabulary from a very early spiritual climate, is capable of expressing what we mean by the word God 'today.'

But is true thought exposed to anachronisms? Is it not perhaps the case that the ideas of a thought worthy of the name rise above their own history, royally indifferent even to their historians? There are perhaps more constants through time than one is led to believe by the differences of language, differences that in most cases come only from the variety of metaphors. And perhaps modernity, that is, the claim of deciphering all the metaphors, is but the creation of metaphors whose wisdom can already be grasped in ancient ways of speaking. Or is that not precisely what is specific to the Talmudic manner? With its ellipses, the unpredictable behavior of its vocables, its figures foreign to all rhetoric, its ostensible non sequiturs, it seems to be a medium marvelously well-suited to permanent interrogation, through which various eras can communicate.

2 The Plan

The text of my translation, copies of which have been distributed to you, almost follows the exotic and eccentric syntax of the original. Is it not too long? As I comment upon its wording, I will probably not be able, in one hour, to exhaust all the points of detail, and certainly not be able to bring out all the broader considerations it suggests.

We may distinguish four parts. Paragraphs 1 through 4 of my translation set forth Queen Esther's request to include, among the liturgical feasts, the memorial of the events in which she and Mordecai are hero and heroine, and to have the scroll on which these events are related written into the biblical canon.

The second part, paragraphs 5 through 7, examines the question of whether the Scroll of Esther is inspired: whether it is – according to the accepted terminology – 'the work of the Holy Spirit.' The work of the Holy Spirit is characterized, paradoxically, as 'making the hands impure.' I shall explain this later. It is a question, then, of determining whether the Scroll of Esther makes the hands impure. In this connection there are further critical considerations as to whether several other texts, whose inspired nature has been challenged, should be admitted into the biblical canon.

Paragraphs 8 and 9 seek signs of the inspired character of the Scroll of Esther in various verses of the scroll. This is the third part.

The last two paragraphs, 10 and 11, seek this sign in two privileged words, the words 'kiyemu vekibelu' of verse 27 of chapter 9 of the Scroll of Esther. A very important part: the conclusion. Although nothing, after all, was ever completely refuted in the preceding considerations, although all remains possible, it is probably a question of essential possibilities.

3 A Place on the Religious Calendar

I read:

> *Rav Shmuel bar Yehudah said: 'Esther sent word* to *the doctors [the doctors of the law]: ''Set me [set my feast] for the [future] generations.'' The doctors sent word* to *her: ''You will stir up [in so doing], violent feelings against us among the nations.''* So *she sent word* to *them: ''I am already written [included] in the chronicles of the kings of Persia and Media.'' '*

The feast of Purim has not yet been instituted and Esther wants to obtain a place in the liturgy. She is told that her request is inopportune. What will the nations say? Are the rabbinic doctors already fearful of anti-Semitism? Do they already think that that Purim affair, in which the Jews had to fight to avoid extermination, will end up saddling the Jewish people with the reputation of being imperialists and ruthless conquerors if the memory of that failed genocide is perpetuated by being brought back every year at a fixed date? Do they perhaps foresee the future indignation of sensitive souls, who in our time are wearied of our commemorations of the *Shoah*? Perhaps. But there is probably another thought in that rabbinic prudence: a doubt as to the universal significance of the event celebrated in the Scroll of Esther. Is it not a chapter of national history – capable, by its particularism, of disturbing the humanity of mankind? The danger of imprudently presenting a national history as Holy Writ! The rabbinic doctors are thus of the opinion that national history would not of itself ensure the holiness of the Bible. They must have already known today's doubts. Is not our Bible, after all, from the story of the Exodus from Egypt on, the particular story of an Eastern people? Is that a Bible for humanity?

Hence Esther's refutation of that fear. My story already belongs to universal history written in the chronicles of the great powers, and it bears significance for that history. It brings truth and peace. You know the beginning of the famous passage in *Esther 9:30.* 'And letters were sent to all the Jews in the one hundred and twenty-seven provinces of the empire of Ahasuerus, as a message of peace and truth, to confirm these days of Purim in their appointed times. . . .' 'Message of peace and truth,' that is the essential. As a matter of fact, in our Talmudic page *Megillah 7a,* Esther does not quote this verse. But the traditional Gemara commentary by Maharsha does so, thinking through to the end – or to the depths, or to the spirit – Esther's answer. And it is so important in the eyes of the rabbinic doctors, that evocation of 'peace and truth,' that in a passage from the same Talmudic tractate, at *Megillah 16b,* it is written: 'Rav Tanshum said (others claim it was Rav Assi who said it): ''The phrase 'words of peace and truth' (which are found in the Scroll of Esther 9:30) teach us that the Scroll of Esther is worthy of being written on the lined parchment as the words of truth of the Torah.''' Rav Tanshum or Rav Assi, alluding to a law regulating the manner in which the Scriptures are transcribed, recognized the inspired nature of the Book of Esther because of the *truth* and *peace* to which the feast of Purim was dedicated.

And this is surely, at the outset of our research on the meaning the Bible may have today, an initial finding. The Bible is inspired because it speaks of truth and peace. The adventure of Esther and Mordecai is biblical because it is a necessary step in the struggle for truth and peace.

4 A Place in the Bible: Closure or Openness

Esther is going to start over. She is going to make another request; or perhaps our page now takes up a different version of Esther's first attempt, a version attributed to a different tradition.

> *Rav, Rav Hanina, Rav Yohanan and Rav Habib – in [the collection of Talmudic texts entitled]* Moed *[feasts], when the group of these four rabbis appears, there is debate about Rav Yohanan by those who name Rav Yonathan in his stead – [these four rabbis] taught this: 'Esther sent word to the Talmudic doctors [of her day]: ''Write me in for the [future] generations,'' but they sent word to her [the verse of* Proverbs 22:20]: *''Is it not for your sake that I committed important maxims* to *writing?'' Three times and not four*!'

The first part of this passage is concerned with establishing the names of those who transmit the account of Esther's appeal to the religious authorities of her time. I have often insisted, in my commentaries, on the importance given in the Talmud to knowing who taught, who stated and who transmitted such and such a truth. I have spoken of the importance which seems to be preserved, in the Torah – of the person of the author in relation to the statement. It is not only to stress the eventually subjective character of all truth, but also to avoid losing, in the universal, the marvel and the light of the personal, to avoid transforming. the domain of truth into the realm of anonymity.

But, in considering this page on which the issue is whether a specific text is or is not inspired, it is important for us, who like to think of ourselves as modern, to observe that the search is not for some supernatural sign that would consecrate that writing. The decision, from beginning to end, remains an affair of human beings, remarkable but concrete – men whose names are known, or at least argued about; men who will have to recognize the word of God in the texts on the basis of their internal meaning. As if the human already carried within itself an echo of that word, or, having perceived the echo before the sound, were equal to the task of recognizing that word by analyzing the texts, though they might exceed by their content what is conventionally understood by religious language. Let me allow myself at this point to recall a *midrash* taken from the *Mekhilta*, commenting on the song of Moses after the crossing of the Red Sea (*Exodus 15:1–19*). 'Here is a king of flesh and blood who comes into a province wearing a crown, flanked left and right by noble warriors, with armies before and behind him. Everyone asks: "Which one is the king?" For he is a man of flesh and blood like all of them. But behold the Holy One, Blessed be He, arising during the crossing of the Red Sea. No one asks that question, all recognize him and say: "Behold my God, and I will glorify Him"' (*Exodus 15:2*). Is not the crossing of the sea of verses as perilous an adventure as that of the Red Sea? And there also God is recognized at first meeting. A meeting without prior acquaintance. With neither crown nor royal train, nor any signs for recognition. In the Hebrew text of *Exodus*, instead of the 'Behold my God' of the translation, we have the more brutal demonstrative: '*Zeh Eli*' – that one is my God.

But let us return to the end of the Talmudic passage we just quoted. The final exclamation, 'Three times and not four!' is quite inappropriate to verse 20 of *Proverbs 22*: 'Is it not for your sake that I committed important maxims to writing?' Unless we read the verse otherwise than required by its obvious meaning. 'Important maxims,' 'chief maxims,' the translation of *Shalishim bemoetsot* of the Hebrew text. Whence the literal meaning: I have written sovereign things for you, things that have the nature of chief in all that is counsel and knowledge. But the rabbinic doctors wish to understand by the word *shalishim* a derivative of the word 'three,' *shalosh*. The verse thus takes on more or less the meaning: 'Is it not true that I have written it three times?' Thus the final exclamation: 'Three times and not four!'

Can one not therefore, in addition to this play of assonance, affirm the rational idea suggested by this play? The sovereign maxims are principles, and consequently imply a certain limit, a 'closure' as we say today, the idea of system; which is also expressed by the number three, not to be exceeded.

Esther's request that her scroll be written into the texts of the Bible and transmitted to future generations met with the response, based upon a biblical verse, that the Scriptures, or the Revelation, were a closed system. The event recounted in the Scroll of Esther – her struggle against Haman, a descendant of Agag – signifies the struggle of Israel with Amalek, the symbol of absolute evil. The metaphysical importance of the Scroll of Esther is indeed, then, immediately obvious. But that struggle with Amalek appears in the Bible three times already. There will be no going beyond that! The thinking is doubtless that the hermeneutics of these three texts suffices henceforth for the full exploration of the problem. The story of Esther would add nothing.

The struggle with Amalek appears in *Exodus 17:14*, where Amalek attacks Israel leaving Egypt; it is repeated in *Deuteronomy 25:17–19*. 'Remember what Amalek did unto thee. . . .' It comes up again in *I Samuel 15*: the war of King Saul against Amalek. Thrice the holy nature of that struggle has been taught, 'three times and not four!' Now that exclamation is in its proper place. It probably expresses a certain conception of the Bible: the Bible as above events. I am not saying – this will become apparent – that this is the sole or definitive thesis of the rabbinic doctors. But it is one of the possible and important theses. To that which has been formulated three times in the Scriptures one does not add the account of a new event that is similar to the others. This is a necessary thesis to protect against certain distortions. Beware of dissidence! Beware of the famous 'times have changed!' The Scriptures are not a history book: they are the *model* of the thinkable, opening onto the depths of *midrash*. The Scriptures confer a meaning upon events: they do not ask for a meaning from them.

This is a position whose rigidity the Torah itself seems to have left behind. And that is precisely what the following portion of our text teaches us. The maintaining of the number 3 suggested by *Proverbs 22:20* – i.e., the idea of closure – can accommodate the lesson of events, and allow for the enriching of the Scriptures by current events.

Verse 14 of *Exodus 17* is cited: 'Write this for a remembrance in the Book.' The verse offers a ternary movement, as if containing three moments of thought into which the essential aspects of the struggle with Amalek would be placed: 'that which is written here,' 'remembrance,' and 'Book.' Three grounds of classification. From which point it becomes possible to discuss what the content of each shall be. Here is the text of the Gemara: 'They sent word to her ... three times and not four.'

Until they found a text favorable to *her [Esther] in the Torah itself. In* Exodus 17:14, *'Write this for a remembrance in the Book'; 'Write this' must mean 'that which is written here,' i.e., in* Exodus 17:8–16 *and* Deuteronomy 25:17–19; *'for a remembrance' must mean 'that which is written in the Prophets' [*I Samuel 15*]; 'in the Book' must mean 'in the Scroll of Esther.'*

The first two texts concerning Amalek, *Exodus 17* and *Deuteronomy 25:17–19*, make up but one and the same moment of thought. Both express the givens of the Torah. As for the story in *I Samuel 15*, it constitutes the prophetic version of the struggle with Amalek. There remains the third category of its essence: the Book. The Book is awaited. It is the Book of Esther. As a teaching of new occurrences, Judaism remains open to it without disavowing, without renouncing, its unity of principle. Within the Scriptures themselves a movement of becoming is assumed. The difference between *Exodus* and *Deuteronomy* is not yet a difference of epoch: it is the special order of the Torah or the order of the letter: 'inscribed here.' That is followed by prophecy – in which the inspiration of the revelation is renewed – and by the Book one cannot read without commenting on it. But to 'comment' on it is only possible in light of the facts, and thus the Scriptures are enriched by the new situations of Holy History, which is not over. Is the relationship between a text and the facts not a reciprocal exchange of illumination rather than a dogmatic legislation of the text in one direction? Both positions, adopted successively by the rabbinical doctors, bear witness to an essential problem of the Scriptures: the relationship between the permanence of recorded Truth and the unceasing newness of the Real. The following paragraph of our passage stresses precisely the profound significance of the problem, which goes back to a venerable discussion, the discussion among the *Tannaim.*

Which is in agreement with the discussion among the Tannaim. *'Write that,' that which is written here [in* Exodus 17:8–16*]; 'for a memorial,'*

9

that which is written in Deuteronomy 25:17–19; *and 'in the Book,"
that which is written in the Prophets [*I Samuel 15*]. Such was the opinion
of Rabbi Yehoshua. Whereas Rabbi Elazar Hamodai said: 'Write that,'
that which is written in* Exodus 17 *and* Deuteronomy 25; *'for a
remembrance,' that which is written in* I Samuel 15; *'in the Book,' that
which is written in the Scroll of Esther.*

Rabbi Yehoshua read even verse 14 of *Exodus 17* as signifying the
closure of the Holy Scriptures. And Rabbi Elazar Hamodai interpreted this
verse in a new way, destined, in his opinion, to authorize the inclusion of
the Scroll of Esther into the canon of the Jewish Bible.

5 Inspiration Put in Question

Paragraphs 5, 6 and 7 of our translation set the background for the
particular problem we are concerned with: How does a text show that it is
God's Word? I shall not give a detailed analysis of the many intellectual
moves reflected in these three paragraphs, nor of the foretaste of critical
modernity of which they are the evidence or the illusion. But the ironic-
sounding form in which the question of the holiness of the text is put (do
these texts have the property of making the hands impure?) must claim
our attention. Presently I shall try to explain it. It brings out specifically
the essential trait of the inspired Scriptures, their constant demand for
hermeneutics, a knowledge of Israel's past and her religious experience.

But let us note first, in this passage, the intellectual courage of a
tradition capable, in its way, of challenging the very texts it transmits, and
of recording that challenge that, never laid to permanently to rest, is
constantly resuscitated, even down to our own day. We have just seen
this, in reading the first paragraphs of the present lesson on the Scroll of
Esther, whose difficult beginnings as biblical canon the Talmud relates. To
these difficulties is now added, in paragraph 5, the account of a teaching
that obstinately denies this scroll the fullness of inspiration, distinguishing
two degrees of holiness: that of the Scriptures properly so called, and that
of holiness that is only conferred through reading or recitation. This latter
is the only one granted to the Scroll of Esther.

*Rav Yehudah has said in the name of Shmuel: '[The Scroll of] Esther does
not make the hands impure.' Would that mean that, in Shmuel's opinion,
the Scroll of Esther does not come from the Holy Spirit, whereas [elsewhere]*

Shmuel does say that the Scroll comes from the Holy Spirit? The Holy Spirit must have recommended that it be read, and not have consecrated its writing.

Does the distinction signify a difference between texts such that some, in their very letter, offer themselves to exegesis and promise rich teachings, while the sense and significance of other texts are fully spent through their liturgical recitation? Does this distinction establish a difference between prophecy and rabbinical decree, attributing (an uncertain thesis) superiority to the inspiration of prophecy over the rabbi's intellect? I leave the question open.

But how can Shmuel uphold the thesis of a lower level of holiness to be attributed to the Book of Esther, while other rabbinical doctors recognize its full biblical sanctity? This will be the objection of the following paragraph, which, precisely for that reason, begins with 'There were objections.' The answer: Shmuel professes the opinion of Rabbi Yehoshua whom the Talmud cited earlier. Yehoshua was the antagonist of Rabbi Elazar Hamodai, and always challenged Esther's place in the Bible. You see – Rabbi Yehoshua's opinion is not just incidental! The Talmud does not bury its problems.

There were objections. Rabbi Meir said that Qohelet [Ecclesiastes] *'does not make the hands impure' and that there is debate as to* The Song of Songs. *Rav Yossi said: '*The Song of Songs *makes the hands impure and there is debate as to* Qohelet.*' Rav Shimon said: '*Qohelet *benefits from the indulgence of the school of Shammai and the severity of the school of Hillel, whereas* Ruth, The Song of Songs *and* Esther *make the hands impure.' [Response to the objection]: Shmuel thinks as Yehoshua does.*

The Scroll of Esther is then not the only text that raises questions, and recognition is not granted by all the rabbinical doctors to the same works of the canon! There are disagreements that are handed down, creating multiple traditions! The school of Shammai, renowned for its rigor, is severe toward *Qohelet*. Hillel's school, reputed more liberal, is favorable to *Qohelet*. But the sanctity of a book is also its ability to 'make the hands impure.' As for the purity of the hands, Shammai's school is less demanding than Hillel's: an amusing and apparently ironic reversal in reputations amidst very serious problems!

But what a striking freedom there is in this whole passage! No one thinks with his eyes closed. It is significant that this deliberation on 'God's word' should be centered on the scrutiny of texts that may appear ambiguous and that, at first sight, do not conform to accepted ideas or to rules of the genre. The fact that a text that has all the appearances of a love song, and that is not devoid, if one may say so, of a certain erotic lyricism, should not be rejected out of hand, and that it can be felt to be the highest discourse (will not Rabbi Akiva say that all the Songs of the Bible are holy, but that *The Song of Songs* is the holy of holies?), and the fact that a prophetic word can be heard and carried in the heart of the often desolate and skeptical philosophy of *Ecclesiastes*: these are signs of a religious thought stirring in all the dimensions of the Spirit. In the following paragraph, inspiration is perceived – refused or recognized – in the place where wisdom and poetry converge. That in this ambiguous zone one must be able to distinguish between religious values and those that are still profane, between the two meanings of the word inspiration, attests to the depth of thought and daring spirit from which Judaism proceeds.

> *We have a baraita. 'Rav Shimon ben Manassa said: "*Qohelet *does not make the hands impure, for it is only the wisdom of Solomon." Someone answered: "Is he not also the author of another wisdom? Is it not written [I Kings 4:32]: 'He composed three thousand parables, one thousand and five poems'?" Furthermore, it is said [Proverbs 30:6]: "Do not allow yourself any addition. ..." What is the purpose of this "Furthermore"?' [Answer]: "It might have been possible to think that he wrote more of them, but that he would write down some, and not write down others. [Hence] the 'Furthermore' means: 'Come and listen. Do not allow yourself to add anything."' '*

6 The Impure Hands

But why would a text that is the work of the Holy Spirit make the hands impure? Here I must leave the tractate *Megillah 7a* and go to *Shabbat 14a*. Why did the Rabbis proclaim 'impurity' on the subject of the Holy Scriptures? Rav Masharsha answered as follows. 'In former times, the *terumah* (i.e., the "food set aside" to be eaten by the priests) was kept next to the Torah. They were kept together, with the thought: "This is holy and that is holy." But when it was observed that by this propinquity the holy scroll was damaged, it was decided to declare it impure.' A purely anecdotal explanation: the scroll of the Torah kept next to the food was exposed, according to the commentators, to the attack of rats, attracted by the *terumah*. The scroll, once it had been declared impure, was no more at risk of being harmed. The *terumah*, which remained pure, was no longer kept together with the scroll, which had been declared impure. It is a simple explanation, which at least allows us to appreciate the value put on the holiness of the Torah. Holier, if possible, than the *terumah*, since it had to be more carefully protected than the *terumah* itself. They went so far as to declare it impure in order to save it from the rats! We might ask ourselves whether, in that whole story, it is just a question of preserving parchments menaced by rats. ... And whether the rodents mentioned by the commentators are the rats of zoology.

But on page 14a of the tractate *Shabbat* the problem of the hands also arises. They are also declared impure because they touch everything. They are *asqaniot* – always busy, taking hold of everything. Indeed nothing is more mobile, more impertinent, more restless than the hand. Moreover we are told that the hand that has touched the Torah cannot touch the *terumah* and becomes impure. The text of *Shabbat 14a* therefore asks the question: 'Are the hands impure because they have been declared impure as hands, or have they been declared impure because they first touched the scroll of the Torah?' The answer is obvious: First the hands that touched the scroll of the Torah were declared impure. If all hands had been declared impure in general from the beginning, it would have been unnecessary to declare specifically that hands that had touched the scroll of the Scriptures were impure.

It is because of the hand that touches the uncovered scroll of the Torah that the hands are declared impure. But why? Is it certain that the nakedness of the scroll only means the absence of a covering around the parchment? I am not sure that that absence of covering does not already and especially symbolize a different nakedness. And is the hand just a hand and not also a certain impudence of spirit that seizes a text savagely, without preparation or teacher, approaching the verse as a thing or an allusion to history in the instrumental nakedness of its vocables, without regard for the new possibilities of their semantics, patiently opened up by the religious life of tradition? Without precautions, without mediation, without all that has been acquired through a long tradition strewn with contingencies, but which is the opening up of horizons through which alone the ancient wisdom of the Scriptures reveals the secrets of a renewed inspiration. Touched by the impatient, busy hand that is supposedly objective and scientific, the Scriptures, cut off from the breath that lives within them, become unctuous, false or mediocre words, matter for doxographers, for linguists and philologists. Therein lies the impurity of these inspired texts, their latent impurity. It was not absurd to warn readers of the dangers brought about by the very sanctity of the Torah, and to declare it impure in advance. Hands off! Contagion, or something of the sort. The impurity returns to and strikes back at the hand from which it came. One may indeed wonder whether the modern world, in its moral disequilibrium, is not suffering the consequences of that direct textual approach whose very scientific directness strips and impoverishes the Scriptures; despite the good reputation attaching to directness in gaining access to the things of the world – things the 'comprehension' of which still means a '*grasping*-together.' It may sometimes be necessary in today's world to 'get one's hands dirty' and the specific merits of 'objective research' applied to the Holy Scriptures must not be belittled. But the Torah eludes the hand that would hold it unveiled. And in the incessant labor of scholars to uncover it there may be heard a sound resembling the gnawing of rodents. Here is, then, a strange commentary: nakedness is not nakedness, the covering is not a covering, the hand is not a hand, the rat is not a rat.

7 Revealing Verses

I now come to paragraphs 8 and 9, which bring us to the heart of the matter. Here are some verses – or parts of verses – whose presence in the Scroll of Esther appears, to four talmudic doctors, to indicate the inspired origin of the entire text; verses that, in various ways, make a case for a transcendence whose traditional formulation has been compromised by our modernity.

> *We have a baraita. 'Rabbi Eliezer used to say: ''The Scroll of Esther is the work of the Holy Spirit, for it is written therein: 'Now Haman said in his heart ...' '' [Esther 6:6].'*

Who could have known the secret thoughts of Haman that the text relates, who but the God who 'reads our thoughts'?

> *'Rabbi Akiva said: ''The Scroll of Esther is the work of the Holy Spirit, for it is written therein: 'And Esther found favor in the sight of all who looked upon her' '' [Esther 2:15].'*

Which also indicates the presence of a God who reads the hearts of men.

> 'Rabbi Meir said: "The Scroll of Esther is the work of the Holy Spirit, for it is written therein: 'Mordecai learned of the plot'" [Esther 2:22].'

Can Mordecai uncover the secrets of a plot without having received a celestial warning? No, so this must be a prophecy in the text of the Scroll of Esther, indicating its supernatural origin.

> 'Rabbi Yossi ben Durmaskit said: "The Scroll of Esther is the work of the Holy Spirit, for it is written therein: 'But on the spoil they laid not their hand'" [Esther 9:15].'

Would the text again indicate that it is not possible in any natural way to ascertain that, throughout the 127 provinces of the Empire of Ahasuerus, the spoils were not touched after the bloody events narrated in the scroll?

But I wonder whether the explanation I have just given of this passage is not a bit too sketchy, despite its appearance of following the text.

Is the significance of the references to the verses quoted limited to an insistence on the supernatural knowledge they are assumed to presuppose? Can the four opinions of the rabbinical doctors recorded in the baraita be reduced to one? Does not the choice of four different verses suggest four different thoughts on the essence of the biblical message, or at least on the spiritual order to which they bear witness and that may yet be meaningful today?

Does not Rabbi Eliezer hope for a humanity in which the inner soul would become transparent to the other person, and cease being the natural seed-bed in which, protected by secrecy, evil designs and probably evil itself germinate? Is that not, after all, the meaning of the revelation of a God who reads the heart?

And does not Rabbi Akiva read in the verse – destined to show him the presence of the Holy Spirit in the Scroll of Esther – the kind reception brought on by the human face in its nakedness, outside all the distinctions of origin, by men of all nationalities? A welcome announcing, perhaps, new interpersonal relations in the future City, but certainly recalling the last pages of *Genesis,* where Joseph, a stranger, slave and captive, 'finds favor in the eyes' of all to whom he appears.

As for Rabbi Meir, does he perhaps catch, in the verse in which he

15

perceives a transcendent voice, the hint of a Messianic light that will succeed in penetrating or dissipating the black thoughts, the darkness darker than that of the secret depths of the souls of others, the secret of secrets of political thought and the terrorism with which it rubs shoulders?

And, finally, the quote from Rabbi Yossi ben Durmaskit is surely not just in praise of a very informative biblical verse assuring us that the spoils have all been relinquished by the victor! It is mainly the account of a defensive combat, free of all attachment to possessions, of all greed, all conquest – the account of Israel's defensive struggle, the disinterestedness of which we still have so much trouble convincing the world; the disinterestedness of a combat that recalls the kingly gesture of Abraham, concerned with freeing persons and renouncing the spoils offered him by the king of Sodom after the former's victory, in chapter 14 of *Genesis*.

But are these wonders enough to convince us, we men of today, of the biblical sanctity of a controversial book, and of its power to make impatient hands 'impure'?

The Gemara itself gives voice to a rabbinical doctor who, in this instance, remains unsatisfied. A modern before the letter. His name is Rabba. The only argument he listens to with approval is that of Shmuel, which is now quoted. Shmuel has not been in dialogue with the four *Tannaim* – giants of the Torah – who for him belonged to an age already past. Rabba is receptive only to Shmuel's argument, which is no longer *tannaitic,* and to which I shall return. Shmuel quotes only three mysterious words, torn away from verse 27 of *Esther* 9: '*Kiyemu vekibelu hayehudim.*' 'Accomplished and accepted, the Jews.'

But first let us read paragraphs 9 and 10 of my translation.

Shmuel said: 'If I had been there, I would have said a stronger word than all those: it is written therein [9:27]: "The Jews fulfilled and accepted ..." It was recognized on high what the Jews had accepted down below.'

Rabba has said: 'In the remark of each one there is difficulty, except in the remark of Shmuel. As for Rabbi Eliezer, it is only a conclusion. Since no one had with the king the favor Haman did, nor was any more honored, one can conclude that he applied to himself [the King's word]. As for Rabbi Akiva, [the text he cites] can be explained, according to Rabbi Elazar: Esther appeared to each as belonging to his nation [cf. treatise Megillah 13a]. As for Rabbi Meir, the text to which he appeals can be explained by what Rav Hiya bar Abba says: ''Bigthana and Teresh must have been from Tarsus.'' As for Rabbi Yossi ben Durmaskit, perhaps the messengers were delegates [in the places where the events took place]. As for Shmuel's position, there is no difficulty with it [it is irrefutable].' Rabba has said: 'That is what the proverb says: ''A speck of pepper is better than a basket full of squash.'' '

8 'They Fulfilled and Accepted'

I shall explain Shmuel's argument presently. Let us first see why Rabba questions the validity of the verses proposed by Rabbi Eliezer, Rabbi Akiva, Rabbi Meir and Rabbi Yossi ben Durmaskit.

Rabba probably has a premonition of our present-day doubts. Is there any need to postulate divine omniscience to know the notorious 'unfathomable depths' of the inner human being or of crime? Can one not sound them by means of drawing conclusions? Human means – methods – will suffice. Has not Rabba already intuited the psychology of the conscious and the subconscious and all they claim to bring into the light from the depths of our human misery? And Esther who wins the goodwill of all who look upon her! Are we dealing here with the end of xenophobia and that hatred of the other man – anti-Semitism? Esther, who concealed her origins, was taken by everyone as a compatriot. Error ensuring friendship among humans! Three cheers for purely 'objective' universality, without people having to overcome their tribal histories and national egotisms! Does it require celestial enlightenment to see through the plots and denounce schemings for reasons of state? Walls have ears, and politology is a science. Rabba is aware of this. All it would take would be for Mordecai to be familiar with the dialect spoken in Tarsus, which was that of the conspirators, to understand their apparently secret language. How great the role of happenstance is in politics, and how resourceful we humans are!

As for those who did not 'touch the spoils,' Rabba suspects the possible presence on the scene of government agents. Can the regime do without their surveillance, and must it not rely on the accuracy of their reports? And is it not their watchful eye and the public order, to which everything they see must 'measure up,' that would be the best incitement and guarantee of generosity and even of disinterestedness?

But we have not yet considered Shmuel's words.

In his view, the sign of the Revelation in the Book of Esther is attached to the three words, '*Kiyemu vekibelu hayehudim,*' which begin verse 27 of chapter 9 of the Scroll of Esther. Here is that verse as it is translated in the Bible of the French rabbinate: '*The Jews recognized and accepted* for themselves, for their descendants and for all those who allied themselves with them, the unalterable obligation of celebrating those two days according to the terms of the writings and on a set date year after year.'[2] The Bible of the Rabbinate stops at the obvious meaning of the verse, suggested by the context of those first three words, translating *kiyemu* by 'recognized' and *kibelu* by 'accepted.' In fact, the word *kiyemu* means rather – and in a very strong sense – 'fulfilled,' 'realized.' Does Hebrew not say, for God living and real, '*El hai vekayam*'? But, since the quoted verse expounds the adoption of a law, the law of Purim, its passage into the liturgy that Queen Esther desired and required to be 'set for generations,' it would be paradoxical that, taken literally, the verse should call for the practice or fulfillment of a law before saying it had been accepted or adopted. That is probably why the rabbinate mitigated the dynamic meaning of *kiyemu* to make it into 'they recognized.' But Shmuel sees, in the inverted order of the terms, 'the Jews fulfilled and accepted,' the invitation to a *midrash.* At least Maharsha, a seventeenth-century rabbi, commenting on page 86a of the tractate *Shabbat,* interprets Shmuel's intervention that way. Here is how that *midrash* may have been formed. If *kibelu hayehudim* means 'the Jews accepted (or adopted),' the dynamic nuance of *kiyemu* would indicate adoption in an eminent sense: the consecration of the law by the 'heavenly power.' What was accepted by Israel on earth had already been in agreement with the divine will. Rabba finds that opinion remarkable, or quite uncommon. 'A speck of pepper is better than a basket full of squash,' he says. Why?

Biblical wisdom and the biblical worthiness of a text, in this view, does not consist simply or solely in modifying, on one point or another, human knowledge or ways of doing things and in announcing modernity and its 'progress.' It means the fundamental aptitude of the human to correspond to the 'absolute will,' through the marvel of inspiration itself, and as the work of a certain History: Prophetic History or Holy History, or the Real History of Israel.

What guarantee is there that the acceptance of the law of Purim and of the Megillah and their entry into the liturgy and the Bible belongs to the order of the absolute? It is the very fact that the acceptance took place in the History of Israel. Shmuel teaches that it is the historical Israel that continues Holy History and ensures the inspired meaning of the texts. (Or at least the holiness of their reading, for let us not forget that Shmuel is not convinced of the literal[3] holiness of the *Megillah*.) The History of Israel and the Passion of Israel through its History would constitute, as it were, the very unfolding of the will of God.

This is confirmed by the last paragraph of our translation, referring specifically as it does to both halves of verse 28 of chapter 9.

Rabbi Yosef deduces [the inspired nature of Esther] from this: 'These days of Purim will never disappear from among the Jews.' Rav Nachman deduces it from this: 'Their memory will not disappear from among their descendants.'

The inspired nature of the Scroll of Esther is ensured by the very permanence of Purim in the History of Israel. The History of Israel in its daily patience, in its Passion and even in its despair and death in the concentration camps, is closely bound – bound by covenant – to the presence itself and the unfolding of the existence of the divine. There is nothing here that resembles the pride of election for which Israel's enemies reproach her. It is, so to speak, as the flaming hearth of all humanity that Judaism experiences itself in that difficult History, with the certainty of continuing to embrace in its apparently post-biblical episodes – down to and including Esther's drama and its resolution – all the just of the nations.

I allow myself now to open page 39a of the tractate *Shevuot,* in which the *kiyemu vekibelu hayehudim* reappears. This page evokes the Jewish people at the foot of Mount Sinai. It is not a particular people: with it there takes place, in the covenant that is concluded, the gathering at the foot of Sinai of the just of all peoples, from all time. Page 39a of *Shevuot* comments on *Deuteronomy 29:13*: 'And it is not with you alone that I make this covenant and this oath, but with those who are placed with us today in the presence of the Eternal our God, and with those who are not here beside us this day.' The Gemara comments: 'When Moses our master bound the children of Israel present at Mount Sinai with the oath of the covenant, he said to them: "Know that I do not bind you by this oath according to your thought (according to your conscience, according to your *kibelu,* according to what you think you are accepting), but according to God's thought and my thought,' for the verse of *Deuteronomy*

29:13 says: 'Not with you alone, but with those who are placed with us today." ' The covenant is in fact made with those present at Sinai. How do I know that it also involves future generations and the *gerim*, the strangers who will be converted? The verse says 'with those who are not here.' I learn the covenant concerning the commandments actually stated at Sinai: How can I know that it also binds me with respect to the commandments that will emerge from Israel's future history, such as the one about the reading of the Scroll of Esther at Purim? Answer: It is written *kiyemu vekibelu*: 'They fulfilled what they had already accepted.' To the history of Israel – the religious history begun at Sinai – and to all that will emerge from that history in the future, all men of goodwill have already consented.

There remains for me, however, an important question, perhaps the most important one of all. 'They fulfilled and they accepted.' Does this give no indication, then, with respect to the content that this Holy History – the history of Israel – is called upon to bring forth? Does Esther's right to a place in the Bible remain purely formal? Is the excellence of Holy History guaranteed by nothing but the formalism of the covenant? Do the Scroll of Esther and likewise the whole of Jewish history tell us nothing of the content that will become the principle of a *law*? In the name of what were the inclusion of the Megillah in the Bible and the institution of the feast of Purim the fulfillment of an absolute? In the name of what did these two events justify the decision of those who adopted their narration as an inspired text?

I believe that the fundamental ethical event narrated in that book is already of itself the confirmation by the Heavenly Tribunal of the welcome the Jews gave to the feast that commemorates it and the Book that relates it.

Remember Mordecai's warning to Esther (*Esther 4:14*): 'If you persist in keeping silent at this hour, then deliverance and relief will come to the Jews from elsewhere, whereas you and your father's house will perish.' Rather than accept the death of others, abandon the others to their death, perish from spiritual loss, Esther prefers her death. Esther will answer (*Esther 4:16*): 'And then I will present myself to the king, and if I must perish, I shall perish.' There is a significant repetition of the identical verb 'perish' in this dialogue to which too little emphasis is given. An ethical advent: the death of the other takes precedence in my concern over my own.

'They fulfilled and they accepted.' This is not simply a *midrashic* interpretation arising from an unexpected order of terms in a text, to affirm the privilege of a history without regard for what it contains. It is rather the saintliness that a book consecrates that allows it to enter into the Holy Scriptures. And we, we men, we recognize saintliness without having been cognizant of it beforehand.

I greatly admired Henri Atlan's talk this morning on the four logjcal figures of rabbinical exegesis, which make it possible to go 'beyond the verse,' and open, perhaps, the very path to transcendence. What was lacking somewhat for me, although this lack was also admirable in that presentation, was the point at which the ethical neutrality of the method is torn asunder.

2
The Translation of the Scripture[1]
From the tractate *Megillah, 8b* and *9a–9b*

Mishnah

Between the [holy] books on one hand and the tefilin *and* mezuzot *on the other, this is the only difference: the books are written in all languages, whereas the* tefilin *and the* mezuzot *only in 'Assyrian' [Hebrew]. Rabbi Shimon ben Gamliel said: 'Even for the [holy] books, they [the masters] have only authorized [by way of another language] their being written in Greek.'*

Gemara

Therefore both these [the books] and those [the tefilin *and* mezuzot*] are similar in their way of being sewn with sinew and in their ability* to *make the hands impure.*

'Books are written in all languages, etc.' [says the Mishnah]. [But we have] a teaching, a baraita [according to which] a Hebrew verse written in Aramaic and an Aramaic verse written in Hebrew and the use of Old Hebrew letters do not make the hands impure [i.e., they strip the text of its religious eminence] and [it is thus] as long as [the text] is not written in Assyrian [i.e., in the letters of Classical Hebrew], in ink and in book form.

Raba answered: 'There is no problem! It is a question now [according to *the Mishnah] of books written in our letters [the Talmudic text says: 'in our body'], now [according* to *the baraita] of books written in their letters ['in their body'].'*

Abaye answered: 'How could you explain that opinion [of the baraita] by saying it concerns the case of books written in their letters? [That doesn't explain] why that opinion [also] covers 'the Hebrew verse written in Aramaic or the Aramaic verse written in Hebrew.' Even a Hebrew verse left in Hebrew, or an Aramaic verse left in

Aramaic is just as [incapable of making the hands impure], since the baraita says at the end [that it does not make the hands impure] as long as it is not written in Assyrian [i.e., Classical Hebrew] letters, in ink and in book form.'

There is [nevertheless] no problem: [for the Mishnah] expresses the opinion of the doctors and [the baraita] the opinion of Rabbi Shimon ben Gamliel.

But how could the baraita express the opinion of Rabbi Shimon ben Gamliel, since the latter allows the writing [of the verses] in Greek?

There is no problem! The Mishnah speaks of books and the baraita of the tefilin and the mezuzot. – Why would one forbid the translation of the tefilin and the mezuzot? Because they [i.e., the verses they contain] contain the word vehayu [and they shall be]. Which means: 'and they shall be always in their initial form.' – But what then is the Aramaic [vocable] in the tefilin and the mezuzot [that might eventually be translated into Hebrew]? Indeed, in the Torah [Genesis 31:47], there is the Aramaic expression Yegar-sahadutha, *whereas there is no Aramaic [in the* tefilin *and the* mezuzot].

There is [however] no problem: in the [baraita] it is a question of the Scroll of Esther, and in the [Mishnah] it is a question of the [other] books.

For what reason [is] the Scroll of Esther [not allowed to be translated]? Because it is written therein (8:9): 'to the Jews, according to their writing, and according to their language.' What is the Aramaic text [that it contains and could be put in Hebrew, thus altering the authenticity of the text]? Rav Pappa said: 'The decree (pithgam) that the king will render.' And Rav Nachman said: 'All the wives show respect (yakar) to their husbands' [Esther 1:20].

(. . .)

Rav Ashi intervenes and shows that the baraita is by Rav Yehudah.

(. . .)

Rav Yehudah said: 'Even when our masters authorized Greek, they only authorized it to translate the Pentateuch. And that was because of the event attributed to King Ptolemy, who gathered seventy-two elders and had them enter seventy-two little houses and did not tell them why he had them enter. Then, visiting each one separately, he told them: 'Write for me [in Greek] the Torah of Moses, your master.' The Lord inspired each one, and they found themselves in the same thought, and wrote for Him:

'God created in the beginning' [and not 'In the beginning created God': *Genesis 1:1*].

'I shall make man in the image and likeness' [and not: 'Let us make man in the image and likeness:' *Genesis 1:26*].

'He ended on the sixth day and rested on the seventh' [and not: 'And he ended on the seventh day': *Genesis 2:2*].

23

'Man and woman He created him' [and not 'He created them man and woman': *Genesis 5:2*].

'I shall go down and confound their language ...' [and not 'Let us go down and confound their language': [*Genesis 11:7*].

'And Sarah laughed amidst her kin ...' [and not 'Sarah laughed within herself': *Genesis 18:12*].

'For in their anger, they slew oxen, and for their passion they demolished the stables' [and not 'For in their anger they slew men, and for their passion they struck oxen': *Genesis 49:6*].

'And Moses took his wife and his children and set them upon that which serves to carry man' [and not 'and set them on an ass': *Exodus 4:20*].

'The sojourn of the Israelites since they established themselves in Egypt and in the other countries had been four hundred and thirty years. ...' [and not: 'since they had established themselves in Egypt had been. ...' *Exodus 12:40*].

'He charged the notable among the children of Israel' [and not 'the young men of Israel': *Exodus 24:5*].

'But God did not let his arm strike those notables of the children of Israel' [and not 'on those chosen of the children of Israel': *Exodus 24:11*].

'I never took from one among them a precious thing' [and not 'I never took from one among them his ass': *Numbers 16:15*].

'It is the Eternal, your God, who has allotted them to shed light on them, to all the peoples under heaven' ['to shed light on them' is not in *Deuteronomy 4:19*].

'Who went to serve other deities ... which I did not command to be worshipped' [the text says simply, 'Which I did not command': *Deuteronomy 17:3*]. They also replaced the word *'Arnebeth'* ['hare': *Leviticus 11:6*] with 'animal with little feet,' because the first name of King Ptolemy's wife was Arnebeth; they feared the king might think that the Jews had intended to make fun of him by writing his wife's name in the Torah.'[2]

[A-propos of the end of the Mishnah], Rabbi Shimon ben Gamliel said: 'Even for the [holy] books, they [the masters] only authorized [by way of other languages] the writing in Greek.' Rav Abu said in the name of Rav Yohanan: 'The *Halakhah* agrees with Rabbi Shimon ben Gamliel's opinion.' And Rav Yonahan said: 'What is the reason Rabbi Shimon ben Gamliel gave [for his opinion]? The verse says [*Genesis 9:27*]: "God enlarge Japheth" [*Yaft le yafet*] "and may He dwell in the tents of Shem!"

– May the speech of Japheth dwell in the tents of Shem.' Rav Hiya bar
Abba said: 'For the following reason: It is written: "May God give beauty
to Japheth." Now, what is most beautiful in the descendants of Japheth is
Greek; may it reside in the tents of Shem.'

As always, I ask your indulgence for the rather ponderous translation
of the Talmudic piece I offer you. It is concerned with getting close to the
elliptical syntax of the text to be commented upon, preserving
intelligibility by additions in brackets. Recourse to periphrasis would no
doubt have made a more elegant translation, but mine will perhaps
suffice for our purposes.

1 Preliminary Considerations

This Talmudic page discusses a *'halakhic'* problem: the conduct stemming
from Jewish religious law. In this particular case, the question is whether
or not that law authorizes the translation of the very verses in which it is
framed, and thus the presentation of the Scriptures, the Hebrew text of
the tradition, in a foreign language, without compromising their dignity
and spiritual significance. Does a translation of the Scriptures retain the
religious qualities of the original? Is it not profanation? Behind the strictly
practical side of the issue, apparently limited to the alternative 'permitted
or forbidden,' looms the question (both more specific and more general)
of the spiritual authenticity of a translation, when it concerns the
revealed thought of monotheism, historically entrusted to the genius of
Hebrew. In one sense it is indeed a specific question. Is a translation
capable of transmitting to the faithful the radiance of the original, and of
confirming their Jewish identity? Through the ages, that confirmation
meant knowledge, the study of the Bible in Hebrew and the
hermeneutics that went along with it. Would not a foreign language
introduce into the traditional text, transmitted with such care, the echoes
of foreign worlds? Does it not lead it imprudently into contexts that
would distort, or at least transform, the initial and sovereign meaning of
an essential message? Yet in another sense it is a more general question,
given the fundamental role played by the Hebrew Bible in the human
genesis of ethical monotheism. In interpreting a *'halakhic'* problem in this
manner I do not think I am distorting its religious and ritual intent. In any
case, I attempt to interrogate the lofty wisdom upon which the Talmud
rests in terms of its universal dimensions, seeking them in the very
conciseness and modulations of the discussions focusing on daily practices

– dimensions that in no way betray the truths and the questions they epitomize or reflect.

The exceptional role attributed, from the beginning of this Talmudic excerpt, to the Greek language – and thus to European civilization – must be emphasized. We should also note the amount of attention given (beyond the semantic difficulties arising from the relative ability or inability of the various languages to correspond with one another on the level of vocabulary) to the purely material aspects of the translated text, aspects concerning translation as a 'written thing,' but also counted among the criteria of its authenticity. These historical givens, a manner of 'local color,' include the distinction between 'classical' Hebrew letters (called 'Assyrian') used in the writing, and 'old' Hebrew letters, the ink in which they are written, the sinew used in connecting or sewing together the written sheets to be made into a book or scroll. Also remarkable is the eventuality, clearly envisaged on this page, of texts in which the translation is written in the same Hebrew letters as the original! Importance is given to all that is called – to use an expressive metaphor of the Gemara – the 'body of the text.' What I have translated by 'our characters' or 'their characters' is in fact expressed in the original as 'in our body' or 'in their body.' These, then, are the elements that link the lines I shall comment upon with the subject of our colloquium: Judaism, Europe, Israel, with 'Israel' to be understood, beyond its spiritual or strictly political meaning, as also the concreteness of a people with its cultural and day-to-day forms.

Other preliminary observations must be made at this point. The commentary on our excerpt from the Gemara raises many problems of erudition. We could inquire into the contingent circumstances to which it refers, the ways and customs of the past, the historical data it evinces. I shall avoid such questions as much as possible. A page from the Talmud, although it can be read as a document from a certain period reflecting a set of historical circumstances, is above all (even in the state of affairs and facts it sets forth) the expression of a teaching of Jewish culture and wisdom. Even if, for example, the account of the history of the translation of the Pentateuch into Greek in the second century B.C.E. – given in the central portion of the piece on which I am commenting – were but a legend, or even if it were merely the repetition, as an eminent historian of the Septuagint has pertinently said, of a 'guidebook blurb' (for tourists and pilgrims visiting the annual festivals at Pharos in Egypt, where the actual act of that translation was celebrated), the miraculous history of this 'guidebook blurb' is, in the Talmud, an apologue or, if you will, a *midrash*. The very fact of its having been collected in the Gemara, the fact that the 'redactors' of the Talmud considered it worthy of remembrance and transmission, and the concise form in which it is presented indicate that beyond its anecdotal value it contains a truth independent of its historical reality and is a teaching. It is this truth that interests us. Background knowledge and historical criticism are not, in my view, devalued thereby, and I shall have recourse to them on one point, as I conclude. But it is impossible to say everything everywhere at all times, and one must not miss seeing the forest for the trees, however interesting their genealogy may be.

A third preliminary question, but one that concerns the fundamental meaning of the excerpt before us: What is the term by which the rabbinic doctors express, in their own way, that religious dignity of the Hebrew Scriptures not to be given up, or to be kept authentic in the translation? It is not called 'sacrality.'[3] The expression that appears from the start is the ability to 'make the hands impure.' I have spoken of it at length in my 1981 Talmudic reading [i.e., 'For a Place in the Bible,' published here as Chapter 1]. Here I shall recall the singular meaning of that formulation, whatever its true origin may be. The reading of the Book of books presupposes not only the current procedures of understanding, which make it possible to grasp a thought in the letters as a hand seizes an object. The reading is enveloped in an older wisdom. A wisdom older than the patent presence of a meaning in the writing. A wisdom without which the message buried deep within the enigma of the text cannot be grasped. It does not let itself be touched by hands that remain bare: as if it might make them dirty. Only books that have lost their inspired message can pass for books that no longer make the hands that touch them unclean. They can without danger fall into the hands of anyone.

2 The Language and the Letters

Let us read the first paragraph of my translation of our Talmudic excerpt. It is called Mishnah. (I don't think it is necessary to explain this word, after so many Talmudic readings.)[4] The Mishnah presents two opinions.

MISHNAH

Between the [holy] books on one hand and the tefilin *and* mezuzot *on the other, this is the only difference: the books are written in all languages, whereas the* tefilin *and the* mazuzot *only in 'Assyrian' [Hebrew]. Rabbi Shimon ben Gamliel said: 'Even for the [holy] books, they [the masters] have only authorized [by way of another language] their being written in Greek.'*

First opinion: Yes, the books of the Bible can be written in all languages. They retain their dignity of Holy Scriptures under those conditions for the Jews themselves. Unlimited universality of the Bible and Judaism! In all languages, the translation keeps its status of book 'that makes the hands impure.' According to this opinion, only the biblical passages consecrated by ritual usage and inserted into religious objects – *tefilin,* phylacteries attached to the arm and forehead of the worshipper at prayer, and *mezuzot* fastened to the doorposts of Jewish homes – must obligatorily remain in Hebrew. It is as if, in order to confer upon these objects their full liturgical weight, the authenticity of the original Hebrew text had of necessity to be added to the meaning of the verse. In addition to the universal Jewish spirit, the Hebrew 'materiality' is needed here. The Hebrew 'body' would appear to be indispensable in this case.

Second opinion: a limitation of that universality. Rabbi Shimon ben Gamliel, in opposition to the first proposition of the Mishnah, restricts the capacity to 'make the hands impure' to the Greek translation of the Bible. A limitation of universality or the presentiment of another type of universality, or of a supplementary universality in Greek, the language of Europe. Does it not possess the excellence of an intelligibility that is, in its own way, privileged? A European language! Does it perfect, or is it equal to, the excellence of Hebrew?

Let us now read further. We already come to a passage from the Gemara, which founds or clarifies or challenges the Mishnah. Here is its first reflection.

GEMARA

Therefore both these [the books] and those [the tefilin *and* mezuzot] *are similar in their way of being sewn with sinew and in their ability* to *make the hands impure.*

The Gemara emphasizes that according to the first opinion of the Mishnah, the 'status' of the biblical books – translatable into foreign languages – is similar to that of the *tefilin* and the *mezuzot* in that they, too, have the ability to 'make the hands impure,' and are sewn with sinew, just as are the parchments bearing the Hebrew verses contained in those religious objects. The Gemara, for the moment, does no more than underscore that resemblance, whereas the Mishnah, in its first opinion, stressed the difference between the Hebrew of the books, which may be translated, and that of the *tefilin* and the *mezuzot,* which may not.

But here is an objection from the Gemara.

'Books are written in all languages, etc.' [says the Mishnah]. [But we have] a teaching, a baraita [according to which] a Hebrew verse written in Aramaic and an Aramaic verse written in Hebrew and the use of Old Hebrew letters do not 'make the hands impure' [i.e., they strip the text of its religious eminence] and [it is thus] as long as [the text] is not written in Assyrian [i.e., in the letters of Classical Hebrew], in ink and in book form.

In ink, because paint could also be used! It is a baraita, a tradition that goes back to the *Tannaim,* but not included in the Mishnah collection established by Rabbi Yehudah Hanassi. It is an 'external' tradition, but one possessing great authority! How is it that it affirms just the opposite of what the Mishnah has just said? In opposition to the Mishnah's universalist stance, which recommends a 'translatable Judaism,' open to the language of the nations, without losing in the process the eminence of a thought that 'makes the hands' of impatient readers 'impure,' we have here an equally venerable tradition that questions the retention of that eminence of the Holy Scriptures once the original language has been touched, be it only to translate its Hebrew verses into Aramaic, or its Aramaic verses into Hebrew, even though the two languages are related. But the baraita also holds that the biblical text is religiously disqualified when the accepted letters have been changed, when the letters of Classical Hebrew have been replaced by Old Hebrew ones. It is also necessary, according to the baraita, in order for the biblical text to keep its status, that it be written in ink in book form. There must be, beyond the Jewish thought of the text, the entire 'Jewish body' of the writing.

There is a particularism in the baraita, according to which there is no universal meaning of Judaism separable from the traditional forms. An untranslatable Judaism. It is indissolubly bound to the letter of the text and the most literal meaning; not only to the singular genius of the original Hebrew and Aramaic that appears in its books, but also to the materiality of the letter, to the rules governing the ultimate materiality of the ink and the form of the book. Is Judaism, viewed in this manner, as a unique humanity, a humanity above humanity, open to conversion to it? Yes, but to a conversion of the whole soul – that is, to its entire culture, ways and customs. The Mishnah said the opposite.

The Gemara will not be content to stop at pointing out the contradiction. It will attempt, in various ways, by the intervention of different rabbinic doctors, to resolve the contradiction. These ways of resolving the contradiction probably indicate, behind their *'halakhic'* meaning and despite the proposed refutations of them, a variety of ways of understanding the relationship of Judaism to the cultures of the nations – especially to European discourse.

Raba speaks first, and tries to lessen the contradiction:

> *Raba answered: 'There is no problem! It is a question now [according to the Mishnah] of books written in* our *letters [the Talmudic text says: ''in our body''], now [according to the baraita] of books written in* their *letters [''in their body''].'*

Raba grants a decisive importance to the 'body' of the text, to the written letters. He thinks that, according to the Mishnah, the translation of the text would not compromise its ability to 'make the hands impure,' provided the letters in which it is written are themselves Jewish, or 'ours.' The recourse to Hebrew letters would thus make translation into all languages possible. (In more recent times, have we not witnessed German in the form of Yiddish written in Hebrew letters, as well as the Arabic of Maimonides?) The baraita disqualifies translation only when the body of writing is foreign. There would thus be no contradiction between the Mishnah and the baraita. The Bible may be translated into all languages, on condition that the body of the translation remains Judaic: the body, i.e., the letters used in the translated texts, the ink and the construction (the form of the book itself). The observance of these 'customs' decides the question of whether the translation retains the power to 'make the hands impure.' It is as if variation in the meaning of the language in the translation mattered less to the spirit when, in its corporality, the text kept to the traditional form. This is a vision of Judaism that was not made up, and is not outdated. Are we wrong in detecting a still current significance in that first position?

But now Abaye challenges that way of reconciling the contradiction between the Mishnah and the baraita.

Abaye answered: 'How could you explain that opinion [of the baraita] by saying it concerns the case of books written in their letters? [That doesn't explain] why that opinion [also] covers ''the Hebrew verse written in Aramaic or the Aramaic verse written in Hebrew.'' Even a Hebrew verse left in Hebrew, or an Aramaic verse left in Aramaic is just as [incapable of making the hand impure], since the baraita says at the end [that it does not make the hands impure] as long as it is not written in Assyrian [i.e., Classical Hebrew] letters, in ink and in book form.'

It cannot, in fact, be argued that the baraita addresses only the question of which letters are to be used in the translation, and that the translation itself is a matter of indifference to it, having no effect on the religious dignity of the text. Doesn't the baraita concern 'the translation of Aramaic into Hebrew and of Hebrew into Aramaic,' which, according to it, would suffice to prevent the text from 'making the hands impure'?

Abaye will try to resolve that contradiction otherwise.

There is [nevertheless] no problem: [for the Mishnah] expresses the opinion of the doctors and [the baraita] the opinion of Rabbi Shimon ben Gamliel.

The opposition of opinions is to be explained, according to Abaye, by the difference in sources. Two doctors, or two schools, are at odds. The thesis of the Mishnah is attributed to the majority of the rabbis, and the thesis of the baraita to Rabbi Shimon ben Gamliel. Is it not Rabbi Shimon ben Gamliel who, in the second part of the Mishnah, upholds the ban on translating the Holy Scriptures into a foreign language other than Greek?

But Abaye's intervention, attributing the opinion of the baraita to Rabbi Shimon ben Gamliel, fails by that very fact: Rabbi Shimon ben Gamliel's consent to Greek translation, in the second part of the Mishnah, does not agree with the baraita's exclusivism, which, in addition, requires Hebrew letters and language in a text that retains the ability 'to make the hands unclean.' Thus the negative conclusion:

But how could the baraita express the opinion of Rabbi Shimon ben Gamliel, since the latter allows the writing [of the verses] in Greek?

Here you see the importance of the possibility even of differing opinions of doctors at the heart of a monotheistic Revelation! 'Both these and those speak the words of the Living God,' according to the Talmud's customary expression. That Law lives through the multiplicity of persons and despite the aspiration to agreement, a hope that is never suspended, but that finds dogma distasteful. But you also see this: again the appearance of Greek. The contradiction remains. Or does it mean perhaps that Greek 'in a Jewish body' is, in the eyes of some, less dangerous to the eminence of a written text that 'makes the hands impure' than is the rendering of Hebrew into Aramaic or of Aramaic into Hebrew!

3 The Incommunicable Judaism is that of the Cult or of Persecution

A new solution is proposed:

> *There is not a problem! The Mishnah speaks of books and the baraita of the* tefilin *and the* mezuzot.

Whose opinion is this? We are not told. Is it not the Gemara itself, that is, the anonymous rabbi who composed it or put it in writing? 'There is no problem' because the Mishnah, which authorizes all translation, speaks of the Holy Scriptures in book form; and the baraita, which forbids it, concerns the verses contained in the *tefilin* and the *mezuzot*. But here is the motivation of the baraita, its justification of the restriction.

> *Why would one forbid the translation of the* tefilin *and the* mezuzot? *Because they [i.e., the verses they contain] contain the word* vehayu *[and they shall be]. Which means: 'and they shall be always in their initial form.'*

The verse containing this word *vehayu*, taken from *Deuteronomy 6:6*, is one of those contained in the *tefilin* and the *mezuzot*. As if that sufficed to explain why the text should be invariable! But the baraita forbids any alteration in the structure of the religious objects! The Hebrew words here must remain in Hebrew, the Aramaic words must remain in Aramaic, the letters must remain 'our' letters. *Vehayu* ('and they shall always be thus') is doubtless a good pretext to make the distinction between cult and culture. The Mishnah is concerned with the books, and not with religious objects. The books retain their meaning in all languages. They must be distinguished from the invariable domain of ultimate and inalterable intimacy. There is, on this view, an unalterable Judaism, that of the synagogue, alongside Judaism's spiritual culture open to all languages, i.e., alongside Jewish literature. There is an unalterable Judaism of the cult, and a Judaism open to modernity.

A possible position, indeed, but one that only *appears* to resolve the contradiction between the Mishnah and the baraita. Here is an insidious question.

> *But what then is the Aramaic [vocable] in the* tefilin *and the* mezuzot
> *[that might eventually be translated into Hebrew]?*

Doesn't the baraita, in its complete formulation, also mention that, in order to 'make the hands impure,' the original text must not present its Hebrew elements in Aramaic, nor its Aramaic elements in Hebrew? Now, the verses that sanctify *mezuzot* and *tefilin* contain not a word of Aramaic!

> *Indeed, in the Torah* [Genesis 31:47], *there is the Aramaic expression*
> Yegar-sahadutha, *whereas there is no Aramaic [in the* tefilin *and the*
> mezuzot].

The expression *Yegar-sahadutha,* two Aramaic words from *Genesis 31:47,* designates the heap raised by Jacob and Laban after their reconciliation, which commemorates the pact of that reconciliation. A most pertinent refutation. The contradiction between the baraita and the Mishnah remains. But this reminder of the purely Hebrew essence of the verses that sanctify the religious objects is quite remarkable. No Aramaic, not a trace of the vulgar tongue, no remembrance of Laban in the intimate words hidden in the heart of the *mezuzot* and the *tefilin.*

But here is a new solution, a variant of the preceding one: the Mishnah and the baraita in their contradiction do not refer to the same biblical text.

> *There is [however] no problem: in the [baraita] it is a question of the Scroll*
> *of Esther, and in the [Mishnah] it is a question of the [other] books.*

The biblical text whose translation would cease 'to make the hands impure' – the text meant by the baraita, a text subjected to all the requirements concerning letters, ink, and the 'form of the books' – must be the Scroll of Esther; whereas the Mishnah would then apply to all the other books, which would thus retain their original meaning in translation, which would 'make the hands impure,' even in the languages of the Gentiles.

Here is the 'argument' that proves this special status of the Scroll of Esther.

> *For what reason [is] the Scroll of Esther [not allowed to be translated]? Because it is written therein (*chapter 8:9*): 'to the Jews, according to their writing, and according to their language.'*

Mordecai wrote to the Jews 'according to their writing and according to their language.'

> *What is the Aramaic text [that it contains and could be put in Hebrew, thus altering the authenticity of the text]?*

There are two places in which the Gemara detects an Aramaic text in the Megillah of Esther.

> *Rav Pappa said: 'The decree (*pithgam*) that the king will render.'*

It is the word '*pithgam*' (*Esther 1:20*).

> *And Rav Nachman said: 'All the wives show respect (*yekar*) to their husbands' (*Esther 1:20*).

There is the word *yekar*, honor, respect, that is also Aramaic.

Thus, the Scroll of Esther is the only book to which the baraita would apply and which, once translated, would cease to 'make the hands impure,' would lose its eminence and its authenticity. What is the meaning of this argumentation, a little forced perhaps, based on bits of verses and words? I do not know what the experienced Talmudists who may be in this room think of it. I myself think that the Scroll of Esther is the only book of the Bible whose dramatic action unfolds in the dispersion among the nations, the only book of the Diaspora. Among the nations! The opposite of the intimacy between God and Israel; and of the confession of the oneness of God (*Deuteronomy 6:4*) that, in the *tefilin* of men, echoes here on earth the consecration of the unity of Israel (*II*

Samuel 7:13) written, according to an apologue in *Berakhot 6a*, in the *tefilin* put on daily by the One God Himself. The Scroll of Esther, a book about persecution, a book on anti-Semitism, is intelligible only to Jews in their language and their writing! The suffering of anti-Semitic persecution can only be told in the language of the victim. It is conveyed through signs that are not interchangeable. It is not, whatever the sociologists may say, a particular case of a general phenomenon, even if all the other problems taken up in the Scriptures are inter-human and can be translated into all languages. This text on the anti-Semitism of Haman and Amalek can only have meaning in a Jewish 'body' and in its original tongue. It is close enough to the real to be interspersed with Aramaic words. Aramaic words, or the residue of Aramaic words, were found there! In the *mezuzot* and the *tefilin*, there is the safe haven of the synagogue! Here, in the Scroll of Esther, there is persecution. That cannot be translated into other languages! Is the word 'holocaust' not too Greek to express the Passion? The name of God is not pronounced in the Scroll of Esther. But it is precisely there that His presence is expressed by His absence, beyond all nomination.

The Talmudic page that is the object of my commentary does not refute this attempt to reconcile the baraita and the Mishnah, but neither does it affirm it.

4 The Privilege of Greek

That is where our Talmudic excerpt introduces an opinion by Rav Ashi, the dialectic of which I omit (as being too complex for an oral lesson). In the translation of the piece at the beginning of this commentary, that omission is indicated by ellipses.

Rav Ashi's opinion leads us toward the interpretation of the Mishnah's second opinion, that of Rabbi Shimon ben Gamliel. It authorizes the translation of the Scriptures solely into Greek, and does not hold that in that language the Scriptures lose their ability to 'make the hands impure.' Rav Ashi finds the names of the doctors who produced the anonymous baraita at the beginning of the Gemara, which we saw to be in disagreement with the Mishnah. A disagreement that had been discussed up until that point. Rav Ashi attributes the opinion of that baraita to Rabbi Yehudah, who is supposed to have repeated the thesis of Rabbi Shimon ben Gamliel that appears in the second part of the Mishnah. Rav Yehudah certainly forbade translation, but made an exception for translation into Greek. That exception only applied to the Pentateuch, and, what is more, the Pentateuch that was translated by the initiative of King Ptolemy of Egypt. An exception, then, that is itself exceptional and unique in history!

But in this way we enter – even if only for a part of the Bible, the Pentateuch – into a new problematic: What is this exceptional relationship between biblical wisdom and Greek?

> Rav Yehudah said: 'Even when our masters authorized Greek, they only authorized it to translate the Pentateuch. And that was because of the event attributed to King Ptolemy, who gathered seventy-two elders and had them enter seventy-two little houses and did not tell them why he had them enter. Then, visiting each one separately, he told them: 'Write for me [in Greek] the Torah of Moses, your master.' The Lord inspired each one, and they found themselves in the same thought, and wrote for Him. . . .

But our Talmudic passage then lists the 'corrections' these seventy-two scholars in isolation made, without communicating with one another, in the text they translated. And there is supposed to have been agreement both on their version of the translation and on the differences with respect to their version of the Hebrew original.

Now the translation of the Pentateuch under one of the Ptolemies of Egypt, perhaps Ptolemy Philadelphus or Soter in the second century B.C.E., is the historical fact of the origin of the Septuagint. It so happened that the miraculous story of the translation and corrections of the seventy-two isolated translators circulated at a certain time in history. But it is also recognized that that story, as taken up by the Talmud, assumes the sense of a sign of divine approval given to the undertaking itself of translating the Pentateuch into Greek – that is, approval of Rabbi Shimon ben Gamliel's position. Divine approval that 'occurs' at a time after the end of prophecy! There is acceptance by the Talmudic doctors of the profound truth of this miraculous account. Our Talmudic text is a *midrash,* the meaning of which is the assertion that the translation of the Pentateuch into Greek retains its ability to 'make the hands impure,' that it is even spiritually necessary, as were the 'corrections' of the original Hebrew version made in the Greek version of the sacred text-corrections whose significance remains to be specified. Do we not have here at least some indication of the sense in which rabbinic Judaism wishes to be a part of Europe?

Here we see a certain 'assimilation to Europe' not rejected by the Talmudic doctors as purely negative! The moment has come in which it would be appropriate to recall some historical information on the extraordinary situation of the Jewish colony in Egypt. It had already forgotten the language of the Torah, including the alphabet, and performed the liturgical reading of the Law in Hebrew transcribed into Greek letters. The royal authority then carried out the plan of giving the Jews living under the rule of the Ptolemies the Mosaic law in Greek, as their national law . The existence of separate, independent law courts and archives for the Jewish community at Alexandria is an established fact. The Ptolemies took a certain interest in the religious affairs of the Jews. The Alexandrian Jews must have rejoiced at this Greek homage to their Torah, and especially, as Father D. Barthélemy (whom I follow on this point in all confidence, and to the letter) writes, it was

> the end of the increasingly distinct divorce separating their daily speech from a previously indispensable language, but one to which almost no one had access anymore.

(Perhaps on this point the current relevance of that situation will justify my recourse to history in the reading of the Talmud!)

The translation of the Septuagint represented, in the eyes of the legal authorities, the definitively approved form of the patronal law of the Jews. Henceforth custom, within the prosperous Jewry of the great capital, granted to the Septuagint of the Law the value of norm. The Greek Bible very quickly replaced the Hebrew one, which was read without being understood in the synagogue. Philo knew no other. But a Jew of Alexandria had a great advantage over his Palestinian co-religionist: he read the authentic text of the Bible in his daily idiom. In Alexandria, you had access to Moses and to the most contemporary culture by the same door. Alexandria was in close communication with Jerusalem, but had long won its emancipation.[5] Emancipation or assimilation? Assimilation, up to a point, into 'Europe.' It is this entrance of Greek into the Bible – this alliance between the Hebrew and the Greek Bible, this assimilation – that page 9b of the Megillah 'authorizes' by relating the miracle of the agreement of the seventy-two translators.

5 The Limits of Assimilation

Assimilation (I choose the most brutal word intentionally), but an assimilation whose limits the *midrash,* in enumerating the corrected verses, marks off with precision. The *midrash* maintains, let us bluntly state, the obligation to learn Hebrew. It requires it first implicitly for the books other than the Pentateuch. This latter is fundamental legislation cut off from all the other texts of the Bible – the prophetic and the hagiographic (which, by a supreme irony, historical criticism often traces to Hellenic sources). But the *midrash* requires that obligation especially – through the corrections recognized as being necessary – for the vast field of rabbinic science, for the entire Law referred to as oral.

Look at our Talmudic text. I have placed the verses as 'corrected' first, and then, in brackets, their translation faithful to the Hebrew. I have numbered these corrections.

1 'God created in the beginning' [and not 'In the beginning created God': *Genesis 1:1*].
2 'I shall make man in the image and likeness' [and not 'Let us make man in the image and likeness': *Genesis 1:26*].
3 'He ended on the sixth day and rested on the seventh' [and not 'And he ended on the seventh day': *Genesis 2:2*].
4 'Man and woman He created him' [and not 'He created them man and woman': *Genesis 5:2*].
5 'I shall go down and confound their language ...' [and not 'Let us go down and confound their language': *Genesis 11:7*].
6 'And Sarah laughed amidst her kin ...' [and not, 'Sarah laughed within herself': *Genesis 18:12*].
7 'For in their anger, they slew oxen, and for their passion they demolished the stables' [and not 'For in their anger they slew men, and for their passion they struck oxen': *Genesis 49:6*].
8 'And Moses took his wife and his children and set them upon that which serves to carry man' [and not 'And set them on an ass': *Exodus 4:20*].
9 'The sojourn of the Israelites since they established themselves in Egypt and in the other countries had been four hundred and thirty years ...' [and not 'since they had established themselves in Egypt had been': *Exodus 12:40*].
10 'He charged the notables among the children of Israel' [and not 'the young men of Israel': *Exodus 24:5*].

11 'But God did not let his arm strike those notables of the children of Israel' [and not 'on those chosen of the children of Israel': *Exodus 24:11*].

12 'I never took from one among them a precious thing' [and not 'I never took from one among them his ass': *Numbers 16:15*].

13 'It is the Eternal, your God, who has allotted them to shed light on them, to all the peoples under heaven' ['to shed light on them' is not in *Deuteronomy 4:19*].

14 'Who went to serve other deities ... which I did not command to worship' [the text says simply 'Which I did not command': *Deuteronomy 17:3*].

15 They also replaced the word 'Arnebeth' ['hare': *Leviticus 11:6*] with 'animal with little feet,' because the first name of King Ptolemy's wife was Arnebeth; they feared the king might think the Jews had intended to make fun of him by writing his wife's name in the Torah.

The fifteen corrections[6] that the Septuagint is said to have made doubtless signify that there is a domain of the untranslatable at the heart of the Pentateuch itself. An interesting study could be made – I shall not undertake it this evening – to determine the various motivations behind these fifteen or thirteen corrections. A study made all the more worthy of being done because in the Septuagint – in the historical Septuagint – of the Pentateuch, only four corrections, out of the fifteen taught by the *midrash*, are to be found! (Numbers 3, 8 and 9 of our list and the correction concerning the word *Arnebeth*.) Among the immediately apparent reasons, there is, surely, an attempt to eliminate anything that might, in the original text, look like a Christian theme (numbers 1, 2 and 5), particularly the plural with the name of God. Corrections that would doubtless be of no use to someone approaching the Pentateuch on the basis of the oral teaching. Also ever obvious, among these corrections, is the (eternal?) fear of anti-Semitism: the inevitable caution necessary for a discourse of the persecuted. Thus the replacement of the word *Arnebeth* (from *Leviticus 11:6*), where 'hare' becomes 'small-footed animal.'

But the Greek translation of the biblical teaching reveals, in its 'corrections' of verses, more subtle reflections. Biblical wisdom is inseparable from *midrash*, the fruit of centuries of spiritual life forming a chain of tradition in which thought is at once transmitted and renewed. This is rather visible, for example, in corrections 3, 8, 9 and 12. The difficulty in the literal or obvious meaning can sometimes – according to a common expression among rabbinic commentators – 'cry out sponta-neously: interpret me.' The difficulty can be overcome by a correction that eliminates it – which avoids a complex *midrashic* preliminary, and, at the price of a slightly inaccurate translation, a serious misinterpretation. What is affirmed by the corrections given in our examples is the very principle of a reading: an order of written meaning exists via a constant appeal to a prior tradition. Writing is intimately bound to an 'oral Torah,' at once preliminary and renewing. This is not a historical contingency but an essential possibility of the Spirit, one of its vocations. The Jewish reading is anything but unbiased, although here being a biased reader means, not the sterility of dogmatic prejudices, but the possibilities and risks of a thought transcending the given; and probably the extraordinary trace that Revelation leaves in a thought that, beyond the vision of being, hears the word of God. The presentation of that Scripture to the Greek reader, whose philosophy and language bring us, beyond its vocabulary and grammar, another marvel of the spirit – the language of an intelligence and an intelligibility open to the unbiased mind – is, for the Torah, a necessary trial. It is a trial that belongs to the very adventure of the Spirit, which cannot lose anyone of its essential vocations. This will be attested to also by the verse commented upon in the very last part of the Talmudic text we are examining, to which I shall return: 'God enlarge Japheth! May He dwell in the tents of Shem' (*Genesis* 9:27). In Rabbi Shimon ben Gamliel's interpretation, according to Rav Johanan, that means precisely: 'May the speech of Japheth dwell in the tents of Shem.' It is certainly a way for us Jews to claim our modernity alongside our antiquity older than all antiquity: the possibility and necessity of being able to express – or trying to express – the Torah also in Greek.

It is the spiritual trial, for the tradition of Shem, of welcoming the speech of Japheth, while at the same time exalting the genius peculiar to the oral Torah (despite the nineteenth century's denial of it) in its infinite richness of new meaning, brought out in the rabbinic reading of the Scripture; the challenge of bringing to the common civilization (whether for the purpose of joining or of judging it) the Greek expression of that creative thought and life. Greek expression, i.e., like that of our academic language of the Western world – even if the latter's unbiased intelligence sometimes runs the risk of remaining naive and there may be something missing in its 'clear and distinct ideas'! A spiritual trial for the tradition to open the tents of Shem for Japheth; tents in which, according to the *midrash,* the study of the Torah takes place. A trial in keeping with the tradition, even if a 'correction' must now and then be made in the pure translation, and if, in a written expression – separated in Greek from its oral perspectives – a modification of meaning is to be preferred to a dangerous misunderstanding of the literal meaning. Even if, despite all the brilliance (or because of all the brilliance) of the unbiased judgment, translation reveals discordances in the text that will one day be explored by philosophy and that, through the *midrash,* were already fecund in another dimension of meaning.

6 Japheth's Beauty

The text ends with a commentary by Rabbi Shimon ben Gamliel that I have already quoted, and that constitutes a venerable written basis for recognizing this role of the Greek language in the Bible, necessary for the understanding of the Bible.

> Rabbi Shimon ben Gamliel said: 'Even for the [holy] books, they [the masters] only authorized [by way of other languages] the scripture in Greek.' Rav Abu said in the name of Rav Yohanan: 'The *Halakhah* agrees with Rabbi Shimon ben Gamliel's opinion.'

The Bible must only be translated into Greek; but perhaps also it *must* be translated into Greek!

> And Rav Yohanan said: 'What is the reason Rabbi Shimon ben Gamliel gave [for his opinion]? The verse says [*Genesis 9:27*]: ''God enlarge Japheth'' [*Yaft le yafet*] ''and may He dwell in the tents of Shem!'' – May the speech of Japheth dwell in the tents of Shem!'

The speech of Japheth? But Japheth had many sons, and how do you know the Bible has Greek in mind? Precisely because of this verb *yaft* that can also be linked to the root of the word *yafeh,* which means 'beautiful'; *yaft*: 'give beauty.'

> Rav Hiya bar Abba said: 'For the following reason: It is written: ''May God give beauty to Japheth.'' Now, what is most beautiful in the descendants of Japheth is Greek; may it reside in the tents of Shem.'

The value of the clarity of the Greek language, of the Greek genius, is recognized by this final text, as is the indisputable contribution of clarity, that is, beauty – the gift allotted to Japheth – to the wisdom of Shem.

And yet – this will be my last point – the text of the Talmud is often very hard on Greek wisdom. On page 82b of the tractate *Baba Kamma* – and it is repeated elsewhere – it says: 'Accursed be the man who has taught his son Greek wisdom.' The statement appears in the context of an act of betrayal committed by an Israelite who had been introduced to Greek culture! I spoke of it one day in one of my Talmudic lessons, entitled, 'Modèle de l'Occident.'[7] The important point in *Baba Kamma 82b* is the objection made to that curse. How can it be said, given the fact that Rabbi (that is, Rabenu Hakadosh, Rabbi Yehudah Hanassi, whose authority is so great), who had gathered and committed to writing the Mishnah, said one day: 'In the land of Israel, it must be either Hebrew or Greek?' Answer from the Gemara (*Baba Kamma 83a*): 'A distinction must be made between the Greek language and Greek wisdom.'

I have made that distinction throughout my elaboration on the privilege of the Greek language. But I have proceeded on my own, of course, in attributing to the Greek language the order, clarity, method, desire to move from the simple to the complex, and especially the unbiased quality of the language of Europe – or at least the language of the university such as it should be, the language a European university professor cultivates, and speaks, even when denouncing the language of the university and rehabilitating the 'savage mind.'[8] I say it again a bit differently – and, for me, this is the beauty of Greece that must dwell in the tents of Shem: the language of deciphering. It demystifies. It demythicizes. It depoeticizes as well. Greek is prose, the prose of commentary, of exegesis, of hermeneutics. A hermeneutic interpretation that often uses metaphors, but also the language that 'demetaphoricizes' metaphors, conceptualizes them, even if it must always begin anew. One must always demetaphorize the very metaphors by which one has just demetaphorized the metaphors, and wring eloquence's neck.[9] It takes patience. But it is that school of patient speech that is also part of what is precious in our Greek heritage.

3

Contempt for the Torah as Idolatry[1]
From the tractate *Sanhedrin, 99a* and *99b*

On the following proposition taken from the Mishnah 90a: 'Among those who have no share in the world to come, there is ... he who says ... ''The Torah is not from heaven.'' '

We have a baraita: [In] the verse Numbers 15:31: 'For having scorned the word of the Lord and broken his commandment, cut off he will be, cut off. . . .' This refers to [the person who says]: 'The Torah is not from heaven.'

Another explanation: It refers to the apikoros.

Another explanation: 'One who scorns the word of the Lord' is a person who interprets the word of the Torah in a way contrary to the Halakhah.

One who has broken His commandment [the commandment of God], is one who profanes the covenant inscribed in the flesh.

'Cut off he shall be, cut off' – this means cut off from this world and cut off from the world to come. Whence the remark by Rabbi Elazar Hamodai: 'He who profanes the holiness of the sacrifices, who disdains the half-holidays, who breaks the covenant of Abraham our father and interprets the Torah without regard for the Halakhah ... who causes the face of his fellow to pale with shame, has no share in the world to come; even if he knows the Torah and has performed charitable deeds, he has no share in the world to come.'

Another baraita: 'For having scorned the word of the Lord' – this refers to one who says: 'The Torah is not from heaven.' And even if he says: 'The whole Torah is from heaven except this verse, which Moses said on his own initiative,' that still means: He has scorned the word of the Lord. – And even if he says: 'The whole Torah comes from heaven, except this deduction, except this a fortiori or this 'proof by analogy,' it is still: He has scorned the word of the Lord.

43

A baraita. Rabbi Meir used to say: 'He who studies the Torah without teaching it is indeed he who has scorned the word of the Torah.' – Rabbi Nathan said: 'It is whoever does not heed the Mishnah' [who has scorned the Torah]. – Rabbi Nehorai said: 'It is whoever has the opportunity to study the Torah and does not do so' [who has rejected the Torah]. – According to Rabbi Ishmael, it is the idolater [who has scorned the Torah]. What indicates that this is the meaning? In the house of Rabbi Ishmael it was taught: 'He who scorns the word of God has already scorned God's word spoken to Moses on Sinai: "I am the Eternal your God" – "Have no other gods," etc.'

Rabbi Yehoshua ben Korha said: 'Whoever studies the Torah without repeating the lesson is like a sower who does not reap.' Rabbi Yehoshua said: 'Whoever learns the Torah and forgets it is like a woman who brings a child into the world only to bury it.'

Rabbi Akiva said: 'To each day its song, to each day its song.' Rabbi Yizhak ben Abudani said: 'What verse teaches that?'

It is said in Proverbs 16:26: 'It is for himself that the laborer labors, for pressing are the demands of his mouth.'

Rabbi Elazar said: 'All men are created for toil for it is said: "Man is born unto toil" [Job 5:7]. I do not yet know if it is for the toil brought about by the mouth itself, or for the toil required by the trade that man is born. Let us turn to Proverbs 16:26. "For his mouth puts pressure on him." – Therefore he is born for the toil imposed upon him by his mouth. But I do not yet know what kind of word is imposed upon man. Does the toil imposed by the mouth mean the toil required by the study of the Torah or the toil required by any speech? "May this book of the Torah not leave your mouth." "It is for the toil required to study the Torah that man was created!"'

That is what Raba said: 'All bodies are containers. Happy those who have been worthy of carrying within them the Torah! "To commit adultery is to be a senseless fool ..."' [Proverbs 6:32]. Resh Laqish said: 'That refers to one who studies the Torah only from time to time. For in Proverbs 22:17 it is said: "Incline your ear and listen to the words of the wise ..." and in Proverbs 22:18, "It will be beautiful for you to keep them in your heart, and to fix them permanently on your lips."'

'And whosoever' [Numbers 15:30] 'has acted high-handedly' – beyad rama – 'among home-born or among strangers, he reviles the Lord! That person will be cut off from his people.' The reference is to King Manasseh, the son of Hezikiah: he would try his hand at interpreting the Torah in a shameless way. He would say: 'Didn't Moses have anything else to write besides 'and Lotan's sister was Timna' [Genesis 36:22] or 'and Timna was a concubine of Eliphaz'

[Genesis 36:12] *or 'And Reuben, having gone to the fields during the days of the wheat harvest, found mandrakes there and brought them* to *Leah, his mother'* [Genesis 30:14]? *Then a voice echoed from heaven and said: 'You sit and speak against your brother; you slander your own mother's son. You do these things, and I should keep silent? Do you suppose that I could be like you? I will reprove you and will put [my grievances] before your eyes.'*

And it is respecting Manasseh that the text of the tradition teaches, saying [Isaiah 5:18]: *'Woe unto them that draw chastisement with the cords of evil, and sin with thick cart ropes.'*

Why with thick cart ropes?

Rav Assi said: 'The evil inclination is like the thread of a spider at first, and at the end like the thick ropes of a cart.'

Since we are on the subject of 'and Lotan's sister is Timna,' what is in fact at stake? Timna was of royal blood. For it is written: Aluf Lotan [Genesis 36:29], Aluf Timna [Genesis 36:40]? *And* Aluf *indicates the dignity of a royalty without the crown. Timna tried to convert. She went to Abraham, Isaac and Jacob. They turned her away. She became the concubine of Eliphaz, Esau's son. She must have said to herself: 'It is better to be a servant in this nation than to have lordly rank in another.' Amalek issued from that union – who causes Israel so much suffering. For what reason? Answer: Timna should not have been turned away.*

'Reuben, having gone to *the fields during the days of the wheat harvest, found mandrakes there and brought them to his mother.'*

Raba, the son of Yizhak, has said in the name of Rav: 'A lesson for the just! May they not stretch out their hand to acquire dishonestly.'

1 The Torah and Idolatry

What is left for me to say after all the research of the last two days to get to the source of the idolatries, to find them in the mystery of their birth, either as cults properly so called – these are perhaps no longer a danger for us, modern as we are, and having read all the books[2] – or (and especially) as hidden, unconscious cults without hieratic rites: as ideologies, fads, mad passions perhaps, in which there must be exposed and condemned some secret closing up of the soul, which is satisfied with I know not what fetish, symbol or representation taken for a concept. Here demystification still has concrete usefulness and is an act of courage.

Therefore I would like to discuss, under the topic of idolatry, the antithesis of idolatry – which had also been the discovery of idolatry or the very constitution of the concept of it, in the dramatic significance it always had for the thought, feeling and history of the West, as the supreme criterion of the value or non-value of spirituality. I would like to speak of the Torah itself, the book of anti-idolatry, the absolute opposite of idolatry! A wisdom that does not permit itself to share the category of the religious with the non-religious or non-gods – whatever may have been their reality, their sociological and ethnographic extension. A wisdom not allowing for any synthesis with its antithesis, nor any neutral zone between itself and its negative. A logical opposition, not tolerating the inclusion of any 'excluded middle.' The cultural intransigence of Israel confessing the message of the Torah as opposed to the 'servants of the stars' – however high and mysteriously the stars may shine – is but the concreteness of that rational necessity.

Thus I would like to speak of the second term of an alternative that humanity has faced since Sinai: idolatry or religion. I shall speak of the term that, as religion, presents itself to us in the form of a book, the book that has denounced not only the morality of statues or adored images, visible to all, but also a deep-seated corruption of morals and the spirit. This is, surely, already its message in the best-known pages, such as *Exodus 22:20–26* or *Leviticus 18:24–30*, to cite almost at random. But I wish to speak of the Torah as desirous of being a force warding off idolatry by its essence as Book, that is, by its very writing, signifying precisely prescription, and by the permanent reading it calls for – permanent reading or interpretation and reinterpretation or study; a book thus destined from the start for its Talmudic life. A book that is also by that very fact foreign to any blind commitment that might think itself virtuous because of its decisiveness or stubbornness, in the sense in which Mr. Kessler[3] was using commitment. The Talmudic life and destiny of the Torah, which is also an endless return, in its interpretation of several degrees, to particular cases, to the concreteness of reality, to analyses that never lose themselves in generalities but return to the examples – resisting invariable conceptual entities. An analysis whose free discussion is ever current.

Thus, to base one's Jewishness on the teaching of a book is to see oneself above all as a reader, i.e., as a student of the Torah, and to turn away from idolatry by true reading or study. The reading or study of a text that protects itself from eventual idolatry of this very text, by renewing, through continual exegesis – and exegesis of that exegesis – the immutable letters and hearing the breath of the living God in them. A

God not incarnate, surely, but somehow inscribed, whose life, or a part of it, is being lived in the letters: in the lines and between the lines and in the exchange of ideas between the readers commenting upon them – where these letters come alive and are echoed in the book's precepts – ordering without enslaving, like truth – to answer in justice to one's fellow, that is, to love the other. Reading and study taking on a liturgical meaning in Jewish culture: that of an entering – rather than a contact – an entering into society, into a covenant with the transcendent will. A liturgy of study as lofty as the obedience to the commandments that fulfills the study. A world to be won or lost, for which the Messianic age, awaited in history, will prove to have been but the final preparation, a world no 'prophet has encompassed nor measured with his gaze,' according to the rabbinic doctors of the Talmud, who (in Judaism, bearer of the Torah) know how to express its [that world's] essence. A future world in which, according to Maimonides, the paradoxical freedom of truth must reign in obedience. Maimonides identifies this freedom with the reign of God, under which the subjection of mankind is called – or means – understanding and love of God. An eschatology of truth (in which the philosopher probably agrees with Greek thought) that various souls intuit differently according to the figures proper to their spiritual levels. A liturgy of study as lofty as obedience to the precepts, but of a never-ending study, for one is never done with the other. Incompleteness that is the law of love: it is the future itself, the coming of a world that never ceases coming, but also the excellence of that coming compared to presence as persistence in being and in what has always been. A world to come, to be conceived in a way different from that of the Greeks. A world to come in which the faithful of the Torah have a share, although the Hebrew preposition expressing that participation, in the Mishnah passage I will comment on (*chelek laolam haba*), raises its ambiguity between the share to be taken in that world (which should have been expressed as *chelek baolam haba),* and the share to be brought to that world, to its very constitution (which is more likely to be expressed as *chelek laolam haba*), a world to come in an inexhaustible future of love itself, an eschatology paradoxically endless or precisely infinite.

2 Contempt for the Torah

Mr. Riveline, in his introduction, quoted a *midrash* according to which the entire Torah would signify nothing but the forbidding of idolatry, so that the various ways of 'scorning the Torah,' of which the text we are now considering speaks, would indicate various ways of incurring the risk of idolatry or of succumbing to it, falling to different depths. Various ways of no longer hearing, or wrongly hearing, the monotheistic Revelation. But in that case, even before the visible forms of idolatry have become manifest to research on mores and institutions – which is not my subject – the latent birth of its nature must already be detectable in Israel's wavering faithfulness to the Torah, and in what is said to be contempt for the Torah, and even in the faulty reading of it. Rabbi Ishmael's position determines the entire first portion of our exposition.

> According to Rabbi Ishmael, it is the idolater [who has scorned the Torah]. What indicates that this is the meaning? In the house of Rabbi Ishmael it was taught: 'He who scorns the word of God has already scorned God's word spoken to Moses on Sinai: "I am the Eternal your God" – "Have no other gods," etc.'

We are going to study pages 99a and b of the tractate *Sanhedrin* more closely – where the Gemara, commenting on the long Mishnah of page 90a of that tractate, discusses the following proposition: 'Among those who have no share in the world to come, there is the one who says of the Torah that it is not from heaven.' This would constitute one of the exceptions to the general rule announced by that Mishnah: 'All Israel has a share in the world to come.' It is a rule excluding idolaters from the world to come. Belonging to Israel implies respect for the Torah. What, then, does unfaithfulness or lack of respect mean? How, by what human behavior, does idolatry surreptitiously slip into what should be Jewish consciousness? The first proposition of our Gemara presents that unfaithfulness as a human questioning of the heavenly origin of the Torah.

> We have a baraita: [In] the verse *Numbers 15:31*: 'For having scorned the word of the Lord and broken his commandment, cut off he will be, cut off. . . .' This refers to [the person who says]: 'The Torah is not from heaven.'
> Another explanation: It refers to the *apikoros*.
> Another explanation: 'One who scorns the word of the Lord' is a person who interprets the word of the Torah in a way contrary to the Halakhah.

The opinions of various rabbinic doctors gathered here do not contradict one another, as is often the case in the Gemara. These opinions specify what the Mishnah means by disdain or scorn for the Torah, whose heavenly origin is challenged, thus causing the challenger to lose his or her share in the future world. The opinions complete one another, but also accentuate the manner in which that disdain for the Torah is essential for each of the doctors. You do not have your share in the future world when you doubt the heavenly origin of the Torah, violating its prohibitions if you are an *apikoros,* or if you interpret the Torah in a way contrary to the *Halakhah* – contrary to the practical law of conduct that is applied traditionally. These are various manners of dejudaization!

What is the meaning of that notion of the heavenly origin of the Torah? In the literal sense, of course, it is a reference to the Sinai Revelation, at the divine origin of the text. There is no question here of putting that meaning aside. But if it is not possible to describe the lived meaning of such terms, one can inquire about the experience in which it is approached. This is not 'spiritualizing' or 'liberalizing' religious notions, it is the attempt to seek for them a translation that the properly religious surplus of truth already presupposes. The Torah must already be from heaven by its content, by its extraordinary teachings, outside the order of the here below. 'The person who says the Torah is not from heaven has no share in the world to come': I am not obliged to understand that judgment as a punishment, to be added to the error of questioning! The Torah is transcendent and from heaven by its demands that clash, in the final analysis, with the pure ontology of the world. The Torah demands, in opposition to the natural perseverance of each being in his or her own being (a fundamental ontological law), care for the stranger, the widow and the orphan, a preoccupation with the other person. A reversal of the order of things! We do not have as much awe as we should at this reversal of ontology into ethics, and, in a sense, the dependency within it of being on the dis-interestment[4] of justice. The word [*parole*] of reversal, whose mood is imperative, the *precept,* and thus precisely the writing of the Torah, a book that dominates the consciousness that follows the affairs and laws of the earth and deciphers the eternity of its present – a prophetic book of alterity and the future.

The identification of one who scorns the Torah with the *apikoros* requires an explanation. In its accepted meaning today, this word designates the unbeliever. It may suggest a follower of Epicurus who disputes the action of the gods in the world. Nothing could be more natural than the refusal of an Epicurean to recognize the giving of the Torah by God. But the Gemara that prolongs the text translated for the present lesson identifies the *apikoros,* disdainful of the Torah, with one who offends his fellow in the presence of a rabbinic doctor. Contempt that does not remain a theological attitude, but immediately becomes contempt for humanity and a defiant challenge to one's fellow.

One who interprets the Torah in a sense contrary to the traditional rules of conduct takes the Torah as a product of culture available for intellectual jousting matches, drawing-room amusement, 'purely theoretical' views devoid of responsibility.

But what does 'breaking a commandment' mean in the text alluded to, *Numbers 15:31?*

One who has broken His commandment [the commandment of God] is one who profanes the covenant inscribed in the flesh.

To profane the covenant inscribed in the flesh means to practice circumcision no longer. But why this specification? Could it be that the human share in the 'world to come' is not attached to the other commandments in the Torah? Does the Talmud not teach us elsewhere (tractate *Avot,* chapter 2): 'Observe as zealously a light precept as a weighty one: for you do not know the recompense attached to each precept'? This also indicates the interrelated nature of the Torah's system of rituals, and the mistrust of choices that, as destructive abstractions, disrupt Judaism's time-tested concreteness. This wisdom is also reaffirmed in the next portion of our Gemara, in Rabbi Elazar Hamodai's enumeration of apparently venial transgressions alongside apparently more serious ones.

He who profanes the holiness of the sacrifices, who disdains the half-holidays, who breaks the covenant of Abraham our father and interprets the Torah without regard for the Halakhah ... *who causes the face of his fellow to pale with shame, has no share in the world to come; even if he knows the Torah and has performed charitable deeds, he has no share in the world to come.*

But the mention of fundamental precepts also underlines the ethical basis of the system: the whole Torah attests to the covenant. Let us read

(*Exodus 24:7*): 'And he' [Moses] 'took the book of the covenant and read it in the hearing of the people.' And the following verse: 'Moses took the blood, and dashed it on the people and said: 'This is the blood of the covenant, which the Eternal has made with you in agreement with all these words . . .' Very significant, this reference to blood, the blood of the sacrifice that still recalls the circumcision. It is linked with the conclusion of the covenant – with the considerable event in the heavenly Torah of a sociality between man and the transcendent, with sociality being accomplished as transcendence. This is a concept essential to Judaism: that the consent to a corporeal wound to be undergone – or to have one's newborn son undergo – places us beyond all pious rhetoric and outside the pure 'inner realm' in which ambiguity, amidst unverifiable 'mysteries,' always finds a convenient shelter.

Also very important is the seriousness attached, in Rabbi Elazar Hamodai's intervention, to the act of putting the other to shame. Elsewhere the act of causing the face of another person to blanch is compared to murder. In *Baba Metsia 58b*: 'Whoever causes the face of his neighbor to go pale with shame in public is compared to an assassin.' The draining of blood causing the cheeks to pale would appear to be as horrible as bloodshed! It is as if the meaning of all the Torah's legalities, from the purely formal prohibitions that seem of little consequence to the 'Thou shalt not kill' of the Ten Commandments, were essentially concerned with respect for the dignity of the human person in the other.

One last point needs clarification in the verse *Numbers 15:31*: the repetition of the verb to cut off.

> 'Cut off he shall be, cut off' – this means cut off from this world and cut off from the world to come.

To the eschatological sanction – which may not be perceived as particularly disturbing – there is therefore added a sanction threatening this present world! Jealousy and violence of an Old Testament? Or the danger of a form of idolatry that worships visible certainty? Attention given to the necessities of history, which never lie! The stability of the world – of all those regimes 'of a thousand years,' built on 'unswerving' physical, political and economic laws – is put in question. A premonition of our crises – our wars, totalitarianisms and unemployment. All idolatry is not always harmless.

3 Historical Criticism: Histories and Prophecies

But contempt for 'the word of the Lord' – contempt for the Torah, the doubting of its heavenly origin – takes on a new meaning with the insistence on the extreme rigor by which another baraita affirms the transcendental origin of the scroll.

> Another *baraita*: 'For having scorned the word of the Lord' – this refers to one who says: 'The Torah is not from heaven.' And even if he says: 'The whole Torah is from heaven except this verse, which Moses said on his own initiative,' that still means: He has scorned the word of the Lord. – And even if he says: 'The whole Torah comes from heaven, except this deduction, except this *a fortiori* or this "proof by analogy,"' it is still: He has scorned the word of the Lord.

Obviously we may read here, on the first level, an absolute negation of all human intervention in the writing of the Torah, and hence a condemnation in advance of all critical exploration of the biblical text on grounds of idolatry. To the point of calling it a betrayal of Judaism to attribute to the human intellect the logical articulations of the teaching contained in the text, beyond the literal meaning!

But are we not, in reading the text in this way, being too impatient? Everything depends on how we understand the unity of a spiritual work, and the spiritual unity of a people who are the bearers of such a work, even if the human may have to intervene in the very formulation of the word of God. Is the human not the very modality of the manifestation and resonance of the Word? Is not humanity, in its multipersonal plurality, the very locus of interrogation and response, the essential dimension of interpretation, in which the prophetic essence of the Revelation becomes the lived experience of a life? 'To be the Torah from heaven': is this its origin going back to a kind of transcendental dictation, or the affirmation of this life in the Torah? And whatever may be the vicissitudes and divisions and traces of 'histories' that the historian's eye discerns in the contributing elements of inspiration, the confluence into a unique, coherent message (one sole Judaism through the millennia) of the many human meanderings of prophecy and rabbinic discussions – is not that confluence as miraculous, as supernatural, as a common origin of sources, imagined to be as unique as the voice of an oracle? I have always admired a *midrash* that traces back to the voice heard at Sinai all that will be said in the way of expositions and lessons, objections and questions, the entire future accumulation of study of the Torah from the Decalogue to our own time, including the questions that the children in elementary school would ask their schoolmasters teaching them the Hebrew alphabet. Revelation in its fullness of life!

Idolatry would be the reduction of these sources to the histories and anecdotes lived by the individuals of the past, instead of sensing in them the prophecy of persons and the genius of a people, and hearing in them the birth of the message for all, and the voice of God in its extreme straightness through the appearance of the tortuous paths it takes.

But then our *baraita* is right after all. It criticizes the historian who, in the voice of Moses, hears only an everyday, private discourse, and who is content to reduce the meaning of a biblical verse to its hither side – the circumstances, dictated by events, leading to its coming to mind; content to seek in the logical configurations themselves in which the verse is developed nothing but the trace of I know not what social or ideological condition of non-narrative historical analysis.

It is not without reason that in chapter 19 of *Exodus*, which recounts the comings and goings of Moses preparing Israel to receive the Torah at Sinai, verse 14, which begins with 'Moses went down from the mountain toward the people' – a very clear, straightforward statement – is nonetheless commented upon by Rashi, and in the following terms: 'This teaches us that Moses did not go and take care of his personal business, but went directly from the mountain to the people.' Nothing private, nothing empirical in Moses – that is the main thing. And already the *Mekhilta,* which Rashi follows in his exegesis, had extended that non-contingency of the prophet to all the words attributed to Moses in the Torah.

4 The Sins of Reading

Respect for the Torah depends on the way it is read. Another baraita informs us of some precautions to be taken.

Rabbi Meir used to say: 'He who studies the Torah without teaching it is indeed he who has scorned the word of the Torah.'

That a right reading of the Torah should include the necessity of teaching what one learns is not a truism. It is interesting to note that study is not the activity of a lone individual and that essentially truth must be communicated, that the 'I think' is sociality, and that that communication of truth is not an addendum to truth but belongs to the reading itself and is part of the reader's concern. But, if it is necessary to teach the Torah in order to perpetuate it, it is probably also necessary that the student should ask questions. The student, being both other and, generally speaking, younger, must come with questions, in the name of the future, and boldly, despite the respect due to the master. The student will ask questions based on what the Torah will mean tomorrow. The Torah not only reproduces what was taught yesterday, it is read according to tomorrow; it does not stop at the representation of what yesterday and today goes by the name of the present.

But also there is a second precaution to be taken.

Rabbi Nathan said: 'It is whoever does not heed the Mishnah' [who has scorned the Torah].

The Mishnah is the tradition of the oral Law which was added at Sinai to the written Torah. But it is also the non-written with all its possibilities – it is that which is beyond the verse, awakening it. The Mishnah is already exegesis stirring within the written and posing the future 'problematic' of the Gemara. It is the Torah in which time and spiritual life through time have rendered explicit or lent new life to the letter – which makes possible, but also impossible, a true transmission. It is the Torah fed by its own flame through time.

Rabbi Nehorai said: 'It is whoever has the opportunity to study the Torah and does not do so' [who has rejected the Torah].

It is one for whom the Torah's entering the world has not transformed the latter drastically. One for whom the Torah exists, self-enclosed like an institution or a sacred object, whereas its essence is opening.

Here, in the Gemara on which we are commenting, occurs – and perhaps logically so – the passage I quoted at the beginning of my exposition. It gives the opinion of Rabbi Ishmael and his school, defining contempt for the Torah as idolatry, and idolatry as contempt for the Torah. Here idolatry can also be taken as idolatry of the Torah.

Here, finally, are two other wrong ways to read the Torah.

Rabbi Yehoshua ben Korha said: 'Whoever studies the Torah without repeating the lesson is like a sower who does not reap.'

Not repeating the lesson means not remembering the Torah; but it also means denying what the first reading – which opens but at the same time covers up – has already hidden. The first reading hides the horizons of the gaze and its relativity. It is content with the first word, the first impression, first-level truths. It takes metaphorical meaning literally, which is the negation of the spiritual and the source of all idolatry. To sow without reaping is also to cease sowing, increasing and renewing the harvest.

Rabbi Yehoshua said: 'Whoever learns the Torah and forgets it is like a woman who brings a child into the world only to bury it.'

A striking image, not only because of its dramatic evocation of the suffering mother. The image suggests the idea that study is not just any activity but a giving birth – and that the result of study is an other me, who answers me, tearing me away from my solitude, and for whom I am answerable.

5 Reading and Song

Rabbi Akiva said: 'To each day its song, to each day its song.'

Is Rabbi Akiva's intervention simply in praise of regular reading and the affirmation of an essential link between the Israelite's time and his or her relationship with the Book? To become a song would indicate a text's being learned by heart, its ever increasing familiarity, and yet the possibility of its being gone over daily without the boredom of repetition. Thus it would seem that we have returned to Yehoshua ben Korha's concern, his fear for those who read without rereading, for those who read without studying. But Rashi, commenting on the word 'song,' also sees it as 'a promise of joy for the world to come.'

Yet I wonder whether within that mention of song by Rabbi Akiva – the most renowned Talmudic master – there is not the recurrence of the problem of being able, in the study of the Torah raised to the level of supreme liturgy, to coincide with the musical or poetic exaltation of the soul, which would come to it not as a promised recompense, but as inherent in that very hearing of the Torah's divine word. It is, perhaps, a problem that haunts the Jewish religious consciousness, the repercussions of which can be perceived in hasidism, in the form in which it entered into a certain eighteenth-century Jewish piety. Ambivalence – or perhaps temptation and ambiguity of the spiritual – such as that attested in the famous *midrash* set forth in the Talmudic tractate *Sota 35a.* King David is said to have dared to claim for his 'songs' the dignity attaching to God's prescriptive word, in saying (*Psalm 119:54*): 'Thy precepts are to me as songs.' Is he not thereby claiming for the singing of the psalms the subtle elevation of the study of the Torah? But God abruptly rejects any confusion of the Talmudic Jew with the psalmodizing one! The *midrash* of the treatise *Sota* accuses the psalmist of 'allowing himself to apply the term song' to the Word, of which *Proverbs 23:5* says (according to an interpretation going back to the rabbinical period) that no sooner has the eye looking at it turned away than it is no longer there. The thread of the dialectic to which the Word is attached need be lost but for a moment, through inattention or fatigue, and the Word will vanish. Nothing is ever definitely gained in it, beyond the living attention of the gaze, which may become weary. The Torah is not simply part of a cultural treasure, like song and the arts. The Word of God, supreme meaning, is without insistence – it flies away like a dream. Perhaps Judaism is, after all, nothing but an accident of history or the miracle of an unflagging attention. Idolatry is real reality, natural reality.

Nevertheless, does not Rabbi Akiva's comment allow us to catch a glimpse, even for the study of *Halakhah* and *Aggadah,* of a kind of severe daily joy in the proximity of this invisible and barely thematizable God, who concerns me, surrounds and obsesses me through the face of my neighbor and responsibility for the other – the imperative nature of which is explicated in the Torah?

6 The Human Vocation and the Book

Where, after all, in Scripture itself, is the foundation for this relationship with the book, the Torah?

Rabbi Yizhak ben Abudani said: 'What verse teaches that?'

The Gemara then refers to a verse in *Proverbs 16:26,* the *prima facie* meaning of which obviously can be translated:

It is for himself that the laborer labors, for pressing are the demands of his mouth.

Common sense would teach us this: the dependency of our human activities in relation to our hungry mouths. A verse capable of explaining our human work in relation to hunger and thirst. The epigraph for a treatise on historical materialism, the preface to an economic interpretation of culture.

The rabbinical reading is open to other possibilities of segmenting the Hebrew statement, which, word for word (a bit more loosely, perhaps), expresses itself in the following way. 'The soul that toils, toils for itself, because on it the mouth has exerted pressure.' The first hemistich is interpreted: the soul toils (to study the Torah) here; it (the Torah) toils for that soul elsewhere. The second hemistich is interpreted: for on the Torah the student's mouth exerts pressure. The toil of one who studies the Torah is a fruitful one, and the Torah itself multiples the fecundity of the toil devoted to it. As if the Torah itself were bringing to a spirit the true spiritual energy, or as if one who studied the Torah released the Torah's rational energy and received more than he brought to it.

The idea of toil being connected with study is essential. It also serves to distinguish clearly between the Torah and song. But is toil a part of man's destiny?

Rabbi Elazar said: 'All men are created for toil for it is said: ''Man is born unto toil'' [*Job 5:7*].'

What is this toil? I do not yet know, the Gemara says, whether man is born for the toil imposed by the mouth or for the toil imposed by the hungry mouth or the work necessitated by it. Is the mouth eating or speech? Our text returns therefore to the second hemistich of *Proverbs 16:26*.

'For his mouth puts pressure on him.' – Therefore he is born for the toil imposed upon him by his mouth.'

The main toil of man – of that man who, according to Job, is delivered unto toil – is the toil of the mouth. The toil of the word. Do we not end up with the classical – Aristotelian – definition of the human being: an animal that has the logos? Not entirely. A moment ago we were tempted to explain man, on the basis of the mouth, in a purely economic way, as an animal who must eat. Now we are already elevated to the level at which the mouth is no longer merely what eats, but also what speaks. It is the logos that is the toil of man. But is it sufficiently high, meaningful and reasonable?

The Gemara continues:

> But I do not yet know what kind of word is imposed upon man. Does the toil imposed by the mouth mean the toil required by the study of the Torah or the toil required by any speech?

A bit of gossip? A conversation? Rhetoric? Eloquent discourse? Is discourse already speech? A verse is necessary to decide: a third verse taken from *Joshua.*

> 'May this book of the Torah not leave your mouth.' It is for the toil required to study the Torah that man was created! [*Joshua 1:8*]

The problem is an important one. Is idolatry excluded from the logos? Is Greek intelligibility sufficient for the human? And is what we have already caught a glimpse of in the intelligibility of the *covenant* and of *sociality* as participation in the future world already assured by language?

Occupation with the Torah is not a distraction. We return to the theme of the difficult freedom it signifies – of the work of the Spirit. But also the danger of the pure logos.

> That is what Raba said: 'All bodies are containers.'

Strictly speaking, what I have translated as 'containers' means 'carriers of mail bags.' Language is the transportation of messages and information at the crossroads of all sorts of influences. The animals that speak are like mail bags carrying messages that are not sayings going from one to another, but wandering words. They toil at the crossroads where all the idolatries find credence.

> Happy those who have been worthy of carrying within them the Torah!

Language that is relation to the other, prescription of responsibility. Whence doubtless denunciation, in the attitude toward the Torah, of the reduction of its writing to pure literature, to being one book among others that are 'full of excellent things' and that help pass the time and amuse from time to time, as products of an 'old culture.'

'To commit adultery is to be a senseless fool ...' [*Proverbs 6:32*]. Resh Laqish said: 'That refers to one who studies the Torah only from time to time. For in *Proverbs 22:17* it is said: 'Incline your ear and listen to the words of the wise ...' and in *Proverbs 22:18*, 'It will be beautiful for you to keep them in your heart, and to fix them permanently on your lips.'

Torah and permanence, Torah and all time. An extraordinary book, calling for the toil of effort, tension – a book distrustful of all leniency toward oneself. Idolatry thus appears, in the 'banalizing' of that gravity, as a degradation. Idolatry is not a childhood of the spirit awaiting the Torah's maturity. The latter, open to all, requires a freedom that would be graven in matter, the stone of the Law.

7 The Scorning of the Scorner

Among the various ways of lacking in faith in the Torah – i.e., in the reading and study of it – we noted, all through the length of our text, openings toward idolatry, however innocent its forms appear. This text will end with the depiction of a deliberate contempt for the Holy Scripture, an outrage against God, committed 'with a high hand.' But this depiction, with its exclusion from the 'world to come,' will also be the pretext for a remarkable passage in which, in addition to a 'complete faith,' the Gemara requires the supplement of an attention to the world from which that faith parted ways.

'And whosoever' [*Numbers 15:30*] 'has acted high-handedly' – *beyad rama* – 'among home-born or among strangers, he reviles the Lord! That person will be cut off from his people.' The reference is to King Manasseh, the son of Hezikiah.

Hezikiah is the king of the line of David who is the most faithful to the Torah. The Talmud mentions a theological tradition according to which the Messiah is not awaited by Israel. The Messiah has already come: he was Hezikiah. Or he could have been Hezikiah, the most pious and just king, the most learned in the Torah – who lacked only one gift, the ability to sing. But Hezikiah was unable to educate his son Manasseh, the most idolatrous king among the kings of Judea! And we learn from our text that he, probably cultured from all points of view (like a modern young man), found in the Torah not things that were contradictory or too severe, but absurd or meaningless things.

He would try his hand at interpreting the Torah in a shameless way.

'He would try his hand' – the man who reads – or the young man who has 'read all the books'![5] 'Revered father . . . father rabbi . . . I myself see things in a much broader perspective. . . . I will say some things that are absolutely obvious. . . . We'll have a good bit of fun!'

He would say: 'Didn't Moses have anything else to write besides "and Lotan's sister was Timna" [*Genesis 36:22*]?'

Genesis contains a genealogy of the descendants of Esau, in chapter 36. Indeed, many names whose reason for being there one may wonder about. Enough to annoy Jacob, in any case, faced with so many princes having carried out precocious political exploits, and already threatening the family of Israel. But what is the purpose, in these cumbersome pages, of information about Timna, apparently Lotan's sister? There is also a second bit of information about Timna.

'And Timna was a concubine of Eliphaz.'

Bedroom gossip included in Holy History! And why so much about Timna in that description?
More apparently useless information decried by Manasseh.

'And Reuben, having gone to the fields during the days of the wheat harvest, found mandrakes there and brought them to Leah, his mother' [*Genesis 30:14*].

What significance could the fact that the mandrakes were gathered 'during the days of the wheat harvest' have for the history of humanity, the vocation of Israel, the coming of the Messiah and the next world? What a hodgepodge there is in this book! Scorn of the Torah with 'a high

hand'! An insult to the Eternal! But especially slander of Moses. A voice
from heaven interrupts Manassah.

> Then a voice echoed from heaven and said: 'You sit and speak
> against your brother; you slander your own mother's son. You do
> these things, and I should keep silent? Do you suppose that I could
> be like you? I will reprove you and will put [my grievances] before
> your eyes.'

A voice protesting first against the slander of a 'brother,' Moses, and
the contempt for his prophecy.

It is a text from *Psalm 50*. It is interesting to recall the context of it, for it
places this 'call from heaven' in the framework of a perfectly 'adult'
theology, in which ethics does not yield before the flattery of the 'pious
gesture,' nor reason before the facile accommodations of common sense.
'Do you suppose that I could be like you?' means, according to Rashi's
commentary on the Psalms, the affirmation of the whole 'order of
mystery open to God' and closed to man. The insignificance of a text
approached without its past and its future in religious consciousness may
prove nothing more than the insolence of a still impatient wisdom. 'I am
not like you. You do not know everything. There are hidden things you
do not know, and of which you would set yourself up prematurely as
judge and critic.'

There is the history of Manasseh. It is the denial of the Torah by one
who says that the Torah is not from heaven, but who also denies its
intrinsic value. He denies it in a fundamental way. It is the prototype of a
whole attitude – with which you are quite familiar – and even of an entire
modernism of good humor.

The text adds:

> And it is respecting Manasseh that the text of the tradition teaches,
> saying [*Isaiah 5:18*]: 'Woe unto them that draw chastisement with
> the cords of evil, and sin with thick cart ropes.'
> Why with thick cart ropes?
> Rav Assi said: 'The evil inclination is like the thread of a spider at
> first, and at the end like the thick ropes of a cart.'

These are apparently indifferent and innocent things that have been
brought out in our analysis – all those cords, even thin ones like the

threads of a spider's web, become as strong as cables to pull a cart – that draw punishment or have idolatry tied to the end.

Will we be convinced by the voice from heaven? What of Manasseh's objections, after all? He was wrong in his denunciation. But is the denunciation justified? The problem remains unresolved.

> 'Reuben, having gone to the fields during the days of the wheat harvest, found mandrakes there and brought them to his mother.'
>
> Raba, the son of Yizhak, has said in the name of Rav: 'A lesson for the just! May they not stretch out their hand to acquire dishonestly.'

Here is the answer to the problem, on which I shall say a few words. The response to the problem of the mandrakes gathered by Reuben, Jacob's son. In the days of the harvest, the field into which Reuben went to gather the mandrakes was already open to passers-by. The Torah – Manasseh's laughter notwithstanding – stresses that even mandrakes are gathered by a son of Israel in a way that rules out any sort of plunder.

But the Timna problem seems more difficult. It is quite essential here.

> Since we are on the subject of 'and Lotan's sister is Timna,' what is in fact at stake? Timna was of royal blood.

But there was no need for her to be mentioned in the series of important individuals among Esau's descendants. Moreover, she only belongs to the population to which Esau attaches himself when he leaves the country of Canaan, which was bequeathed to his brother Jacob. But how do we know that she was of royal blood?

> For it is written: *Aluf Lotan* [Genesis 36:29], *Aluf Timna* [Genesis 36:40].

Both Lothan and Timna were *Alufim.*

> And *Aluf* indicates the dignity of a royalty without the crown.

Something like a duchess or grand duchess. What does that teach us?

> Timna tried to convert.

The Gemara says what the text of the Torah does not say: that Timna had already gone to Abraham, Isaac and Jacob (Abraham lived a long time!) to ask for a husband from among Abraham's descendants.

They turned her away. She became the concubine of Eliphaz, Esau's son.

Eliphaz is in fact of Abraham's blood. He is Esau's son. Timna, then, would seem to have consented to enter the family of Abraham, Isaac and Jacob, even if only as a concubine to Eliphaz, Esau's son!

She must have said to herself: 'It is better to be a servant in this nation than to have lordly rank in another.'

Better the spiritual greatness of that line than membership in a great nation in which there are wars, victories and conquests! But the text also teaches us that:

Amalek issued from that union – who causes Israel so much suffering.

The moral? The Gemara gives it.

Timna should not have been turned away.

I then tried to discover, through the commentators on page 99b of our Gemara, how it came about that Abraham, Isaac and Jacob could have rejected Timna's demand and contributed to the birth of Amalek. I found answers that do not satisfy me – according to which Abraham, Isaac and Jacob may not have been sure that, behind the pretext of being attached to the house of Abraham, Timna was not just looking for a husband!

I prefer the Gemara's harsh moral. It comes very well at the end of all this text, with all its exactions of pure spirits, all its superb and admirable rigor. To this admirable rigor, this superb spirit, a movement of openness must be joined. Failing which the high-mindedness of the Torah becomes haughtiness of spirit. Idolatry of the Torah? But it is still the Gemara – i.e., the living Torah – that instructs us and puts us on our guard against that ultimate contempt for the Torah, that final denial of its celestial origin.

4
Beyond Memory[1]
From the tractate *Berakhot, 12b–13a*

Mishnah

The exodus from Egypt is recalled also at night. Rabbi Eleazar ben Azariah said: 'Here I am like a seventy-year-old man, and have not seen the exodus from Egypt recalled at night. It took Ben Yoma's coming to teach it through a midrash. It *is said:* [Deuteronomy 16:3]: *''In order that you may remember the exodus from Egypt all the days of your life.'' ''Days of your life'' – that means the days; ''all the days'' means the nights.' As for our sages, they have taught: ' ''The days of your life'' means the entire duration of this world; ''all the days of your life'' implies the Days of the Messiah.'*

Gemara

Let us recall a baraita. Ben Yoma said to our sages, 'Will the remembrance of the exodus from Egypt still be obligatory in the Days of the Messiah? Is it not said [Jeremiah 23:7–8]: *''In truth, the days will come, says the Eternal, when they shall say no more: 'May the Eternal live, who brought up the children of Israel out of the land of Egypt' but, 'May the Eternal live, who brought up and led the seed of the house of Israel out of the north country, and from all the countries into which I had driven them.' '' ' The sages answered: No, that does not mean that the exodus from Egypt 'loses its place,' but that the freeing from subservience to the empires will be the primary thing and the exodus from Egypt the secondary one. In the same way that* [Genesis 35:10]: *'You will not be called Jacob, but your name will be Israel' does not mean that Jacob 'loses his place,' but that Israel will be his primary name and Jacob his secondary one.*

Does it not say in Isaiah 43:18, *'Remember former things no more, nor consider the things of old'?* 'Remember former things no more, *is [the emancipation] from subservience to the empires;* 'Nor consider the things of old' *is the exodus from Egypt. And what is the meaning of [*Isaiah 43:19*]: 'Behold, I will do new things – See, they are already unfolding'? Rav Yosef taught: 'It is the war of Gog and Magog.'*

To what is it comparable? A man was going along and came upon a wolf – and got away. After that, he told nothing but wolf stories. He came upon a lion, and escaped: then he told the story of the lion. He encountered a snake – and got away. There he is, having forgotten both of them [the wolf and the lion] and telling nothing but the story of the snake. So *with Israel: the most recent hardships eclipse the earlier ones.*

In I Chronicles 1:27: *'Abram – the same is Abraham.' He first became the father of Aram; he became in the end the father of the whole world. Sarai – the same is Sarah. She was first a princess among her people; she finally became the princess of the whole world.*

Bar Kapra taught: 'Whoever calls Abraham Abram breaks a positive commandment, for it is written in Genesis 17:5*: ''But thy name shall be Abraham.'' ' Rav Eliezer said: 'He breaks a negative commandment [an interdict], for it is said: ''Thy name shall no longer be Abram.'' Henceforth, to say Sarai to Sarah does it violate an interdict? [Answer] There* [Genesis 17:15], *it was to Abraham that the Holy One, Blessed be His Name, said: ''Sarai thy wife, thou shall not call her name Sarai, but Sarah shall be her name.'' But what of he who continues to call Jacob Jacob? [Answer] Here there is a difference! The Scripture itself returns to [this name of] Jacob* [Genesis 46:2]*: ''And God spoke unto Israel in a vision during the night and He said: ''Jacob, Jacob.'' '*

Rabbi Yossi ben Abin, and, according to others, Rabbi Yossi ben Zevida, objected. '[Do we not find] ''It is You, Eternal God, who chose Abram'' [Nehemiah 9:7]*?' He was answered: 'Here [it is different]: the prophet is enumerating what constitutes the glory of the Merciful One. He begins by [telling] what was at the beginning.'*

1 The Conscious and the Memorable

The proximity of God is experienced in Judaism through memory, and consequently in the prevalence of the past and of the events and imperatives foundational to Holy History, which is usually understood as elapsed time. It is a sensibility in which the past plays a central role in the Jewish psyche, to the point of resonating with, and telling itself in, the actuality of every lived present. A consciousness that is immediately narration, an interiority in which some story stirs, giving the present its meaning. Consciousness is not, in this case, just the actualizing of the new, but also the narration of the past by which consciousness is sustained and ordered.

The going forth from Egypt – the Exodus – and the evocation of that exodus in which freedom was given to a people, the coming to the foot of Mount Sinai where that freedom culminated in Law, constituted a privileged past, the very form of the past, as it were. But by the same token it is a thought virtually obsessed by the theme of freeing slaves – whence, perhaps (despite their particularism and tentativeness), the texts from *Exodus 21*, destined to their many sublimations in the rest of prophetic scripture. Here we have a dimension of the memorable and as it were the spirituality – or the respiration – of consciousness, which already, in its content of presence, is memory of affranchisement, and lived concretely as the soul of freedmen. The Jew is free *qua* affranchised: his memory is immediately compassion for all the enslaved or all the wretched of the earth, and a special flair for that wretchedness that the wretched themselves are prone to forget.

This past of the Exodus and the Law forms the heart of the Jewish weekday morning prayer. Or, more precisely perhaps, this memory is already prayer, morning prayer, prayer of awakening, awakening as prayer. The first proposition of the Mishnah that I am commenting on innovates: it introduces this daily morning recollection of the Exodus into the evening liturgy.

The exodus from Egypt is recalled also at night.

What is the importance of that innovation?

The recalling of the Exodus, the memory of which is so important to Jewish religiosity, is not the utterance of just any statement among others. It has a context in the liturgy in which gestures and thoughts contained in this memory are brought together concretely. It comes about in the last part of the recitation of the famous *Shema Israel,* in which the Jew confesses his belief, and which comes back to him in all his martyrdoms: 'Hear, O Israel, the Eternal is our God, the Eternal is the Only One' (*Deuteronomy 6:4*). That formulation is followed by the one inviting us to love the One God. But that appeal to feeling becomes more concrete in the reminder of the commandment to take up the words of the Torah unceasingly, to let ourselves be penetrated by them, to transmit those words to our descendants and to respect the Law and the symbols it institutes. That sequence is followed by another, from *Deuteronomy 11:13*, in which faithfulness to this monotheism and its obligations is affirmed as the very condition of the Jew's sojourn on earth, and even of his sojourn on the earth as *his* land, and in which the earth – the element of being – is raised, by virtue of being the locus of a human sojourn, to the fullness of its ontological accomplishment. The third biblical sequence constituting the *Shema* is taken from *Numbers 15:37–41*. It prescribes the wearing of *tzitzit*, the well-known fringes at the four corners of the shawl. The sight of the *tzitzit* should remind (again a reminder!) the Jew of his obligations. A sight that awakens obligation. A privileged sight, protecting the faithful from the temptations and seductions of sight itself, and from the supposed innocence of his uninformed heart. This text ends with a formulation of the 'signature': 'I am the Eternal your God, who brought you out of the land of Egypt, to be your God.' *Liheiot lakhem lelohim*: In order to be God for you. That is doubtless the place – beneath that signature evoking the signatory's main title and where, if I may make so bold as to say, the divinity of God takes on meaning for a man – in which the daily recollection of the Exodus or the liberation occurs. It is the passage that consecrates the intimacy between the faithful and God who will be God *for* him or her. An intimacy that means obeying the commandments and serving God – but that remains freedom, or ensures freedom, by surmounting the very dependence that, formally, such a relation seems to imply. In the sight of the fringes, this passage expresses the elevation of sight, and the knowledge derived from it, to the ethical order.

This is a remarkable conjunction, in which the principal moments of Judaism are in harmony. An interesting detail: in verse 39 of *Numbers* 15, which relates how 'the sight of the fringes is protection from the waywardness of the eyes and the heart,' the fringes are designated by a personal pronoun in the singular. The singular refers back to the blue thread that is added: not 'You will see *them*,' but 'You will see *it*.' The rabbinic commentary: in looking at the fringes, you will see God. Through the recollection of the acts commanded by the Law, contemplation of the invisible God! A 'vision' of the invisible God in the respect for the Torah's ethical obligations! A vision of the invisible God in the fringes, linked to the remembrance of the going forth out of Egypt, of the past of the Exodus.

2 The Unheard-of Is Possible

In the threads of the fringes, a vision of the invisible God. But then the story of the Exodus, linked to the sight of the fringes, would be linked to daylight, to the awakened consciousness. Whence the novelty of the first sentence of our text, 'The exodus from Egypt is recalled also at night,' when the *tzitzit* are not normally visible. Henceforth the past of the Exodus, the remembrance of the going forth from Egypt, will enter into our nights as it opens our days.

> Rabbi Eleazar ben Azariah said: 'Here I am like a seventy-year-old man, and have not seen the exodus from Egypt recalled at night. It took Ben Yoma's coming to teach it through a *midrash*. It is said [*Deuteronomy 16:3*]: "In order that you may remember the exodus from Egypt all the days of your life." "Days of your life" – that means the days; "all the days" means the nights.'

The time of remembrance is, then, both night and day! An innovation that Rabbi Eleazar ben Azariah apparently learned late in life from Ben Yoma. 'Here I am like a seventy-year-old man': would this mean that Ben Yoma's lesson was unheard-of, or that Rabbi Eleazar ben Azariah was not as old as he looked? Let us consider the anecdote on this subject on page 28a of our treatise *Berakhot*. It is the account of Rabban Gamliel's dismissal by force. Rabban Gamliel, head of the rabbinic academy, was too strict a master. He was dismissed for that very excess of severity. A replacement is sought, and Eleazar ben Azariah is designated. He possesses wisdom, material independence and nobility – being descended from Esdras in the tenth generation; responsible for an exceedingly glorious spiritual heritage. Everything seems to portend an eminent role for him. But he is only eighteen years old – without one white hair. Can one teach without innovating? But can one innovate without reference to a tradition, without remaining the contemporary – real or apparent – of the discourse of the past? A miracle was needed! Eighteen rows of white hair appeared on Eleazar ben Azariah's head – who, at the age of eighteen, henceforth looked seventy, in order that all innovation should derive from earlier forms.

This extension of memory to the totality of a human life, regardless of the alternation of night and day – Ben Yoma derived it from the unsaid, suggested by a word that seemed merely supplementary in an early verse.

But this word, according to the Talmudic sages, contains more. The audacity of *midrash*!

> As for our sages, they have taught: 'The days of your life' means the entire duration of this world; 'all the days of your life' implies the Days of the Messiah.

The exodus from Egypt – original past – does not remain a memory dominating the time of persons and their finite duration. It punctuates the time of the total history of humanity, right up to the point of its eschatological denouement. The liberation from the Egyptian yoke is, from this perspective, the dominant event of Judaism and of the human. Its influence extends even to the Days of the Messiah. The Israelites, in their Egyptian enslavement, touched the depths of the human condition. Their deliverance anticipated the salvation of humanity itself. The past of their memory carries the future within it. This would be the structure of history, and the foundation of the sages' position.

Is it the sages' position? Let us move toward the Gemara.

'Let us recall a *baraita*,' i.e., a Tannaitic text – a text of high authority, though omitted from Rabbi Judah Ha-Nasi's collection.[2] The baraita teaches:

> Ben Yoma said to our sages: 'Will the remembrance of the exodus from Egypt still be obligatory in the Days of the Messiah? Is it not said [*Jeremiah 23:7–8*]: "In truth, the days will come, says the Eternal, when they shall say no more, 'May the Eternal live, who brought up the children of Israel out of the land of Egypt,' but, 'May the Eternal live, who brought up and led the seed of the house of Israel out of the north country, and from all the countries into which I had driven them.' "'

Ben Yoma, who thus extended the memory of Egypt to the entire duration of time lived by persons both night and day, now glimpses the time of Judaism, and hence human time, beyond the limits of memory. Its meaning comes from elsewhere. Judaism and humanity as a whole (when thinking of Judaism, one must always catch sight of humanity as a whole in it, just as it is appropriate to anticipate in Abram Abraham, the father of many nations) open themselves to a future more – or otherwise – significant than slavery and emancipation from slavery. They open themselves to a freedom freer and more human or perhaps more tormented than the one that comes down to breaking free from the will of the other man, and more miraculous than the miracles of the Exodus. Neither the wonders nor the horrors of the human vocation are yet exhausted, in Ben Yoma's view. There are those that take place upon the return from exile and dispersion. But there is perhaps also, in the exile and dispersion, the inhumanity of an ordeal more inhuman than slavery. A universality through Israel, more universal than the one that remains marked by the particularism of Jacob – though it is questionable whether Jacob's hardships can ever be effaced from history. I shall return to this question. That greater universality is certainly what Ben Yoma intuits and what is about to be suggested by the mention of Abraham: a history beyond the one that is compounded of memories and could be contained therein. A history overflowing memory, and, in this sense, unimaginable. A history, as yet entirely novel, that has not yet happened to any particular nation.

Ben Yoma has thus asked the question: Can one not draw from the verse in Jeremiah the hope of an unheard-of future, of a prophetic history – putting an end to the fascination with memories?

The sages answered: No. . . .

But they also answered: Yes.

That does not mean that the exodus from Egypt 'loses its place,' but that the freeing from subservience to the empires will be the primary thing, and the exodus from Egypt the secondary one. In the same way that [*Genesis 35:10*]: 'You will not be called Jacob, but your name will be Israel' does not mean that Jacob 'loses his place,' but that Israel will be his primary name and Jacob his secondary one.

At the point we have come to, the sages appear more prudent than Ben Yoma. There is a meaning of Israel that is broader than that of Jacob, but Jacob, a secondary or second name, remains the name of a living being. The Exodus cannot be forgotten, remains an ineradicable event. Surely there remains a question to be examined later. What does that secondarity mean? It is not that of a lapse of validity, like an 'Old Testament,' nor any kind of 'prefiguration.'

3 Future and Trial

But here, announcing something beyond memory, is a message far more explicit than the text from Jeremiah.

> Does it not say in *Isaiah 43:18*, 'Remember former things no more, nor consider the things of old?' 'Remember former things no more,' is [the emancipation] from subservience to the empires; 'Nor consider the things of old' is the exodus from Egypt. And what is the meaning of [*Isaiah 43:19*]: 'Behold, I will do new things – See, they are already unfolding'? Rav Yosef taught. . . .

What are these new things? After the exodus from Egypt and the miracles that overturn the order of nature, are the liberation from subservience to the empires and the return of the exiled sufficiently new? But what an extraordinary text! Rav Yosef sees in it an unheard-of, totally new event.

> Rav Yosef taught: 'It is the war of Gog and Magog.'

Not *a* war, but *the* war: total war. Beyond any memory! There is deliverance in Isaiah's promises and the end of subservience to political power – to all political power, not just that of Egypt. But the only part of the absolute newness of the message Rav Yosef perceives – and understands positively – is the superlative evil heralding the end. Might it be that the 'may the Eternal live' of the ultimate future will be announced by the inhumanity of the war that precedes it? As Rav Haya bar Aba sees it: 'All the prophets have only foretold the Days of the Messiah; as for the world to come, no eye has seen it, except Thine, O Eternal! And it is made for those who wait.' Those who wait without foretelling. Those who wait, therefore, in the suffering of long-suffering, in patience and suffering. The prophet foretells only historical time. Does not the wisdom of the rabbinical doctor reach further, measuring the best in terms of the worst that will be transcended? Does not wisdom thus exceed the prophet's foretelling? What Rav Yosef is designating are the inhuman trials preceding the 'unheard-of' of the ultimately awaited.

But Israel's new trials and tribulations, whose end is perhaps always prematurely proclaimed (and who knows if even today that should not be a concern), may be, in their mysterious eventuality, the very modality

71

without which a spiritual transcendence is concretely impossible, and the challenging of the remembered past in which 'all has been accomplished.' Israel – or the humanity of the Human – has not yet finished compounding its memories. Israel's cup of suffering has not yet been drunk dry. 'Mysterious eventuality' – the popular term for it is perhaps 'threat of anti-Semitism.' The memories of a prodigious past in which a parted sea let the freed tribes pass through and swallowed up their pursuers take on an ambiguous meaning. ... *Zekher*[3] ceases to indicate the meaning of History! And is that not the true meaning of the parable with which our text continues?

> To what is it comparable? A man was going along and came upon a wolf – and got – away. After that, he told nothing but wolf stories. He came upon a lion, and escaped: then he told the story of the lion. He encountered a snake – and got away. There he is, having forgotten both of them [the wolf and the lion] and telling nothing but the story of the snake. So with Israel: the most recent hardships eclipse the earlier ones.

That is the form in which the history of Israel is forgotten! And that is the way in which the future preceding the ultimate 'deliverance' is announced: by the appearance on the road of two wild beasts and a snake, one after another. Each new encounter with wildness eclipses the horrors of the preceding ones. Wolf, lion, snake – a triad recalling that of *Amos 5:19*: 'It will be as when a man flees from a lion and finds himself face to face with a bear, enters his house and is bitten by the snake.' The wolf of our Talmudic passage is, in Amos, a lion (which is no less wild) and Amos's lion is a bear in our text. The snake that ends the trials of the story is the same. The wolf and the lion, like the lion and the bear, are visible, foreseeable threats. The snake 'comes crawling' and 'attacks the heel,' according to *Genesis 3:15*. On page 98b of the treatise *Sanhedrin*, Resh Laqish deciphers these zoological signs of *Amos* and clarifies our text: 'I will show you an example of it in the world of today. When a man goes to a field, and meets a government surveyor, is it not as if he had met a lion? Here he is back in the town, and he bumps into a tax collector. Is it not as if he had met a bear? He returns home and finds his sons and daughters dying of hunger. Is it not as if he had been bitten by a snake?' This is the deciphering of an apologist, but it requires further deciphering. The government surveyor challenges your title to the land you are working, the tax collector always finds you owe money – these are civil servants or states questioning your illusory rights as a citizen. The Diaspora of Israel in lands that, always foreign, continually trample, beneath the tread of lions, wolves and bears, the very legal order that made them inhabitable. But this is still the domain of history, a structural realm in which it is possible to walk, to wander or to flee. Savagery and wasteland, the memory of which may yet fade. But the death of the starving children thrusts us into the snake pit, into places that are no longer places, into places one cannot forget, but that do not succeed in placing themselves in memory, in organizing themselves in the form of memories. We have known such pits in this [the twentieth] century!

And about the ultimate deliverance that this cataclysm, too over-powering for thought, precedes – about a deliverance before which the memory of the Exodus would pale – about the new humanity that will emerge from that trial, all that is said are the negative and formal structures of 'transcendence,' in a text that presents itself as being prophetic: it is Jacob who becomes Israel, it is Abram, the father of Aram (the father of a people) who becomes the father of all nations. In Abraham and Sarah a universal and united humanity is announced.

> In *I Chronicles 1:27*: 'Abram – the same is Abraham.' He first became the father of Aram; he became in the end the father of the whole world. Sarai – the same is Sarah. She was first a princess among her people; she finally became the princess of the whole world.

Were all those woes – the 'war of Gog and Magog,' those snake bites, that starvation of children, all that Passion of innocents, that Passion of Israel – necessary in order for a reconciled humanity to be thinkable? Here are some specifics – content incorporated to introduce *Halakhah*: commandments and interdicts. To use the term Abraham is, according to Bar Kapra, a positive commandment. Not to call him Abram is an interdict, according to Rav Eliezer.

> Bar Kapra taught: 'Whoever calls Abraham Abram breaks a positive commandment, for it is written in *Genesis 17:5*: "But thy name shall be Abraham." Rav Eliezer said: 'He breaks a negative command-ment [an interdict], for it is said: "Thy name shall no longer be Abram."'

73

Interdicts and commandments. Unless we are to divine: Hear, through the relative present, bold anticipations of an absolute future! Hear, in the present's uncertainty, in Israel's misery, Abraham, the father of human universality, hailed as such, invoked as such! Time to accept universality! The anticipated is already irreversible! Israel – historians know it – has lived through its long centuries of persecution in this sort of ambiguity. Obligatory thoughts in waiting! But here is the interdict: Do not conceive of Abraham in terms of Abram! Do not constitute the future from traces of memory, mistrusting new things and even the miracle required for universal peace.

Henceforth, to say Sarai to Sarah – does it violate an interdict? [Answer] There [*Genesis 17:15*], it was to Abraham that the Holy One, Blessed be His name, said: 'Sarai thy wife, thou shalt not call her name Sarai; but Sarah shall be her name.'

Is this a new interdiction? A related side issue? Or, on the contrary, an essential problem for 'a time that overflows memories?' Will the woman's condition for ever remain inseparable from the possessive that contains – or deforms – the second syllable of a word meaning, in the case of Abraham's wife, the sovereignty of a princess?[4] The sovereignty of a princess or of a human person! But also the sovereignty of a woman, who, in a masculine world, always runs the risk of being taken as a thing to be owned. The dramatic ambiguity of the feminine, which has won her only the folklore supremacy of the woman celebrated in a song, but already owned; sung, but a plaything – incapable of validation as humanity rising above the local setting to be a princess for all humanity. The dramatic ambiguity of the feminine that vanishes in the world of Abraham exceeding the past. Henceforth, dignity of the person that has regained her fullness and accedes to the highest vocations of the human. This ontological correction is announced by God precisely to the husband. Abraham will soon hear (*Genesis 21:12*): 'And in all that Sarah says to you, obey her voice.' In prophecy itself, a possible subordination of the male inspiration to the female.

Absolute names, absolute language, absolute vocations and the imposition of forgetting – all that is necessary for the awakening of Israel in Jacob.

But what of he who continues to call Jacob Jacob? [Answer] Here there is a difference! The Scripture itself returns to [this name of]

Jacob [*Genesis 46:2*]: 'And God spoke unto Israel in a vision during the night and He said: ''Jacob, Jacob.'' '

An awakening to Israel in Jacob, to be sure. But how many awakenings are but insomnia! 'Visions of the night,' nocturnal truths in which God speaks to Israel, but calls him Jacob, as formerly. It is the insurmountable intimacy of the exile that still continues, and in which the language of accomplishment reverts to that of pure promise. It is memory surviving forgetfulness. A tired man, opposing the violence and lies of the earth, having had many misfortunes, continues the struggle. The greatness of Israel is still in Jacob! God calls and encourages him in *Genesis 46:2*, at the precise moment when Israel is going to find his son Joseph in Egypt at the height of his princely glory, but also at the moment when, leaving the Holy Land, Jacob leads the children of Israel toward slavery in Egypt. Henceforth the promise made to the Patriarchs will be kept only as a hope of the exiled. The exiled, of whom the Eternal, as during Jacob's sojourn with Laban, will only 'know' the 'humiliation' and 'work of the hands' (*Genesis 31:42*).

One last difficulty! Does not Scripture itself commit a transgression? Does it not, in *Nehemiah 9:7*, refer to Abraham as Abram?

Rabbi Yossi ben Abin, and, according to others, Rabbi Yossi ben Zevida, objected. '[Do we not find] ''It is You, Eternal God, who chose Abram'' [*Nehemiah 9:7*]?' He was answered: 'Here [it is different]: the prophet is enumerating what constitutes the glory of the Merciful One. He begins by [telling] what was at the beginning.'

Is Scripture, then, only a historical work concerned with seeing that the rights of a certain past are respected? Is it not Holy History, telling, in the election of Abraham, of the miracle of temporality – or of temporality as miracle – and showing the greatness (by recalling an inglorious beginning) of the marvels of lovingkindness, that is, of the Spirit?

In the Talmudic page we have just examined I have been especially sensitive to a Judaism that overflows memory, that attempts to conceive of it beyond the Exodus, and senses an unforeseeable future ('no eye has seen it'), but also a future opening up through a new mode of trial, new dimensions of suffering.

Of that future of Judaism our page traces only the formal traits. In Israel's destiny, human universality transpires and is being accomplished!

Abraham, the father of many nations (after the passage through a night, a war dubbed of Gog and Magog, but in which the *ahavat Israel,* the love for Israel, may be the original tenderness for the other, the compassion and mercy in which lovingkindness arises), must have been stirred in the suffering in which the last hopes stand out against a world of promises belied. That is doubtless their very mode of appearance, and the last chance for merit that is unaware of itself. What a paradox Holy History is – in which the announcement to Abraham implies the certainty of the cruelty of the Pharaohs. An eschatology through the Passion of Israel among the nations. Passion of Humanity bleeding through the wounds of Israel.

4 Vasily Grossman

That war of Gog and Magog may have already begun in this [the twentieth] century of *Shoah.* Do the first great books of our time not testify to it?

I would like in closing, almost by way of conclusion, to bring to bear the remarkable novel by Vasily Grossman, *Life and Fate.* It seems to me of prime importance.

Grossman, who died in 1964, was an assimilated Russian Jew, to whom Pushkin or even Nekrasov were, since childhood, necessary for the inner life – as they had already been to his mother. This Soviet writer certainly believed, in October of 1917, that he had entered into the times of eschatological events, so to speak. His work prior to *Life and Fate* expressed that hope and that faith with talent and sincerity.

In *Life and Fate,* which is about the defense and victory of Stalingrad, Grossman expressed ample homage to the glory of the Red Army and the Russian people, and recognized the truth of that glory in its abnegation and sacrifice. But *Life and Fate* did not appear in Russia. The manuscript was seized and all its copies, including the typewriter carbons, were confiscated. By some miracle the text found its way to the West and was published. In its writing, at once cold and inspired, the Stalinian reality, in all its horror, was blended with the Hitlerian horror. Its style, wedded to its essence, attests a world that is no longer a place. An uninhabitable world in the abyss of its dehumanization. The breakdown of the very basis of European civilization. An uninhabitable world of people who have been degraded, stricken in their dignity, delivered to humiliation, suffering, death. A dehumanized humanity, surrounding institutions that were nonetheless the outgrowth of an initial revolutionary generosity and concern for the rights of man – a humanity transformed into camps or, everywhere where that was not the case, menaced by camps in which the 'I' is no longer sure of its identity.

A humanity described by Grossman as surrounding the despotic central anti-Semitism of Hitler's Germany and its extensions – or reverberations or resurrection – in Stalin's Russia. Grossman's book, by its realism, can also pass for a masterpiece of reporting, recording all the forms of concentration – camp horror, and of life, still outside the barbed wire, but already damned at every level, every moment. A war of Gog and Magog too strong for memories, pictures, texts. Is the reality not there, unimaginable, preceding all prophecy, emerging from no story? Grossman does not quote any Hebrew verses. Do they still exist somewhere? Did this assimilated Jew ever read any?

But we must listen. From one end to the other of that inhuman apocalypse, from out of its depths, there can be heard the muffled stirrings of a persistent, invincible humanity. The 'I' of men, forced by suffering back into the shackles of the self, breaks forth, in its misery, into mercy. What I called *ahavat Israel* earlier rises, before hope, from the abyss of despair. Cannot despair of the human be reduced to – or raised to – Jewish consciousness? The possibility, in a senseless world, of a meaning that is insufficient, nonetheless, to ensure the establishment of a world. But invisible forces in that weakness can be heard in the night, related by Vasily Grossman through 800 pages that, though sustained by no verses, articulate in the ineffable the fable of a novel and develop a plot.

Through the inhuman, extraordinary promptings of mercy survive, from one human uniqueness to another, independently of, and as if in spite of, structures – political or ecclesiastic – in which they were always exhibited.

The long-standing Western confidence in rational practices being generated from political and religious institutions and meant to foster man's being a neighbor to the other – belief in the human institutions through which the *good* would succeed in *being* – is shaken. There is, in this book, a constant pessimism with respect to the possibility of saving man in this manner. Will the war of Gog and Magog, the twentieth century and its nuclear future or fear, deliver the final blow to the maturity or senescence of us moderns, formed by the promises of the philosophers of history, and of progress and Messianism? Or will we be consoled by the invincible but unarmed goodness of the just and the saints, a goodness claiming to be better than 'the memory of the Exodus'?

Would not such a form of wisdom be the equivalent – in the words of a character from *Life and Fate* who remains an unrepentant man of action – of the naivety of those who believe in the 'old saw about the goodness of little old ladies' and who want to 'douse the worldwide conflagration with a syringe'? Can mercy have any meaning if there does not remain – be it only secondarily – the firmness of justice, as was the wish of the prudent sages of our Gemara? Despite the prophecies announcing a prodigious future following the inhuman trials that would introduce it, these sages held firmly to the memory (even if only of secondary importance) of the Exodus, and hence to the 'strong hand' and 'outstretched arm' of which *Exodus* speaks.

Nevertheless, the sovereignty of that primordial goodness or mercy that evil cannot overcome (a goodness uncovered in the turmoil, the sign of a God still unheard-of but who, without promising anything, would seem to assume meaning beyond the theologies of a past shaken to the point of atheism) is perhaps the conclusion reached by *Life and Fate.*

But if so, it is not a conclusion that is formulated, in that work, by the author himself. It is not stated by any of the active protagonists of the novel. It is expressed in the extraordinary utterances of a marginal character named Ikonnikov, a 'feeble-minded person' who is also an inspired mind – one who in Russian is called a *yourodivyj*; the son of a priest, but without theologically orthodox faith. Perhaps the only character capable of expressing bold truths. Were these truths lying dormant in a forgotten corner of some letters or syllables of the Scripture – only to awaken as Word of God in the Jewish and non-Jewish suffering of the twentieth century, in a time without promise, time of a God without succor?

Here are a few excerpts from Ikonnikov's words and notes.

Don't make fun of me. . . . I did not come up to you to make jokes. Last year, on September 15, I saw twenty thousand Jews – women, children and old people – executed. On that day I understood that God would not have allowed such a thing. It seemed obvious to me that God did not exist. . . . When violence is carried out, calamity reigns and blood flows. I was there for the great suffering of the peasants (the anti-Kulak struggle) and yet the goal of the collectives was good. . . . I do not believe in the good, I believe in kindness. . . . Not even Herod shed blood in the name of evil; he shed it for his version of the good. Herod's good. A new power was born that was a threat to him: to his family, his friends and favorites, his kingdom, his army. Now, what it was was not an evil, but Christianity.

Humanity had never yet heard those words: 'Judge not, that ye be not judged, and with what measure ye mete, it shall be measured to you again. ... Love your enemies, do good to them that hate you. Bless them that curse you. Pray for those who curse you. As you would have others do unto you, do the same to them also, for that is the Law and the prophets. ...'

What did that doctrine of peace and love bring to humanity? The tortures of the Inquisition, the struggle against heresies in France, Italy and Germany, the war between Protestants and Catholics. ...

I have been able to see in action the implacable force of the idea of social good born in our country. I saw it again in 1937; I saw that in the name of an idea of good as humane as that of Christianity, people were exterminated. I saw entire villages starving; in Siberia I saw the children of deported peasants dying in the snow. ...

There exists, side by side with this so terrible greater good, human kindness in everyday life. It is the kindness of an old lady who gives a piece of bread to a convict along the roadside. It is the kindness of a soldier who holds his canteen out to a wounded enemy. The kindness of youth taking pity on old age, the kindness of a peasant who hides an old Jew in his barn. It is the kindness of those prison guards who risk their own freedom, smuggle the letters of prisoners out to wives and mothers. That private goodness of an individual for another individual is a goodness without witnesses, a little goodness without ideology. It could be called goodness without thought. The goodness of men outside the religious or social good. ...

That goodness has no discourse and no meaning. It is instinctive and blind. When Christianity gave form to it in the teachings of the Church Fathers, it became tarnished – the wheat became chaff. ... It is as simple as life. Even the teachings of Christ weakened its power! Its power resides in the silence of the heart of man. ...

The history of man is the struggle of evil trying to crush the tiny seed of humanity. But if even now the human has not been killed in man, evil will never prevail.[5]

5

The Nations and the Presence of Israel[1]
From the tractate *Pesahim, 118b*

Rav Kahana said: 'When Rabbi Ishmael, the son of Rabbi Yosé, fell ill, Rabbi sent word to him, asking: "Tell us two or three [more] things that you had told us in the name of your father." He sent back to him in response: "Here is what my father said: What is the meaning of 'Praise the Eternal, you, all the peoples ... [for His mercy has been great toward us' [Psalm 117:1–2]? 'The peoples of the universe, what do they have to do with it?' Here is what the text means: 'Praise the Eternal, you, all the peoples, for the wonders He has shown in their [your] presence.' How much more so we ourselves, 'since it is toward us that his mercy has been great.' " ' '

He also told him another thing: 'Egypt will bring a gift to the Messiah in the future. He thought he should not accept it, coming from them, but the Holy One, Blessed be He, will say to the Messiah: "Accept it from them; [after all] they took in our children in Egypt." Whereupon "important persons will arrive from Egypt" [Psalm 68:32]. Cush [Ethiopia] applied an a fortiori reasoning to its own case: For them who had reduced them to slavery, it is thus [and their gift was accepted]; I who have not reduced them to slavery, even more so. The Holy One, Blessed be He, therefore said [to the Messiah]: "Accept it from them." Whereupon "Ethiopia will hasten to stretch out its hands to God." ' '

The criminal Roman Empire [in turn] applied an a fortiori reasoning to its own case: 'If for them who are not their brothers it is thus, we who are their brothers, even more so.' The Holy One, Blessed be He, then said to the angel Gabriel: 'Rage against the wild beast of the reeds [community of the brave ones]' [Psalm 68:31] [which may be read as follows]: 'Rage against and repel the wild beast, and keep for your own possession the community [of Israel].' Another interpretation: 'Repel the wild beast of the reeds, who lives among the reeds [in the forest] since it is written: ''The boar of the forest devours it and the beasts of the field feed upon it'' ' [Psalm 80:14]. *Rabbi Hiyya, the son of Abba, said in the name of Rabbi Johanan: 'Repel the wild beast, all of whose acts are written with only one pen.'*

'Community of the brave ones with the calves of the peoples,' they slaughtered the brave like calves without masters. 'She opens her hand for freewill gifts of silver': they reach out their hands to receive [bonuses] of silver, but they do not use it in keeping with the desires of those who gave it. 'He has scattered the peoples who delight in battles.' What caused Israel to be scattered among the peoples of the earth? It is the reconciliation he wanted to bring about with them.

Rabbi Ishmael sent Rabbi yet another teaching [that he had received from his father]: 'There are three hundred and sixty-five streets [or large squares] in the great city of Rome; in each one there are three hundred and sixty-five towers [silos]; in each tower, there are three hundred and sixty-five storeys; and in each storey there is enough to feed the whole world.' Rabbi Shimon, the son of Rabbi, asked Rabbi (others say it was Rabbi Ishmael, the son of Rabbi Yosé, who asked Rabbi): 'For whom is all that?' – 'For you and your fellows and acquaintances, as it is said: ''The product of her trade and her ill-gotten profit will eventually be consecrated to the Eternal; they will not be treasured or laid up, for it will be for them that are seated in the presence of the Eternal'' [Isaiah 23:18]'. . . . [2]

1 The Choice of the Text

To excerpt from a Talmudic treatise (from a Gemara that comments on or develops a Mishnah) a passage that lends itself to a study on the problems addressed in these meetings or colloquia is a hazardous enterprise. The very idea of excerpting from the Talmud is a difficult one. The limits of the excerpt always remain uncertain. It is uncertain whether the different sequences of each treatise, apparently connected to one another in many cases by the accidents of compilation, may not have a deeper coherence not visible at first. It is not impossible that some other passage, taken for the beginning of a development, may only be the consequence or continuation of an argumentation invisibly preceding it in the logic of the given page as a whole. To a more vigorous dialectic than that of even the well-informed reader – always a possibility in this lofty science – the premisses and conclusions of a sequence of reasoning may not be where the unprepared, unguided look expects or looks for them.

I cannot remedy that situation this evening. At least I will inform you, as I attempt to isolate my excerpt and study it, of the treatise from which I have taken it, the chapter to which it belongs and the Mishnah that precedes the Gemara in which it occurs. My theme – our theme today, still current: Israel and the nations – is a theme that turns up throughout the texts of Jewish thought. I sought it in the treatise *Pesahim*, devoted to the ritual and laws related to Passover, which the great Rabbi Salzer of Marseille has admirably translated into French and provided with commentaries. I have directed my inquiry to chapter 10, in which the Mishnah of page 117b specifies the rites of the third and the fourth cup during the *Seder* ceremony. The second sentence of the *Mishnah* states: 'fourth cup – over which he (he who is giving the *Seder*) will finish what remains to be said of the *Hallel*, ending with the Benediction of song.' *Hallel*, songs of praise, the Blessing of song, notions that are discussed or worked out in the Gemara that follows that *Mishnah* and constitutes the context of the sequence from which we have chosen the passage for study here. It begins precisely with the song of the nations glorifying or praising the God of Israel. I have determined the beginning and end of the excerpt to be commented upon with full consciousness of the arbitrariness involved in such editing, as I said in my opening words of excuse. Our excerpt goes from the end of 118b to the beginning of 119b of the treatise *Pesahim*, pages 369–72 of the translation by the great Rabbi Salzer.

2 The Oral Torah and its Transmission

Rav Kahana said: 'When Rabbi Ishmael, the son of Rabbi Yosé, fell ill, Rabbi sent word to him, asking: "Tell us two or three [more] things that you had told us in the name of your father."'

The teaching given in our excerpt is presented in a form that often characterizes the transmission of rabbinic wisdom revivifying or renewing the terms of Scripture, seeking the unsaid hidden within the said. An ambitious task: our text seems to insist on wisdom's way of passing from generation to generation like a family heritage, the testimony of a type of reflection that remains personal in a setting in which the father-son relationship seems secondary to that of master-student. Yet it is a teaching that, despite the intimacy, belongs fully to the public order. Rabbi is anxious to question the dying Rabbi Ishmael, in order to confirm or clarify the teaching that Rabbi Yosé, Rabbi Ishmael's father, had left to his son – as if the concern not to lose the whole truth, the fear that Rabbi Ishmael might take it with him to the grave, were as important as questions of health that might be asked in the home of the sick Rabbi Ishmael. Thus there are four names connected with the statement of a teaching from the outset: the deceased Rabbi Yosé, the dying Rabbi Ishmael, Rabbi, who asks questions of the dying man about that wisdom, and Rav Kahana, who is already teaching it.

Who are these doctors? Without losing ourselves in the 'chronology of rabbinic doctors,' and without attaching as much importance to it as does a certain group of young Parisian Jews,[3] it is interesting to note that Rabbi Ishmael is not the same one as the famous Rabbi Ishmael who is best known for having given a fixed form to the logical figures for the interpretation of the Torah. Our Rabbi Ishmael belongs to the rabbis of the transitional period, going from the *Tannaim* to the *Amoraim*. But Rabbi Yosé, his father, was still among the students of Rabbi Akiva – which is a very elevated title.

3 The Problem and the Plan of the Talmudic Excerpt

He sent back to him in response: 'Here is what my father said: What is the meaning of: "Praise the Eternal, you, all the peoples … [for His mercy has been great toward us" [*Psalm 117:1–2*]? "The peoples of the universe, what do they have to do with it?" Here is what the text means: "Praise the Eternal, you, all the peoples, for the wonders He has shown in their [your] presence." How much more so we ourselves, "since it is toward us that his mercy has been great." '

The messenger who was sent to get from the mouth of Rabbi Ishmael the last thoughts of his father, Rabbi Yosé, returns with the latter's thoughts concerning *Psalm 117*. The two verses that constitute this psalm raise, one might say, a problem. The first verse calls upon the nations to glorify the Lord; the second explains that call for praise by the kindness God had shown toward Israel, but not at all, as would seem natural, by any divine grace toward these nations themselves. Rabbi Yosé resolves the difficulty. According to him, *Psalm 117* is an *a fortiori* argument. If the nations praise the Eternal for a grace not directed toward themselves, Israel, the beneficiary of His favor, should all the more glorify the Lord our God. *Psalm 117* is, on this view, a way of admonishing Israel: a sermon.

A wisdom surely extending beyond the sermon. It teaches us a wonder of the human heart: the nations, praising God for a kindness He showed toward Israel through Holy History, are able to experience their condition as simple witnesses of that kindness, and to testify to it by songs of gratitude. By songs of gratitude, but also no doubt by a liturgy of good works and lofty, generous historic acts. And what could be the meaning of this increased praise that Rabbi Yosé makes incumbent upon Israel? Where is the devotion of this extra faithfulness? This is a teaching of important problems. They involve the very relation of humanity to the election of Israel, and the meaning of that election, and the significance of Israel in the spirituality of the Human.

Rabbi Ishmael is said to have revealed to Rabbi two other things taught by his father. First, the future fate of the nations at the time of the Messiah awaited by Israel and the constitution of a new humanity surrounding it: Egypt, Cush (or Ethiopia), Rome. The prototype of nations and nationalism. All the nations will want their share in the Messianic world. Perhaps we will learn, in this second message of Rabbi Yosé's, in which the histories of the nations are judged, the significance and meaning of the allegiance to the Lord beyond the glory of praises and song.

The third thing transmitted by Rabbi Ishmael also takes us back to Rome. Rome appears in the guise of a monstrous city of countless skyscrapers, the rabbinic doctors' futuristic nightmare of the Western world in its twentieth-century American realization. A city heaped with riches, a tiny fraction of which would suffice to feed the entire world. The accumulation of useless wealth. Nothing circulates, nothing is distributed. A magnificent science is concretized or suffocates in a technology of matter metamorphosed into walls. A city without men – 'For whom is all that?' An evil spell to be broken. By those who have never slept. By those who are sitting – always sitting – in the house of study – which is *yeshiva*[4] – before a Book in which all things are ceaselessly renewed. Faithfulness most faithful!

4 The Nations and the Days of the Messiah

He also told him another thing: 'Egypt will bring a gift to the Messiah in the future. He thought he should not accept it, coming from them, but the Holy One, Blessed be He, will say to the Messiah: "Accept it from them; [after all] they took in our children in Egypt." Whereupon "important persons will arrive from Egypt" ' [*Psalm 68:32*].

This is the second teaching of Rabbi Yosé, transmitted to his son, Rabbi Ishmael, and communicated by the latter to Rabbi and proclaimed by Rav Kahana: The nations are determined to take part in the Messianic age! It is a recognition of the ultimate value of the human message borne by Judaism, a recognition reflected in or called for by the verses of *Psalm 117*. Has not the history of the nations already been in a sense that glorification of the Eternal in Israel, a participation in the history of Israel, which can be assessed by the degree to which their national solidarity is open to the other, the stranger? A recognition of the Torah before Sinai? The entire examination of this problem is tacitly related to a verse not quoted: *Deuteronomy 23:8*. 'Thou shalt not abhor an Edomite, for he is thy brother; thou shalt not abhor an Egyptian, because thou wast a stranger in his land.' Fraternity (but what does it mean? Is it not, according to the Bible, a synonym of humanity?) and hospitality: are these not stronger than the horror a man may feel for the other who denies him in his alterity? Do they not already bring back a memory of the 'Word of God'?

The Talmud will not enumerate all the nations – not even all those that appear in the Scriptures – and decide on their possible association with the Messianic universe. The three nations or states or societies mentioned – Egypt, Cush and Rome – represent a typology of national life, in which, through the forms of existence that are pure history, there can be seen the inhuman or the human. An allergy to or an aptitude for truth, without pretending to the title of bearer or messenger of the Torah.

Egypt is mentioned first. Egypt – an essential point for universal history, but the very crux of Holy History. The Exodus is the liberation *par excellence* leading to Sinai before the Promised Land. It is the country of servitude, but also the place where Abraham and Jacob found refuge in time of famine; where Joseph was able to assume universal political and economic responsibilities at the very core of Holy History; and where, at the hour of exterminating cruelty, Pharaoh's daughter saved Moses from the waters. ...

The Messiah, to whom Egypt, or the 'Egyptian,' presents a gift, cannot forget that servitude and wants to reject the sign of allegiance offered to him. But God requires him to accept the gift, reminding him of the shelter offered Israel by the country of Egypt. Shelter that will become a place of slavery – but first a place offered to the stranger. Already a song of glory to the God of Israel! Verse 32 of *Psalm* 68 is alluded to in our Gemara. 'And then the *hashmanim* – the remarkable people – will arrive from Egypt.' This is from *Psalm 68*, which, like *Psalm 117*, invites the nations to song. 'Sing unto God, ye kingdoms of the earth; O sing praises unto the Lord' (*Psalm 68:33*).

A decision by the Eternal to accept Egypt's homage. The Bible renders that foreseeable in *Deuteronomy 23:8*, a verse the Messiah himself, despite his justice, must have forgotten. One belongs to the Messianic order when one has been able to admit others among one's own. That a people should accept those who come and settle among them – even though they are foreigners with their way of speaking, their smell – that a people should give them an *akhsaniah*,[5] such as a place at the inn, and the wherewithal to breathe and to live – is a song to the glory of the God of Israel. Simple tolerance? God alone knows how much love that tolerance demands. It is impressive and beautiful that, in the relations between Israel and the nations, this should count for so much in Jewish thought.

To shelter the other in one's own land or home, to tolerate the presence of the landless and homeless on the 'ancestral soil,' so jealously, so meanly loved – is that the criterion of humanness? Unquestionably so. And despite the slavery forced upon these strangers, is it still a homage to the Most High of Israel and the right to a share in the Messianic world? The Messiah obeys the order of the Lord. He accepts the gift from Egypt. But on his own, he was going to refuse! No peace without superhuman pardon!

> Cush [Ethiopia] applied an *a fortiori* reasoning to its own case: For them who had reduced them to slavery, it is thus [and their gift was accepted]; I who have not reduced them to slavery, even more so. The Holy One, Blessed be He, therefore said [to the Messiah]: 'Accept it from them.' Whereupon 'Ethiopia will hasten to stretch out its hands to God' (*Psalm 68:33*).

The acceptance of Egypt despite the slavery it had imposed upon the children of Israel – and doubtless the acceptance of all the nations similar to Egypt – produces a strong impression on Cush and all the nations or states resembling it. A country of black men with nothing to reproach itself for, nor anything to congratulate itself for. According to the Bible, at least, it is never the theater of important events. A purely geographical reference. Reference, for example, to the empire of Ahasuerus – 127 units or provinces, says the Book of Esther, reaching 'from Hodu[6] to Cush.' In Holy history as well as in universal history – without an active role, a bit marginal. Neither friendly nor hostile to the message of Israel. A third or a fourth of mankind – is not its very silence and neutrality a natural goodwill of 'the noble savage?' But then also perhaps praise for the Eternal of Israel? Given the success of Egypt, who had enslaved Israel, Cush, whose hands remained clean, is welcomed under the auspices of an *a fortiori* argument in which the peoples who do not have a complicated history are assigned with ease, within the corruption of the civilizations, a philosophy of history. This success is attested by *Psalm 68:32*: 'Cush shall hasten to stretch out her hands unto God.' Cush, and doubtless countries similar to it! Are they not called upon to praise the God of Israel? Read *Psalm 68:33*: 'Kingdoms of the earth, praise God, sing before the Eternal.'

> The criminal Roman Empire [in turn] applied an *a fortiori* reasoning to its own case: 'If for them who are not their brothers it is thus, we who are their brothers, even more so.'

The third nation to be named, Rome. The third order or political category, or the third possible destiny of the human. A criminal empire. Rome, destroyer of Israel, burner of the Temple; Rome the villain, both here and on page 10a of the Talmudic treatise *Yoma. Romi harshaah*.[7] But also the Rome of universal history – violent, warlike, imperialistic. Now here she is, wanting to associate herself with the Messianic order, and justifying her ambition by an *a fortiori* reasoning. Powerful and unjust, yet claiming brotherhood with Israel. Is she making an implicit appeal to *Deuteronomy 23:8*? 'Thou shalt not abhor an Edomite, for he is thy brother; thou shalt not abhor an Egyptian, because thou wast a stranger in his land.' Chapter 36 of *Genesis* abundantly relates the relationship between Esau and Edom, and it so happens that history tells us of close ties between the country of Edom, south of Judea, and the Roman Empire. Whence the strange and ambiguous identification of Rome with Esau and the brotherhood of Israel and Rome. Perhaps Isaac and Abraham, the father and the grandfather, did not entirely fail in the paternity of Esau? Brotherhood or antagonism of warring brothers, feared and condemned in the Bible, beginning with Cain and Abel in this pure bond of blood always about to end in bloodshed, but that can – from unique to unique – reveal itself as love ordered by the word of the Most High. Antagonism or ambiguity? Israel cannot forget the verse *Deuteronomy 23:8*. The West is Israel's brother. We must, at least, recall the ambiguity of *Shabbat 39b*, and of *Avodah Zarah 2b*. We must be sensitive to the text of *Bereshit Rabbah 9:13*, perhaps less ambiguous. There verse 31 of *Genesis*, chapter 1 ('And God saw everything that He had made, and, behold, it was very good') is commented on. What does this 'very good' mean, the rabbinic doctors wonder. They decide it means Rome. Rome, *very good*? Is it possible? But she, at least, of all the creatures, requires obedience to a law and acts with justice. The page we are now in the process of analyzing will give us an impressive picture of Rome. The distant West, a future America. Enough to feed mankind from all quarters!

Did Rome fully grasp the word of the Lord, consecrating fraternal bonds of love between beings? Is her share in the Messiah's world not compromised by the inhuman tenor of ethics and politics in actual everyday Roman life? The merely formal brotherhood Rome is in a position to invoke annuls, in the arguments it produces, the very force of its *a fortiori*. It is as a 'wild beast' that Rome is, in our text, delivered to the angel of chastisement set against her by the Holy One, Blessed be He. The bestiality, the savagery, of the wild beast are immediately evident in Rome's crimes. Can it still be hoped that the lion will lie down with the lamb? Whence the exclamation of verse 31 of *Psalm 68*: 'Rage against the wild beast of the reeds.' This cry is addressed to the angel Gabriel called upon to rage in this verse, which is sandwiched in between the image of kings bearing their offerings to Jerusalem, the chosen ones of Egypt going up from their country, and the impatient hands of Cush raised to God. A verse of refusal, between two of chanted affirmation.

> The Holy One, Blessed be He, then said to the angel Gabriel: 'Rage against the wild beast of the reeds.'

A condemnation of Rome, of a certain Rome, a certain political and ethical model. The verse of *Psalm 68:31* is longer than this first sentence, and its meaning – even its literal meaning – is complex and difficult to translate with precision.

The text of the Talmud that begins with that sentence is apparently at once the addressing of the angel ordered to rage against Rome and the interpretation of various elements of that address made up of expressions borrowed from *Psalm 68:31*, but also using verse 14 of *Psalm 80*. It is an interpretation, but one that intervenes already at the level of the literal reading itself. Here we see the freedom and boldness typical of *midrash,* discovering within Hebrew words surprising roots and affinities, hence new resonances, new dimensions of meaning, punctuating the statements, accentuating the words in function of truths intuited in an inspired text – more demanding than the syntax and vocabulary. That addressing of the angel becomes a characteristic Talmudic piece, drawing upon a hermeneutics in which Rome – or the fraternal West – appears in a guise that excludes it from the triumph of the Messianic peace. It is a Talmudic text whose odd nature is further emphasized by the French language. The verse it interprets doesn't even appear as a unified proposition: its diverse articulations are dispersed in the commentary. It seems to me helpful to group these scattered pieces beforehand. Here is this verse of *Psalm 68:31* in the translation of the great Rabbi Salzer: 'Rage against the wild beast of the reeds, community of the brave ones, with the calves of the peoples – she opens her hand for freewill gifts of silver. He has scattered the peoples who delight in battles.'[8] We shall see that this translation is a bit different from that of the French rabbinate, published under the direction of the great Rabbi Zadoc Kahn, which is probably neither more nor less accurate than the one I have chosen to follow: 'Scold the beast crouching in the bulrushes, the herd of powerful bulls mixed in with the steers of the nations who come to humble themselves, bearing silver ingots. [God] scatters the peoples who love battles.'[9] [Still four parts to be distinguished in the text, without any obvious connection between them.] The difference in the translations attests to the obscurity of certain parts of this verse, especially in the next to last part, concerning silver, rendered in the Catholic translation of the famous 'Jerusalem' Bible (of well-established historical and philological soundness) as 'that she humble herself, bringing gold and silver.' She: 'the beast of the reeds' or the 'band of brave ones?' Who knows?

> ['Community of the brave ones'] [*Psalm 68:31*] [which may be read as follows]: 'Rage against and repel the wild beast, and keep for your own possession the community [of Israel].' Another interpretation: 'Repel the wild beast of the reeds, who lives among the reeds [in the forest] since it is written: ''The boar of the forest devours it and the beasts of the field feed upon it'' [*Psalm 80:14*].' Rabbi Hiyya, the son of Abba, said in the name of Rabbi Johanan: 'Repel the wild beast, all of whose acts are written with only one pen.'

'Community of the brave ones with the calves of the peoples,' they slaughtered the brave like calves without masters. 'She opens her hand for freewill gifts of silver': they reach out their hands to receive [bonuses] of silver, but they do not use it in keeping with the desires of those who gave it. 'He has scattered the peoples who delight in battles.' What caused Israel to be scattered among the peoples of the earth? It is the reconciliation he wanted to bring about with them.

Psalm 68:31 – the literal interpretation of which verse is not easy – is, in its direct meaning, or in what the rabbis call the *pschat,* subjacent to this Talmudic text. It is thus a verse that is suitable and sufficient to express criticism of Roman (or other) violence, and anger toward Rome and its civilization ('Rage against at the wild beast,' etc.) and to exclude them from the Messianic universe to which they claim a right. Violence whether it be of Rome or another: this verse only concerns Rome (the name does not occur in the Old Testament) because of the 'great anger' it expresses. But what matters for our own study is the opinion of the rabbinic doctors on the refusal – or acceptance – of Rome by Judaism according to its most authentic thought, and the way in which, through *midrash,* that thought seeks an emphatic mode, as it were, of that *pschat,* the concrete terms of which are transfigured and transcended in essential metaphors – while losing neither their original meaning nor their original significance[10] – in view of an absolute meaning of the whole.

The verse already attempts through imagery to express its direct meaning, portraying the savagery of the beast that a humanity deserving the anger of chastisement would resemble. Possibly depraved by its very nature; a humanity implanted in the soil, and that (can one ever be sure?), through the landscapes of field and forest and through the arts that celebrate them, has a taste for the strong savor of the native soil, like a 'beast crouching in the bulrushes,' as in the rabbinic translation of the verse, differing from the one I have adopted, but that I quoted. Peoples thus taking part in all the merciless necessities of the 'struggle for life.' This is the direct thought of verse 31 of *Psalm 68,* which then proceeds immediately to another image, comparing the human deserving of that angelic ire to a herd, or to powerful animals – 'bulls' according to the translation of the French rabbinate, 'brave ones' according to that of the great Rabbi Salzer – bulls or brave ones mixed in with weaker or more common bovines – a situation suggesting the idea of violence. To this the third part of the verse adds the idea of financial abuses – the rich humiliating the poor. The verse ends with a prayer asking for the dispersion of a collectivity destined to violence by the kind of society it is and fond of war. This links war to an internal societal disorder – a thought perhaps already less simplistic than anti-militarism without sociology. In all this the reader should see the impressions of a first reading of a difficult verse to decipher, but impressions of an entire unsettling aspect of our Western world, its so often bloody history, with its cult of heroism and military nobility, its nationalistic exclusionism, its racial, social and economic injustice. Nothing of its science, logic, technological potential – which is, however, in my opinion, at issue in Rabbi Yosé's third teaching, handed down by his son Rabbi Ishmael to Rabbi, and taught by Rav Kahana. The impression of a first deciphering of verse 31 of *Psalm 68*, to be sure. But are we not already under the influence of its *midrashic* meaning sought by our Gemara, and which will be more specific? The translation of the Talmudic text that follows and is inspired by verse 31 of *Psalm 68* – a verse that is quoted in fragments in the course of the interpretation itself – is also rather difficult. The Talmudic text transposes and tends to think further the inspired words of the Psalmist: 'Rage against' or 'Repel' or 'Scold.' Can Gabriel, the angel of God, whose name means precisely strength and courage – but as attributes of the Most High – strike without loving, destroy without building? Therefore we must, according to the rabbinic doctors, read the 'Rage against' or the 'Repel,' in inserting into the biblical text a 'And keep for thyself as a possession the community of Israel.' The struggle against Rome is the preservation of Israel, the chance of a regenerate humanity!

Does the biblical text authorize, does it tolerate this interpolation? But it is as if the words of the verse signified for the *midrash* both through their usual or main meanings, which are confirmed by their insertion into the context, but also by their secondary or even occasional meanings – which they take on, for example, by their proximity, or association, elsewhere in the vast expanse of the Bible's pages, with another verse, and other circumstances. And this in spite of the syntactic structure that, in the verse we have been examining, orients the evocative word in its own direction. What the great Rabbi Salzer translates most appositely as 'community of the brave ones,' but the Bible of the rabbinate also has its reasons to render as 'herd of bulls,' is said in the Hebrew text in terms justifying both meanings. 'Community of the brave ones' may well call to mind the community of Israel, but do not these terms belong logically to the second part of verse 31 of *Psalm 68*? What does it matter? The *midrash* allows one to think it – to feel its proximity – from the first part of the verse. The *midrash* also reads, in the consonants of the Hebrew word *qaneh,* meaning cane or reed – and without considering the vowels – the imperative of the verb 'to acquire.' It thus obtains: 'Acquire' or 'Keep for your own possession the community of Israel.' This proposition, grasped in its echoes, so to speak, is nonetheless essential to the spiritual meaning of that struggle of the angel with Rome! The commentary that Rashi adds in the margin of this 'Keep for yourself as a possession the community of Israel' of our Talmudic selection underscores this concern to express the positive reason for that struggle against Rome and the elevation of that reason. Rashi reminds us that there is a rabbinic tradition that under-stands Egypt and Cush as being included in the 'community of Israel,' already saved in this battle of the angel Gabriel, and admitted into the Messianic order. It is the entire new humanity of redemption that is protected by the anger directed toward the wild beast of Rome.

This is a remarkable freedom of interpretation, a freedom of the spirit that is willfully misunderstood when called 'prisoner to the letter.' It is as if the reverberation of each term from Scripture, the resonance of the divine word gathered up in these twenty-two signs of the holy Jewish language, were progressively more completely and better understood as the reading continued – with its repetitions – keeping the soul awake and lending itself, through the entire length of these venerable pages, to parallels and minute distinctions in order to form, as in musical chords, the discourse of a kind of thought testing itself by reason.

But the Hebrew word *qaneh,* where we just read 'Acquire' or 'Keep for your own possession,' is read by Rabbi Johanan, in keeping with a tradition handed down by Hiyya ben Abba, as *qalam,* meaning 'pen,' in the singular, and hence as the future rise of a whole literature written by a single pen – a whole literature that is essentially tendentious and thus anti-Jewish, but doubtless also beyond anti-Semitism – and spread by the same microbe, the poisoned press of totalitarian regimes, the temptation of the Occident. And then, after this, there is the return to the usual meaning of *qaneh,* the *qaneh* properly so called – reed or cane – and hence its reading as an allusion to the *forest,* which authorizes the mention of *Psalm 80,* which speaks of a forest, but first of a vine 'plucked up out of Egypt' (*Psalm 80:9*), expelling the nations, a vine that 'took deep root' (verse 10), 'equaling the cedars of God' (verse 11), surrounded by fences which, once broken down, leave the vine open to the forest, where 'the boar of the wood doth ravage it' and 'it serves as a pasture to that which moveth in the fields.' The wild beast of the reeds is identified with the boar, or wild pig. The metaphor is perhaps not arbitrary. Elsewhere the Talmud insists on the symbolic nature of the pig, whose flesh is forbidden as food, but who, though he does not chew the cud, yet has a cloven hoof. The appearance of *kashrut,* of purity! He is thus capable of a show of acceptability. The respectable veneer of evil, hypocrisy of evil – the good intentions of our bloodstained annals! Other commentators identify it with the beast of *Daniel 7:7* 'with powerful teeth of iron, devouring and grinding,' who ruthlessly 'stamped the residue with its feet.' Rome as the apocalyptic beast of the vision of Daniel!

What can I say of the mysterious or enigmatic or simply obscure images or metaphors of the third part of verse 31 of *Psalm 68*? 'To open one's hands for freewill gifts of silver' or 'the powerful bulls' who come 'to humble themselves, bearing silver ingots?' Do they represent the solicitation of silver or the exaction of sums of money from private citizens – the prey to representatives of Roman power – in exchange for promises not kept? Do they denounce the very structure of the abusive state, the political order of Rome in ethical disorder or arbitrariness?

Another very impressive feature is the *midrashic* variant brought to bear on the literal meaning of the last part of our verse, announcing, requiring or beseeching the dispersion of the state founded on war, or denouncing – this would already be a Messianic criticism – the false appearance of a social equilibrium established through warfare. Does the *midrashic* variant teach that, beyond the cruelty of combat, there is good reason to fear rapprochements 'at any cost,' pure assimilation? Facile virtue of the West, hypocritical pretext of the colonizers? It can also be the cause of dispersion and deportation. The words 'battle' and 'proximity' are written with the same consonants![11] The *pax romana* is not yet peace. And the broken fences of *Psalm 80:13*, which let the boar into 'the vine of the Lord, plucked out of Egypt' – were they not to some extent the fences of certain forms of Jewish particularism?

It seems unnecessary to comment further on the second part of verse 31, *Psalm 68*. It is the prophetic vision, through the apparent grandeur of the Roman West, of the community of Israel reduced to a herd, in which the brave are delivered up to death – throats cut like calves without masters, reduced to anonymous flesh.

5 Toward a New Humanity

> Rabbi Ishmael sent Rabbi yet another teaching [that he had received from his father]: 'There are three hundred and sixty-five streets [or large squares] in the great city of Rome; in each one there are three hundred and sixty-five towers [silos]; in each tower, there are three hundred and sixty-five storeys; and in each storey there is enough to feed the whole world.'

This is the third teaching of Rabbi Yosé handed down by his son, Rabbi Ishmael, to Rabbi, and taught to all by Rav Kahana. It, too, involves Rome. The cruelty and voracity of the boar repelled by the angel Gabriel exhausts neither all the potential nor all the threat of the Graeco-Roman order that was to become modern humanity. The Graeco-Roman order – for I add Greece to Rome, encouraged by our text that in a moment, in citing the prophet Isaiah (*Isaiah 23:18*), will refer to a chapter that relates to Tyre, Phoenicia, and thus the whole area of the cradle of our fraternal Europe. Here, then, is Rome, with all its strange but indubitable and irresistible greatness of a colossus. Universal legality, though lacking in nuance and cumbersome, unloving, merciless, unpardoning. Still, we recognized it earlier as 'very good,' because better than the arbitrary. A stretch of vast areas brought together as an empire: all this is reflected in the imagery of those skyscraper walls, containing such great stores of food and wares on every storey. One storey would hold enough to feed the entire world! Rome suffocating beneath what humans need! Stone towers, ruled by numbers that echo one another – and no doubt by more mathematics than these numbers reveal. A petrified mathematics. In the bulk of those walls, a science blinded by the rules it has dictated. An economy of the wealth of pure accumulation. Things that have become useless, as if reverting to their raw materials. Things separated from man, things that have become things-in-themselves. Is it still – by science, technology and wealth – a hymn of praise that the peoples sing, praise measuring His goodness revealed to humanity through Israel? Or would these superhuman affairs not be rather as inhuman as the wild beast of the forest?

> Rabbi Shimon, the son of Rabbi, asked Rabbi (others say it was Rabbi Ishmael, the son of Rabbi Yosé, who asked Rabbi): 'For whom is all that?'

For whom is all that? For there is no longer anyone. There are no more men.

There is Rome, in its wealth and power, like a 'crisis of humanism'! Death, the end of man. The son of Rabbi asks Rabbi: For whom is all that? But was Rabbi himself able to give an answer? He must not have gotten any answer from Rabbi Yosé on this question, since Rabbi Ishmael, Yosé's son, appears to have asked Rabbi the same question.

Whatever the case may be, the answer comes to Rabbi from Isaiah, whom he quotes.

> For you and your fellows and acquaintances, as it is said: 'The product of her trade and her ill-gotten profit will eventually be consecrated to the Eternal; they will not be treasured nor laid up, for it will be for them that are seated in the presence of the Eternal' [*Isaiah 23:18*].

This is a response that does not opt in favor of the private self-satisfaction of any individual as opposed to a crisis-ridden humanity. A response in which the rays of Messianic light shine through the thought of the prophet Isaiah. They do not leave us in the dark; they do not neglect the abstract architecture of the numbers and concepts arising round about our Mediterranean nor the abundance of bread and ideas, indispensable and true, respectively, to this or that group, that it bears or brings. But those rays break the evil spell of *having* by which being insists on being. They offer a glimpse at a future suspension of the heaping up, the amassing, the accumulation by which, for being – in the advent of its being – it is ever and again a question of its own being. A forgetting, a failure to recognize the other! A piling up, amassing, unending totalization of the objects and money that mark the rhythm and essential structure of the perseverance of being in its being. Its concrete modes: stock-piling and banks. But also men at war. A suspect ontology!

That 'consecration of possessions to God' spoken of by Isaiah – circulation of goods, distribution and gifts – is the designation of the other adventure pursued by the peoples collectively: peace. Categories of the 'otherwise than being.' Consecration to God. To God, whose most glorious title, recalled in verse 6 of *Psalm 68*, so amply quoted in our Talmudic excerpt – but which appears throughout the Bible – is: 'Father of orphans and defender of widows.' Consecration to God: his epiphany, beyond all theology and any visible image however complete, is repeated in the daily Sinai of men sitting before an astonishing Book, ever again in progress because of its very completeness.

6
From Ethics to Exegesis[1]

The texts brought together in this volume are not based on any local particularism that would require explanation as they cross the linguistic border from French. True, they are all centered upon the age-old fact of Israel, with its Scriptures and their interpretations. But they do not belong to the literature of religious archaeology or the saga of a private or marginal history. These essays themselves lay sufficient stress upon the remarkable role that devolves upon the reality of Israel, in its very exception, as a formation and expression of the universal; but of the universal insofar as it unites persons without reducing them to an abstraction in which their singularity of unique beings is sacrificed to the genus; universality in which uniqueness has already been approached in love.

But my work, which is situated in the fullness of the documents, beliefs and moral practices that characterize the positive fact of Judaism – in its empirical and historical content, which is constantly enriched and renewed by the ongoing contributions of the religious experience, lived, yet unpredictable; bearing exegetic traits, but new – attempts to return to the structures or modalities of a *spiritual* that lends itself to, or consents to, or even tends toward, such treatment. These structures or modalities are hidden beneath consciousness, which is representative or conceptual, already invested in the world, and hence absorbed in it. They are hidden, but can be discerned by a phenomenology attentive to the horizons of consciousness, and in this sense (despite its use of biblical and Talmudic documents and formulations) it is a phenomenology prior to a theology that would use what it has borrowed as its premises.

The fact of Israel, its Scriptures and their interpretations (but also the tortuous line winding its way through history, traced by the Passion of Israel, by its permanence, in faithfulness to inspiration or to the prophetism of its Scriptures) constitute a *figure* in which a primordial mode of the human is revealed, in which, before any theology and outside any mythology, God comes to the mind. The challenge of an ontological reversal! The original perseverance of being in its being, of the individualism of being, the persistence or insistence of beings in the guise of individuals jealous for their *part,* this *part*icularism of the inert, substantivized into things, particularism of the enrooted vegetable being, of the wild animal fighting for its existence, and of the soul, the 'owner and interested party' Bossuet speaks of, this particularism exacerbated into egotism or into political 'totalities,' ready or readying themselves for war – is reversed into 'Thou shalt not kill,' into the care of one being for another being, into non-in-difference of *one* toward *the other*. Non-in-difference toward the other, the unique of its kind, as if toward the absolutely other, the other person. Alterity becomes proximity. Not distance, the shortest through space, but initial directness, which extends as unimpeachable approach in the call of the face of the other, in which there appears, as an order, an inscription, a prescription, an awakening (as if it were a 'me'), responsibility – mine, for the other human being. The face of the other, in its defenseless nakedness – is it not already (despite the countenance this bareness may put on) an asking? A beggar's asking, miserable mortal. But at the same time it is an authority summoning me to 'appear,' summoning me to respond. A mortal whose death 'regards me,' beyond my own. It is an original obligation to which I am, in guise of *me*, devoted and elected, I am ordered *me*. 'Thou shalt love thy neighbor as thyself,' or 'Thou shalt love thy neighbor, that is what thyself is.'

Non-in-difference to the other, approach to its otherness in the face of others; non-in-difference that, beneath the hatred it may turn into, was already a primordial love in the irrepressible attention of meeting. 'Thou shalt not kill' or 'Thou shalt love thy neighbor' not only forbids the violence of murder: it also concerns all the slow and invisible killing committed in our desires and vices, in all the innocent cruelties of natural life, in our indifference of 'good conscience' to what is far and what is near, even in the haughty obstinacy of our objectifying and our thematizing, in all the consecrated injustices due to our atomic weight of individuals and the equilibrium of our social orders. The entire Torah, in its minute descriptions, is concentrated in the 'Thou shalt not kill' that the face of the other signifies, and awaits its proclamation therein. The life of others, the *being* of others, falls to me as a duty. In the *thou* of this commandment, the *me* is only begun: it is for the other in its innermost nucleus. Rupture of being *qua* being. At the heart of the ultimate intimacy of the identification of the *me* with the *oneself*, there is the rupture of immanence: the Other passes before the Same. 'Please, after you, sir!'

Thou shalt not kill. Is this not, through the face of others, the very significance of the word of God, the unheard-of significance of the Transcendent that immediately concerns and awakens me? Revelation – circumstances or kenosis – in which the 'abstract' truth of monotheism is thought concretely, without the imagery of representation, the 'place' into which the Infinite descends from the 'heavenly heights' – from its absoluteness or from the mythology of its worlds behind the world – precisely the place in which 'It comes to mind.' There is a disproportion in the idea into which God has entered! And this produces a guilty conscience. But this is precisely how it happens that the subject does not rest with a clear conscience in adequation with being. This is an inadequation that lets an uneasy feeling filter through: the feeling of having infringed on someone else's territory in positing oneself.

Our awareness of this disproportion between the idea and its *ideatum* goes back to Descartes! But in this way there is an original authority. An origin of the imperative mood of verbs, in the Word of God. The hearing of that imperative would then already be obedience. Does not *Exodus 24:7* end with a 'We will do and we will hear,' a verse in which the Talmudic doctors make much of the *do* preceding the *hear?* Is it a freedom that abdicates, or an obedience in which goodness already makes its appearance: the *for-the-other* that already is born or awakened in the substance penetrated by an infinite verb, undoing the *conatus essendi*? But the Talmudic rabbis do not speak in these terms when they discern angelic tones in *Exodus 24:7*!

Does not prophetic inspiration, then, retain the secret of this intervention thanks to which God's Torah is expressed – according to the Talmudic doctors – in the *language of human beings*, while in that same Torah, within the obvious meaning of pure information, there is included a semantics that is absolute, inexhaustible, ever renewable through exegesis? Further, according to these same learned doctors, nothing is worse for a believer than to make a distinction, in the Pentateuch, between the 'Mosaic' and the 'divine': so strong is the principle according to which the prophetic intervention of Moses is the concreteness of the Revelation without mediation. But 'The Eternal has spoken, who would not prophesy,' as is suggested in *Amos 3:8*. Is not the prophetic gift latent in all inspiration, and is not inspiration the sublime ambiguity of human language? And is it not so that our 'national literature' – and even the folklore of 'savage minds' – by their *manners of speaking*, their *how*, their *art* (modalities of expression we are content to describe as quiddities: beauty or poetry), outmaneuver the scrupulous univocity of informational language, in recalling or intuiting the reverberation of some enigmatic verb yet to be spoken or translated: 'My Name is fearsome among the nations' (*Malachi 1:14*)?

It is an inspired verb, whose meaning takes even the speaker by surprise. A speaking that can already be *read* in the spoken word and that can be distinguished by a certain completed quality of the articulated verb, which is already a proverb, verse or versicle, quotation-like. Completion and authority, the disproportionate voice of a God addressing human beings in the prophetic or poetic tongue. This is an ascent within words, be they the most recent ones, to I know not what antiquity that is already to be translated, already to be deciphered. A dead language to be resuscitated, in order that its innumerable intentions may be reawakened! The latent birth of Scripture, of the book, of literature, and an appeal to interpretation, to exegesis, an appeal to the sages who solicit texts. A solicitation of solicitation – Revelation. An appeal to the Talmud and to the infinite renewal of the Word of God in commentary, and commentary on commentary. There is a prophetism and a Talmudism preceding theological considerations: its *a priori* (for it is doubtless also the very process of the coming of God to the mind) in the face of the other man.

Torah or divine teaching, but also prophetic word, making itself manifest in Judaism as the wisdom of the commentary of the masters in which it finds renewal, and in the justice of the laws that are always subject to the review of love, in which the uniqueness of none can be forgotten. A difficult universality: in the fraternity necessary for the 'logical extension' of a genre such as that of humankind. The notion of the human, henceforth, was conceived and interpreted as it had one day been interpreted in the Torah by the Westerner – the future Christian. Irreversibly, in the Torah, he recognized himself and chose himself, even though he has sometimes contested or detested the severity of the letter and the detail, and has not yet been able to face the end of mythologies.

The Inhuman watches and awaits its chance before these denials, hatreds or negligences – as before an imprudent pastime: it keeps coming back. That is the dramatic destiny of this time of the [twentieth] century's closing, a time that calls itself and likes to think of itself as a 'time of peace.' A time of quotidian presence, like an everlasting today: a synchrony of becoming called modernity, in which 'work' and 'vacation' alternate, despite the millions of unemployed. But it is the presence of the foreseeable and the hope invested in the programmable, in which being on the scale of reason is offered only to human satisfaction; temporality in which all is possible, and all the possible is permitted. But is it not also a time that is misunderstood, a time between the formidable shadows already projected by the very future of our glorious science in its triumphant and destructive technical mastery, on one hand, and on the other, a past that refuses to be forgotten? A past of world wars and the camps of the twentieth century: Concentration and Death. A past of the Passion of Israel under Adolf Hitler.

7
Judaism and Kenosis[1]

1 Greatness and Humility

There is probably no need, here, to remind ourselves that the idea of divine incarnation is foreign to Jewish spirituality. The Talmudic doctors, whose thought, discussions and even differences of opinion are vital to the formulation of that spirituality and to the interpretation of the Old Testament in its meaning for Israel, draw many teachings from verse 16 of *Psalm 115*: 'The heavens are the heavens of the Lord; But the earth hath He given to the children of men.' Among these teachings there is that of the tractate *Sukkah 5a*, which comments upon that verse as follows. Never has the 'presence of God' come down to the ground level of the earth; never did Moses or Elijah, in their ascension, reach the very height of the heavens.[2] This is a daring interpretation, which modulates the straightforward meaning of verses such as *Exodus 19:18, 19:20, 33:23*, and, in *II Kings*, verses *2:1* and *2:11*.

But the fact that kenosis, or the humility of a God who is willing to come down to the level of the servile conditions of the human (of which St Paul's Epistle to the Philippians [2:6–8] speaks), or an ontological modality quite close to the one this Greek word evokes in the Christian mind – the fact that kenosis also has its full meaning in the religious sensibility of Judaism is demonstrated in the first instance by biblical texts themselves. Terms evoking Divine Majesty and loftiness are often followed or preceded by those describing a God bending down to look at human misery or *inhabiting* that misery. The structure of the text underlines that ambivalence or that enigma of humility in the biblical

God. Thus, in verse 3 of *Psalm 147*, 'He who healeth the broken in heart, and bindeth up their wounds' is the same one who, in the following verse, 'counteth the number of the stars, and giveth them all their names.' *Psalm 113* sings of 'the elevation above all nations and the glory above the heavens' of 'our God that is enthroned on high'; but He 'looketh down low upon heaven and upon the earth.' The psalm ends with God's care for the barren woman, whose despair is deeper than that of the poor person whom God 'causes to rise up out of the dunghill.' As if to say that exaltation were at its height in these very acts of humbling! The importance of these verses for Judaism is emphasized by the fact that they have become part of Judaic liturgy.

But what is significant for Jewish 'theology' as such is the express Talmudic attestation of that importance: there is an inseparable bond between God's descent and his elevation. Let us begin by citing an adage from the treatise *Megillah 31a*, which explicitly affirms: 'Rabbi Yohanan has said: Wherever you find the power of the Holy One, Blessed Be He, you find his humility'; that is written in the Pentateuch (in the Torah), and said again in the *Prophets,* and repeated a third time in the *Writings*.[3] Written in the Pentateuch: 'For the Lord your God, He is God of gods, and Lord of lords, the great God, the mighty, and the terrible; no respecter of persons and not to be bribed' (*Deuteronomy 10:17*); and, immediately following: 'Who doth execute justice for the fatherless and widow, and loveth the stranger, in giving him food and raiment.' It is said again in the *Prophets*: 'For thus said the High and Lofty One that inhabiteth eternity and whose name is Holy: I dwell in the high and holy place, but also with him that is of a contrite and humble spirit, to revive the spirit of the afflicted' (*Isaiah 57:15*). It is repeated for a third time in the *Writings*: 'Sing unto God, sing praises to His name; extol Him that rideth upon the skies' (*Psalm 68:5*), and immediately thereafter: 'The Father of orphans, the protector of widows' (*Psalm 68:6*)'. Most remarkably, here, that humility means mainly the proximity of God to human suffering. Elsewhere in the Talmud it is a reference to the performance of functions that pass for very modest ones. The treatise *Sotah* (*24a*) teaches: 'The Torah begins and ends with acts of charity, since it is written at the beginning: "And the Eternal God made for Adam and for his wife garments of skins, and clothed them" (*Genesis 3:21*); and at the end it is written: "And he buried him in the valley"' (*Deuteronomy 34:6*). The alpha and the omega of the Divine, in the performance of the functions of tailor, clothier and gravedigger!

But this theme of the conjunction of elevation and descent, of the greatness of humility or the humility of greatness, seems to me also to be treated in the parable of 'The Moon that makes itself little.' This parable approaches the theme without hiding the ontological or logical 'upsets' latent in the kenosis. Page 60a of the treatise *Hulin* expresses its purpose (as is often the case with rabbinic wisdom) in a slightly amused tone, which shields the important problematic from a declamatory style; while its openness is preserved by leaving some of the meaning implicit.

The parable, cast in the form of a dialogue between Eternal God and the Moon, is supposedly motivated by a contradiction brought out in *Genesis 1:16*, which announces the creation of 'two great lights,' but right afterward refers to 'the greater light' and 'the lesser light,' as if, between the first and second half of the same verse, one of the great lights had diminished. The contradiction is set in relation to *Numbers 28:15*, which specifies the sacrifices to be performed for the new moon. It says: 'And additionally one he-goat for a sin-offering in honor of the Eternal shall be offered besides the continual burnt-offering, and the drink-offering thereof.' This text appears to present no difficulties – but the problem arises out of the ambiguity of the Hebrew, in which 'a sin-offering in honor of the Eternal' can also be read to mean 'a sin-offering on behalf of the Eternal,' as if the Eternal One (God forbid!) had committed a sin to be atoned for by the sacrifice of a goat. A goat-offering for God's atonement! And so here we see how, on the basis of the letter of the text, the rabbis cause problems – as if to justify their bad reputation for not being attentive to the spirit of the Scriptures, beyond the letter. But first let us enter into the play of imagination and thought that has been set in motion in this manner. On page 60b of the treatise *Hulin*, Rabbi Shimon ben Pazi tells an edifying story based on the contradiction pointed out in *Genesis 1:16*. Immediately after the creation of the two great lights, one of them, the Moon, said to the Creator: 'Sovereign of the world, can two kings wear the same crown?' And God answered: 'Go, therefore, and make yourself smaller!'

Was the Moon unable, out of pride or vanity, to share the greatness she had received with the Sun? And was not the order she was given, 'to make herself smaller,' the just punishment for such pretentiousness? Or was the Moon, troubled by a precocious philosophical concern, affirming the necessity of a hierarchical order in being? Did she already intuit the 'negativity' between equals and discern that greatness cannot be shared – that the sharing of greatness is war? Rather than commanding a punishment unjustly imposed, perhaps what the voice of God proposed was the greatness of smallness – of humility, of the abnegation of night. The nobility of the best ones: smallness equal to greatness, and compatible with it.

The Moon, however, does not see it that way. 'I just expressed a sensible idea: is that any reason to make me smaller?' says the Moon in answer to the Master of the World. Hierarchy is necessary, but I already see that it is necessarily unjust. The ontology of the creature is contradictory. It is dangerous to utter truths! As for the greatness of smallness, I do not at the outset see it as being as great as greatness. Is not the 'glorious lowering' a scandal to reason?

The Moon's argument is then taken into account. 'Thou shalt reign day and night,' says the Lord, 'while the reign of the Sun will be limited to the day.' A discreetness in light – is this already a decline? There are lights without brilliance whose luster the Sun cannot dim: there are insights of the intuitive mind that systematic reasoning, in its glorious clarity, cannot refute.[4] The wisdom of the night remains visible during the day.

'What would be the advantage of shedding light in full daylight?' says the Moon. The role of second brilliance cannot heal the wounded ego. And the civilization of triumphant science will one day invalidate all instinctive knowledge and all truths without proof. This is an antimony on the essence of the intellect, between God and the Moon!

The dialogue continues. 'By you,' the Eternal says to the undaunted Moon, 'Israel will be able to reckon the days and nights.' This consideration opens a new dimension, which makes the inevitable hierarchy fairer, and helps the Moon understand the possible greatness of making-oneself-little. The Sun and Moon are not just lights, but movement, time – history. To the solar calendar of the nations is added Israel's lunar calendar: universal history, and individual history. The biblical history of Israel: drawn in upon itself, lateral, yet Messianic history. Perhaps it was necessary that among the categories of ontology – or despite these categories – the category 'Israel' should arise, in order that the notion of a smallness as great as – or greater than – greatness should take on meaning.

But the Moon does not give in, and the antimony persists. 'It is impossible,' she says, 'to reckon the cycle of the seasons without recourse to the Sun. Does not Scripture say in *Genesis 1:14*: They (Moon *and* Sun) will serve as signs to mark the seasons, days, and years?' The Moon is questioning the possibility, for Israel, of doing without universal history in the long run. Does not its ethics claim politics for its own? Does not its biblical history look to visible history for fulfillment?

Perhaps it is true that neither the light of thought nor the glory of history can tolerate the alleged greatness of humility. Perhaps its majesty has meaning only in the holiness of the person, where, as exaltation of renunciation in the justice of the just, it is the humanity of man and the image of God! Hence the Creator's last attempt to console the Moon, offended by her title of 'lesser light.' 'The names of the just evoke your title: Jacob, called little in *Amos 7:2*, Samuel the Little (a holy rabbi of the Talmudic period), King David, called Little David in *I Samuel 17:14*.'

'The Moon has since then remained without any arguments. But Eternal God sees that she is not satisfied.' A dissatisfaction without arguments, a dissatisfied silence! This is perhaps the residual ambiguity that surrounds the greatness of the saintly and humble who risk being taken for failures! The residue of the stubborn contention of a nature persevering in its being, imperturbably affirming itself. To this there is no response, but for this, precisely, Holiness takes on the responsibility. Here is the humility of God assuming responsibility for this ambiguity. The greatness of humility is also in the humiliation of greatness. It is the sublime kenosis of a God who accepts the questioning of his holiness in a world incapable of restricting itself to the light of his Revelation. This explains the end of the dialogue between the Eternal and the Moon, and verse 15 of *Numbers 28*. Rabbi Simeon Ben Laqish will say: 'In what respect is sacrifice of the goat at the time of the new moon so unusual that the text (*Numbers 28:15*) says on this subject: For the expiation of the Eternal? The Holy One, Blessed be He, says, in effect: The goat must serve for me to be forgiven for having reduced the size of the Moon.'

2 A Traditional Culture

But I do not intend to limit myself to abstract statements, of whatever authority, that remain aloof from Judaism in its historical process of becoming, and would constitute invariable validation of a multimillennial Israel. It is a process of becoming that was admittedly from an early date conscious, perhaps too conscious, of its originality. But it is a process that may have received a great deal, it will be pointed out, from its surroundings – even while rejecting its surroundings. I therefore propose to seek the testimony of a period during which that height of a God who comes down to the level of human beings as if He had need of them – a time imbued with the idea of a humility in God's very height – marked Jewish sensibility and was accentuated within the enclave of a piety and a theology that were cut off from external influences, and tapping their own root.

I have always attributed special significance to the Judaism of the years during which Jewish religious life, in the Diaspora, seemed to be nourished – already or still – by purely traditional elements. It was a time when that tradition seemed to renew itself from within. This period, marked by the prestigious master Eliahu, the *gaon* of Vilna, one of the last Talmudists of genius, who lived during the second half of the eighteenth century (1720–97), seems to me to constitute a vital moment in that religious history.

I find testimony of what is called kenosis (which, as I have just said, transpires through the letter and spirit of many verses of the Old Testament, to the attentive reader) most notably in a book over a century and a half old that I read frequently. It was published posthumously in Vilna, in 1824. It was written by a Lithuanian rabbi, Haim of Volozhin (1759–1821), a remarkable disciple of the *gaon* of Vilna. It is titled *Nefesh Hahaim* (The Soul of Life).[5]

The era of the *gaon* of Vilna comes just before the renowned *Haskalah,* or Jewish Enlightenment, during which period the close-knit East European Jewish communities began (a little later than their West European counterparts) to assimilate the indispensable and liberating elements of modernity. It was an era of a high culture – but a culture that flourished within the framework and strictures of an exalted tradition; an era of traditional Judaism zealously protected by the *gaon.* The *gaon* even protected this traditional form of Judaism from the Hasidic movement, which diverged from certain tendencies of the tradition – though no actual schism developed.

It is possible that that tradition may have borne, unbeknownst to itself, the remote traces of contacts between Judaism and the Graeco-Roman or Christian world, during the centuries when the Talmud itself was being formed at the beginning of our era – even though these contacts may have been only polemical. Similarly, it would be unreasonable to deny the philosophical contributions that enriched the Jewish intellectual heritage during the Middle Ages. Did not the Greeks, through medieval philosophy, enter Judaism? But the *gaon* rarely cited Maimonides. And aside from these possible traces of paganism (or of contact with paganism) included in the age-old tenor of Judaism, no external influences were present during the *gaon*'s time; nor was there anything to revive heterogeneous memories.

This traditional culture consisted in the pure glorification of the Torah, a glorification celebrated in the form of study to be pursued along the lines of problems intrinsic to the Torah. This study, by its dialectical vigor and rigor, had taken on a liturgical significance. From a religious point of view, that is the highest kind of significance! It was not just study that pursued the acquisition of knowledge necessary for the practice of the Law, and of rites, but study that was considered valid as *association,* as covenant, as sociality with God – with his will, which, though not incarnate, is inscribed in the Torah.

The *yeshiva*, or house of study, was the high place in that world. And the author I propose to present, Rabbi Haim of Volozhin, is called of Volozhin because it was in a little Lithuanian town called Volozhin that he founded a *yeshiva* that became famous and exemplary.

Of course, it was the study of the Torah as elucidation and commentary on Scripture. But it was a reading of those texts through the problematic and the hermeneutic of the Talmud, using the kabbalah of the *Zohar* and that of the sixteenth century (which is called the kabbalah of *Safed*) as points of reference. And there is nothing in that study that comes from modern philosophy! A few hundred kilometers from Königsberg and Jena, and scarcely two centuries after Descartes and Malebranche, we find ourselves in the presence of a Judaism that lives according to an intellectual and practical tradition that the faithful know to be irreducible and specific: a tradition that, within its boundaries, remains to an astonishing degree spirituality and life, and the intellectual effort of daringly subtle speculation. Its argumentation, it is true, most often takes the form of exegesis of verses and the stating of oral traditions whose authority rules reason; yet it is a dogmatism within which, in the course of the dialectic, ideas are brought out – ideas whose meanings enlighten or challenge the intelligence, and that open up a way of thinking undaunted by the singularities of an exotic, strange exegesis with promising perspectives and horizons.

But it is also a form of argumentation that either does not know or does not value the historical perspectives to which perhaps the very material to be interpreted harks back. From one end to the other the material is commented upon as a synchrony, as an absolute. All is co-eternal in Scripture and in the commentaries. But there is also renewal and a continual broadening of the obvious meaning into various dimensions of meaning, and continual discovery. This renewal and extension is from within, surely emerging from religious life itself which is lived in contact with the texts, which are also alive within their enclosure. That religious life is lived in contact with 'an inscribed God.' It is a religious life carried by and carrying these texts; in which it agrees with the ancient parable of the wise men of Israel. They say the Levites who carried the Holy Ark of the Tabernacle across the desert were also carried by that Ark: a parable that is probably the true figure of inspiration.

This defenseless inner life of a civilization would soon be overcome by the rise, so close at hand, of the modern world, impelled by the Industrial Revolution. The proximity of that irresistible invasion is attested, as early as the end of the eighteenth century, by the well-known escape of the Jewish genius and anarchist Salomon Maimon to the Germany of Immanuel Kant. Of the world he was escaping he saw no more than the minor externals and ruins. Yet it had an inner life profound enough to endow East-European Judaism, which had opened itself up to Europe, with the consciousness of a rare sense of belonging – a sense in which the survivors of the *Shoah* were to seek some elements of a lost wisdom to be recovered.

3 Everything Depends On Man

Rabbi Haim of Volozhin's book, which, strictly speaking, is devoted to the above-mentioned identification of the highest form of religious life with the traditional study of the Torah, lays out theological perspectives in which two aspects of God are affirmed. On one hand we have the notion of God designated (if the term designation can be used here) by the unsayable tetragram, expressed or translated by the kabbalistic term *Ein-Sof*, Infinite, the absolute of a God affected neither by the created world nor by its history; on the other hand, and at the same time, the same God understood as master of the world, source of all power and all justice, called *Elohim* – who, like a soul of the world, maintains the existence, light, power and holiness of the world, in the form of continuous creation. But it so happens, according to the doctrine presented in this work, that this God, master of power, is powerless to associate himself with the world he creates and recreates, enlightens and sanctifies and maintains in being by that very association, without a certain behavior of man – a being created, but ontologically extra-ordinary. The vocation, or *raison d'être*, of humanity is precisely to provide the necessary conditions for the association of God with the worlds, and thus for the being of the worlds ('being' that also means holiness, elevation and light), as if being could not, *qua* being, in its pure persistence-in-being, constitute its own justification for being, such as would suffice in the eyes of God. And so it is that, in the cosmology of *Nefesh Hahaim* (if one may call its ordering of the world a cosmos), the power of the master of all powers is subordinate, to a certain extent, to the Human, as if omnipotence were not yet the privilege of the Divine! As if the master of all powers depended, in the words of *Nefesh Hahaim*, on a 'food provided by man,' a food made of actions reflecting the will expressed in the Torah. This is a metaphor, *recognized as such* and probably intended to be suggestive, by recalling the cult of sacrifices, called 'bread of the Lord' in numerous verses of the Pentateuch; especially since, according to the anthropology of the author, food maintains the presence of the living soul in the human body, without the soul's having to eat it. But to some degree, in relation to the human will, the Divine is then subordinate. There is kenosis in this 'sub-.'

In order to elaborate on that idea, with Rabbi Haim of Volozhin' s book as my starting point, I shall develop two points. One takes up the cosmology or general ontology of *Nefesh Hahaim*, and the other concerns the more specific problem of the meaning of prayer. I will consent, of course, in setting forth these points, to use a certain language whose formulations are not to be taken literally; to the degree that it is possible, I shall try to disengage these points from the terminology I reproduce.

The mastery of *Elohim*, master of all powers, expresses itself in the very act of creation *ex nihilo* of a world, or more precisely a countless number of worlds, and it also expresses itself (as their maintenance in being) by his *association* with these worlds. His association with these worlds confers being, which is also called power, light, purity and holiness: I have already emphasized this permanent link between being and value. Let us note the plurality of the worlds. Whatever its origin may be, in the categories of the Kabbalah or in the author's terminology, the positing of myriad entities lends itself to a less abstract meaning. I suspect, behind this plurality of worlds, individual persons, collectivities and ideal realities. In this pluralism there is the possibility of being-toward-being, of alterity. 'All the others' have, for each one, the objectivity of beings who are others. Hence, perhaps, without any cosmology as a system, the legitimacy of the word 'world' to designate the other entities in relation to the identity of the identifiable in the form of the human 'I.'

Among these entities or worlds there is a hierarchic order. It is a hierarchy of holiness and dignity, and thus an intertwining or a concatenation with strands of the holiness and light of God, who is the summit and principle of that concatenation. In this order, the higher is the soul of the lower: the height is the animation, the depth the 'body' or 'clothing' of the height. The height is also called the root of the depth: the roots, in this case, grow upward, so to speak. The height is the inside, and the upper is what gives movement to the lower. Movement is not, as used here, a mechanical principle.

Elohim, at the top of the hierarchy, is the soul and animation of all the worlds; through their hierarchical interconnection, the master's energy is transmitted to all, by lowering itself from the higher to the lower, but also by raising the lower toward the higher. There is an expansion of 'energy,' which is also, as in a continuous creation, ongoing every moment. This is the truth behind *Nehemiah 9:6*: 'Thou giveth life to all beings.' The present of the verb 'to give,' in this verb, is to be taken literally.

But the creature is not reducible to that hierarchy in its simplicity, in which it might still resemble a Greek cosmos. Elevation, if it is thought through to the end (and consequently, the same is true of the being, holiness and purity of a world) does not depend solely on its place in the cosmological hierarchy. In that intertwining of the high and the low, man – each one in relation to all the others, each man as a subject – occupies an exceptional place. Paradoxically, everything depends on him – he whose body is at the lowest level, located within the order of action and work, at the level of matter. Everything depends on him, even the outpouring of God, which confers being and light on the entire hierarchy of worlds. The last to be created and raised to the highest by the divine breath that gives him life, he carries within his being a residuum of all the levels of the creature. He has in some way drawn off something from all the worlds, from their light, their holiness and their being. The human is in affinity with the totality of the real. Thus he is both located in the lowliest site and linked with all the levels of the creature. But his soul, which *Genesis 2:7* calls divine breath, remains near the Throne of God, around which are gathered all the souls of Israel, i.e., (we must accept this terminology!) all the souls of the authentically human humanity, which is conceived in Haim of Volozhin as being subsumed beneath the category of Israel. This divine breath is still breathing in the higher part of the soul – man being still in loving communication with God – as if, by that higher part of his soul, outside his body, man were above himself. Thus he is both at the nadir and the zenith of the hierarchy, under the Throne of Divine Presence.

Hence, there is a privileged relationship between the human soul, the soul of Israel, and God. There is a connaturality between man and the manifold entirety of the creature on one hand, and a special intimacy between man and *Elohim* on the other. This intimacy is characterized both by *Elohim*'s superiority to man, who is a part of creation, and by the dependency, intended by *Elohim,* of *Elohim* on man with respect to everything concerning the association of *Elohim* with the worlds, i.e., everything concerning the very existence and devotion of the worlds. Man, by acts in agreement with the Torah, *nourishes* the association of God with the world; or, by his transgression, he exhausts the powers of that divine association. The growth of the holiness, the elevation and the being of the worlds depend on man, as does their return to nothingness (see *Nefesh Hahaim*, book 2, chapter 17).

What a remarkable ontology there is in this cosmology! The meaning of human action is not reduced exclusively to its natural finality in the present circumstances of being; it is, in man (as 'myself,' always chosen), that which ensures being, elevation and holiness in the *other than myself,* in 'the worlds,' depending upon whether man is or is not in accordance with the will of God as written in the Torah. God associates with or withdraws from the worlds, depending upon human behavior. Man is answerable for the universe! Man is answerable for others. His faithfulness or unfaithfulness to the Torah is not just a way of winning or losing his salvation: the being, elevation and light of the worlds are dependent upon it. Only indirectly, by virtue of the salvation or downfall of the worlds, does his own destiny depend on it. As if through that responsibility, which constitutes man's very identity, each one of us were similar to *Elohim.*

This is, for Haim of Volozhin, the source of the ultimate meaning of the famous 'to be in the image of God' of *Genesis 1:26* or *5:1*, in which, for Judaism, the human being is defined, as distinct from the 'rational animal,' as the philosophical tradition would have it. Man is, like the Creator himself, at the apex of the hierarchy of the worlds, the soul of the universe. The last part of the Hebrew verse, *Genesis 2:7*, which tells of the breath of God entering a body 'molded from the clay of the earth,' does not translate literally as 'man became a *living being,*' but rather 'a *living soul.*' The literal meaning is more profound: man is the soul of all 'the worlds,' of all beings, all life, like the Creator himself. And this, not in the name of any pride or diabolical pretension, but by the will of God himself, who did not recoil from that equality with the human, or even from a certain kind of subordination to the human, a God who states in *Isaiah 51:16*, 'And I have put My words in thy mouth, and I have covered thee in the shadow of My hand, that I may plant the heavens and lay the foundations of the earth . . .'. God must have put his creative word in man's mouth, then! Thus, the end of *51:16*, 'And that I may say unto Zion: "Thou art my people".' Thou art my people, *'ami atah,'* which the rabbinical exegesis, being 'insensitive' to the vowels, has no difficulty in transforming into *'imi atah,'* thou art *with* Me, i.e., thou art with Me in the act of creation. The acts, words and thoughts of man have some power over the created world and the forces of creation!

This is the ethical meaning of human activity: its conformity with God's order in the Torah, or the transgression of that order, has a significance that transcends, of course, the natural effects of the act, as well as whatever it could mean, morally, for a self. It counts first and foremost for the others. That is its gravity. It causes 'to live or to die' not just myself, but others besides myself. In his acts, man is responsible for all the other worlds and men. The association of God with the worlds, or his distance from them the being or non-being of the creature – depends on me.

What I have already said about the connaturality of man and the worlds must be repeated here. That connaturality is conceived through the kabbalistic image of worlds making up, collectively, a human stature, formed in such a way as to correspond to the bodily organs, which, in turn, correspond to the positive laws and interdicts of the Torah. Thus, according to the Torah, the life of the human individual sustains and gives life to the cosmos, and the Torah, in being given to mankind, is given to the universe! Being *is,* through ethics and man. Thus, man is responsible for the universe. He makes and unmakes worlds, elevates and lowers them. God's reign depends on me. God has subordinated his efficacy – his association with the real and the very presence of the real – to my merit or demerit. And so God reigns only by the intermediary of an ethical order, an order in which one being is answerable for another. The world *is,* not because it perseveres in being, not because *being* is its own *raison d'être,* but because, through the human enterprise, it can be justified in its being. The human is the possibility of a being-for-the-other. That possibility is the justification of all existing. The world is justified in its being by human dis-interestment, which concretely signifies consent to the Torah, and therefore surely already study of the Torah. More important than God's omnipotence is the subordination of that power to man's ethical consent. And that, too, is one of the primordial meanings of kenosis.

Here is a fundamental text on man's responsibility as implied in that kenosis.

'Let no one in Israel (please God!) say: "What am I and what can I accomplish by my humble acts in the world?" Let him understand, on the contrary, and let him fix in his mind: that no detail of his acts, his words, his thoughts of every instant, is lost. Each one of them goes back to his root, on high, to take effect in the height of heights, in the worlds and among the pure lights of the high places. The intelligent man who understands this according to the truth will fear and tremble in his heart, thinking of the points to which his bad actions reach, and the corruption and destruction determined by even a slight fault. This destruction is incomparably greater than that brought on by Nebuchadnezzar and Titus (destroyers of the Temple of Jerusalem). For these latter could not be the cause of any evil, any destruction in the heights; being pagans, they have neither any part in the upper worlds, nor roots in those worlds. Those worlds are beyond their reach, whereas, through our sins, the force of the supreme power is diminished and worn.'

'Our acts, our words, our thoughts' – three levels of human being. Thoughts proceed from the divine breath, already or still, above the body. By thought 'man transcends man,' as Pascal would say. An anthropology of an already human humanity, with unlimited responsibility, called Israel. I have already explained this use of the word Israel. Nebuchadnezzar and Titus, simple pagans, do not have that cosmic responsibility. The evil or good they may do does not yet have the significance of the human going beyond the human. They act only within the limits of natural causality. Or, in an evocative phrase, 'they can only grind grain that has already been ground.' The awesome election of humanity in Israel. 'Let the heart of the holy people tremble; it contains in its stature all the forces and all the worlds . . . for it is they who are the Holiness and the Sanctuary of on high. Down below, in this world, reality is at the mercy of a Nebuchadnezzar and a Titus, masters of the earth. But when a

113

true man has an impure thought in his heart, a thought of lust, it is as if he were to bring a whore into the Holy of Holies of the Sanctuary of on high.'

4 God Needs Man's Prayer

This sudden reversal of human subjectivity, which can no longer be defined as an *in-itself*, or as a *for-itself*, which is defined as a forgetting of self in 'fear and trembling' for the other, for the worlds and the other human beings (an abnegation which also expresses a God giving up his omnipotence and finding satisfaction only in the for-the-other), is expressed by Haim of Volozhin, in a remarkable manner, in his analysis of prayer. At no time is prayer an entreaty for *oneself*; properly speaking, it is not an entreaty, but an *offering of oneself*, an outpouring of the soul. At least that is what true prayer is meant to be in Jewish piety, according to *Nefesh Hahaim*.

I shall avoid exegetic details (of the Talmud and the Kabbalah) that form the context of Rabbi Haim of Volohzin's description as he attempts to determine the ontological status of prayer. In his view, the essence of prayer is the benediction, will and origin of abundance, in its function of generous offering, for the purpose of associating God and the world – the fact of being 'food' in the sense developed above. A prayer composed of words of the Israelite ritual, carefully chosen by the 'men of the Great Synagogue,' which was made up of 'sages and prophets,' – by those who, after the Babylonian captivity, carried on the traditions unbroken by exile – the link between prophecy and the rabbinate: a key moment in the spiritual history of Israel. These words chosen by the men of the Great Synagogue were endowed with unparalleled spiritual power, 'conducting thoughts to their purity of intention and extreme elevation.' This gave them the special privilege of possessing a marvelous refinement, eliminating all vain thoughts, all vain ideas that would hinder purity of thought and intention. 'To pray,' the author adds, 'is to strip the soul of its clothing, the body.' Or, better yet, it is 'to pour out one's soul.' Is it not written in *I Samuel 1:15*, apropos of the prayer of Hannah, the future mother of the prophet Samuel: 'I poured out my soul before God.' Is not prayer the soul itself? 'Thou shalt love the Lord thy God with all thy soul' (*Deuteronomy 6:5*): does this verse not refer to the inner service of God, indicating prayer? A whole series of verses is cited that must be taken literally, in keeping with this perspective of rabbinic exegesis, in which the literal meaning leads further than the metaphor. Far from being a demand addressed to God, prayer, in this view, is the soul's rising upward like the smoke of sacrifices, the soul's delivering itself up to the heights – dis-inter-esting itself in the etymological sense of the term. God desires prayer in accordance with the literal sense of *Proverbs 15:8*: 'The prayer of the upright is his desire.' He needs prayer, just as he needs those who are faithful to the Torah, in order to be able to associate himself with the worlds, for their existence and elevation. Here we again come to the central theme of the book discussed earlier. The worlds cannot continue *to be*, simply by virtue of the energy of their substance: they must be justified in their being, they need the ethical mediation of man, they need man and man's prayer, which are *for the others*. Thus, prayer, called 'the service of the heart' or even 'the labor of the heart' (again, the expression is a literal one), is the edification of the worlds or the repairing of the ruins of creation. To pray signifies, for a 'myself,' seeing to the salvation of others instead of – or before – saving oneself.

True prayer, then, is never for oneself, never for one's own needs. Rabbi Haim explicitly asserts this. Having been instituted by the men of the Great Synagogue to replace the daily sacrifices in the Temple (now destroyed or far away) how could these prayers have come to be associated with human demands? The sacrifices that were made every day in the Temple – were they not daily holocausts? And the flesh offered up in the Temple – was it not to be burned completely away, leaving nothing behind for the giver of the sacrifice? Can the individual, then, speak in prayer of his or her selfish needs, when that would compromise the pure dis-inter-estment of the burnt-offering?

And should we ask in prayer for our human suffering to be abated? Is not suffering the atonement for sin? 'No suffering without sin,' the tractate *Shabbat* (*55a*) says.[6] Would we want the sick to renounce their medical treatment and let the poison flow into their afflicted members just because the medicine is bitter and the surgeon's intervention painful? Would we prefer sins for which there can be no atonement?

But doesn't the Talmud itself recommend that we add supplications for our personal hardships to our prayers glorifying the Eternal? That is permitted only in the case of hardships that strike us through the distress of all Israel, a danger threatening the people of the Revelation, a people persecuted, despised. Is not Israel the very manifestation, among men, of divine glory and the divine message? Is Israel not the bearer and subject of Holy History? And is not the persecution of Israel the profanation of the Most High? Can one keep from calling on His Name, when His Name is being humiliated? My self is not a sufficient reason for my prayer. It is by reason of the glory of Holy History and its truth that supplication is authorized for myself, without the relationship to God being reduced to a concern for myself.

Is the human suffering of the individual condemned to silence? Does the Talmudic authorization to pray for oneself absolutely exclude all requests of the unhappy self? According to Rabbi Haim of Volozhin, praying for relief from one's own misery is never the ultimate aim of a pious prayer – the prayer of the just. The goal of all prayer remains the need of the Most High for the prayer of the just, in order that he may make exist, sanctify and elevate the worlds. But to the degree that the suffering of each person is already the great suffering of God who suffers for that person, for that suffering that, though 'mine,' is already his, already divine – the 'I' who suffers may pray, and, given God's participation, may pray for himself or herself. One prays for oneself with the intention of suspending the suffering of God, who suffers in my suffering. The self need not pray to mitigate its own suffering: God is already with me, before any asking. Is it not said (in *Psalm 91:15*): 'I am with him in suffering'? And does not *Isaiah 63:9* speak of God who suffers in the suffering of man? The suffering self prays to alleviate the 'great suffering' of God who suffers, to relieve the suffering of God, who suffers both for man's sin and for the suffering of his atonement. And in that suffering of God which is greater than his own, and toward which, in his prayer, he rises, man's own suffering is assuaged. Man no longer feels his own pain, compared to a torment surpassing his own, in God. Precisely therein lies atonement: in that measure in which God's suffering exceeds my own. It is in God's suffering that the redemption of sin is realized – to the point of abridging suffering. A holy feat: bitterness sweetened by bitterness!

In concluding, I would like to recall a note written by Rabbi Haim of Volozhin, which in a certain way emphasizes that kenosis of a God who, though remaining the One to whom all prayer is addressed, is also the One *for whom* the prayer is said. The note has the characteristic rabbinic style of a commentary on the Scripture and even a renewal of commentary.

The note first takes up the prayer that remains a request, but remains legitimate in view of the distress of Israel, bearer of the Torah, persecuted for its very faithfulness. In this case, the profanation of God's name is attested and carried out in every individual's private misfortunes. It is a prayer for oneself, but it is justified by that intolerable profanation. First, the author alludes to the aggression of Amalek, who attacks Israel just barely come out of Egypt. Chapter 17 of *Exodus* relates that first war with Amalek, who has become the symbol of evil, the sworn enemy of Israel, of its religious calling, and of its Torah. *Deuteronomy 25:17–19* orders a war without quarter against Amalek. Among the essential traits of that first aggression there is the spiritual role played by Moses, who is established on a hill. And *Exodus 17:11* tells us: 'And when Moses held up his hand, Israel prevailed; and when he let down his hand, Amalek prevailed.' The Talmudic treatise *Rosh Hashanah 29a* comments on this verse. It is notably suspicious of the magical effect attributed to this raised arm, even if it is the arm of Moses. Here is the opinion it expresses: 'Was it the arm of Moses that made war or withstood the attack? Surely not. But this passage teaches us that when the people of Israel looked heavenward and served its Heavenly Father with all its heart, it was victorious; otherwise it was defeated.'

Rabbi Haim of Volozhin interprets the apparent meaning of the preceding Talmudic text in a different manner. The arm of Moses, which, during the people's distress, reminds them of the Most High to whom true worship is directed and on whom victory depends, becomes in the new interpretation the arm that recalls to men in their distress the humiliation of a God disgraced, *for whom* prayers are said. Thus Rabbi Haim justifies the prayer of a sinful self *for* itself; but it is the prayer of a self no longer hateful.[7]

The end of Rabbi Haim's note is in reference to the continuation of the Talmudic passage just quoted, which is on *Numbers 21:4–9*. It is the story about the snake-bites when Israel was crossing the desert! These snake-bites had nothing to do with either Amalek or Israel's message. But there was a case of human suffering, the suffering of sinners. Let us suppose at least that there is no suffering without sin. And Moses intervened with God. Here is verse 8 of chapter 21: 'The Eternal said to Moses: Make thee a (brass) serpent and set it upon a pole; everyone that is bitten, when he seeth it, shall live.' The Talmudic passage from the treatise *Rosh Hashanah*, page 29a, is again suspicious of magic!

'Is it really the serpent that brings about life or death? This should be thought of otherwise: When the Israelites turned their eyes heavenward and served their Heavenly Father with all their hearts, they were cured; otherwise, they died of poison.' The serpent on a pole was then no more

117

than a reminder of the Most High toward which all 'service of the heart,' all prayer, must go.

So indeed; but here again Rabbi Haim of Volozhin renews the Talmudic thought he comments upon. The brass serpent atop a pole is the reminder of a God who is already suffering because of the sins committed by men on earth, as well as because of the snake-bites that kill them. But it is as prayer *for this God* who suffers that men's prayers can become 'prayer for oneself.'

8
The Bible and the Greeks[1]

What is Europe? It is the Bible and the Greeks. The Bible: an ontological inversion? The original perseverance of realities in their being – the inertia of material objects, the enrootedness of plants, the struggle between wild animals, the war among 'owning and interested' men, as Bossuet calls them – is inverted in the man announced to humanity in Israel. Thus, for being that is dedicated to being, for being that has no other purpose than to be, the human self might also signify the possibility of interrupting its *conatus essendi*, the possibility of answering for the other, who 'is none of my business,' who is nothing to me. 'Thou shalt not kill,' that is to say, 'Thou shalt love thy neighbor.' This is an odd recommendation for an existence summoned to live at all costs.

There is this possibility of a responsibility for the alterity of the other person, for the stranger without domicile or words with which to converse, for the material conditions of one who is hungry or thirsty, for the nakedness of the defenseless mortal. Where is the person who would not come toward me in that essential misery, whatever countenance they may put on? The other, the one separated from me, outside the community: the face of the person who asks, a face that is already a request, but also the face of one recognized in love as irreplaceable, unique. Or, in that fragile uniqueness outside the extension of the concept, the face of one commanded. In that weakness there is the commandment of a God or an authority, and, despite all they say, there is a renouncing of the force of constraint. And from that moment forth, in this self persevering in being, there emerges mercy and the overturning of being's tautology of pure 'being *qua* being.'

In *Genesis 24*, Abraham's servant, having come from afar in search of a wife for his master's son, asks Rebekah, the future mother of Israel, for a drink of water from her pitcher. But Rebekah also waters the camels of the caravan, 'until they have all done drinking.' She waters the camels who cannot ask to drink. According to the rabbis who wrote commentary on this passage, as soon as Rebekah came out to meet him, the waters in the deep rose above their natural level. Is this a miracle, or a parable? The waters, which were there on the morning of the first day of creation, before the first light shone, and were still a purely physical element, still part of the first desolate *tohu vavohu*, finally rose. They rose in the service of mercy. They took on meaning. *Genesis 24* also relates the thankfulness of Abraham's servant. He gave Rebekah 'two bracelets for her arms of ten shekels' weight of gold.' Two bracelets weighing ten shekels, or two tables of the Law? The Decalogue? The rabbinic doctors make the association. In their view, Abraham's servant recognized Sinai. It is a prefiguration or an enactment of the revelation in the responsibility for the first person to come our way – even if it is a beastly creature, so to speak:[2] a responsibility exceeding the demand heard by myself in the face of the other.

But 'the first person to come along' for myself and the other person would also constitute the third party, who joins us or always accompanied us. The third party is also my other, also my neighbor. Who would be the first to speak? Where does the priority lie? A decision must be made. The Bible requires justice and deliberation! From the heart of love, from the heart of mercy. One must judge, one must reach a conclusion. There must be knowledge, verification, objective science, system. There must be judgements, the state, political authority. The unique beings recognized by love, which are extrinsic to all genera, must be brought into the community, the world. One must bring oneself into the world. Hence the first violence within mercy! For love of the unique, the one and only must be given up. The humanity of the human must be set back within the horizon of the universal. Oh, welcome messages from Greece! To become educated among the Greeks, to learn their language and their wisdom. Greek is Europe's inevitable discourse, recommended by the Bible itself.

Greek is the term I use to designate, above and beyond the vocabulary, grammar and wisdom with which it originated in Hellas, the manner in which the universality of the West is expressed, or tries to express itself – rising above the local particularism of the quaint, traditional, poetic or religious. It is a language without prejudice, a way of speaking that bites reality without leaving any marks – capable, in attempting to articulate the truth, of obliterating any traces left by it – capable of unsaying, of resaying. It is a language that is at once a metalanguage, careful and able to protect what is said from the structures of the language itself, which might lay claim to being the very categories of meaning. A language which intends to translate – ever anew – the Bible itself; a language which, in the justice it allows to take root, cannot for ever offend the uniqueness of the other, nor the mercy that uniqueness appeals to, at the very heart of the subject, nor the responsibility for the other, which only loosens the clenched teeth to respond to God's word in the face of the other person.

There is a memory of the Bible in the justice borne by that word. This means, concretely, in Europe, the endless requirement of justice hidden behind justice, the requirement of an even juster justice, more faithful to its original imperative in the face of the other.

And yet the history of modern Europe attests to an obsession with the definitive. In opposition to the established order, there is an obsession with an order to be established on universal but abstract rules – i.e., political rules, while underestimating or forgetting the uniqueness of the other person, whose right is, after all, at the origin of rights, yet always a new calling. The history of modern Europe is the permanent temptation of an ideological rationalism, and of experiments carried out through the rigor of deduction, administration and violence. A philosophy of history, a dialectic leading to peace among men – is such a thing possible after the Gulag and Auschwitz? The testimony of a fundamental book of our time such as Vasily Grossman's *Life and Fate*,[3] in which all the systematic safeguards of justice are invalidated and the human dehumanized, sees hope only in the goodness of one person toward another, the 'little kindness' I have called mercy, the *rahamim* of the Bible. An invincible goodness, even under Stalin, even under Hitler. It validates no government, but rather bears witness, in the mode of being of our Europe, to a new awareness of a strange (or very old) mode of a spirituality or a piety without promises, which would not render human responsibility – always my responsibility – a senseless notion. A spirituality whose future is unknown.

9
Moses Mendelssohn's Thought
Preface to the translation of *Jerusalem* [1]

Dominique Bourel, a philosopher and intellectual historian interested in the way in which Enlightenment thought was expressed by Jewish writers in eighteenth-century Germany, has translated the philosopher Moses Mendelssohn's *Jerusalem: or On Religious Power and Judaism (Jerusalem, oder Über religiöse Macht und Judentum)* with care and erudition. The translation is well introduced and very usefully annotated. The notes are particularly helpful in this 200-year-old work, with all but forgotten proper names and allusions to contemporary events.

These pages formulate the philosophy (or the ideology, or the charter) of the emancipation of the Jews scattered among the modern nations, in which they were still, two centuries ago, without political rights. That emancipation, hoped for and initiated in the years leading up to the French Revolution of 1789, was pursued with confidence and exaltation throughout the entire nineteenth century. Integration with the nation – states of the West – political assimilation – was not (at least according to Mendelssohn's doctrine) supposed to rid Jews of their particular historical identity, which was interpreted as being essentially, even exclusively, religious. Mendelssohn conceived of the religious as circumscribing a domain regulated by freedom of conscience, in which only inner promptings were valid. It was an area free from the imposition of the state, and even of the Church: the latter could only legitimately affect the conscience through education. Religious convictions would not, within the state, justify the making of any exception that would remove any citizen's legal rights or equality, nor would they confer political privilege on anyone. At least half of Mendelssohn's book is taken up with reflections on the freedom of conscience and its relation to the powers of church and state, on natural law and the social contract. It contains an entire political philosophy, but it also bears witness to the desire or ambition of Western Judaism to be a part of the European nations. The positive side, and noble inspiration, of this important moment in Jewish history must not be underestimated, despite the bitter disappointments of the twentieth century. Emancipation, which was both a great moment in modern political philosophy and essential to the Jewish collectivity, appeared important at the level of universal thought, and was recognized as such as soon as this work was published. Kant read it with 'admiration for its penetration, finesse and intelligence.' He considered it the harbinger of a great reform, which was 'imminent, though slow in coming, and relevant not only to Israelites, but also to the other nations' (letter to Mendelssohn, August 16, 1783). Traces of Kant's reading of Mendelssohn's book can be found in Kant's *Über den Gemeinspruch: Das mag in der Theorie richtig sein, taugt aber nicht für die Praxis* (Concerning the common saying: This May Be True in Theory But Does Not Apply in Practice). As for Hegel, he knew and had studied *Jerusalem* in the theological writings of his youth, but already with an unfavorable attitude toward Judaism.

Beyond his theoretical reflections on the equality of the various religions before the state, and beyond his protest against the loyalty oath regarding certain dogmatic truths that the state was supposedly justified in requiring of citizens called to serve in public office, Mendelssohn championed an idea of freedom that was more radical than that of many of the legal scholars of his day. Professor Alexander Altmann of Harvard University (editor of Mendelssohn's *Complete Works* and author of his biography), in a beautiful article, 'The Search for Freedom in Mendelssohn's Political Philosophy' (*Daat* 5, summer 1980, published by Bar-Ilan University in Israel), analyzes the fundamental ideas underlying the concept of natural laws used by Mendelssohn as follows. The freedom of natural law cannot be limited by any social contract; that he considered to be an impossibility inscribed in the essence of man. That quasi-ontological impossibility of relinquishing one's freedom appears to Altmann to be characteristic of Mendelssohn's thought. For man, freedom was both a right and an obligation: an obligation that would take precedence in the eventuality of any conflicting obligations. Although the individual might restrict his natural rights in the interests of peace and security in the social order, the freedom of conscience could bear no such restrictions on the basis of those arguments. Peace and security were not the ultimate goal of the social contract and the state. The state's vocation was the furtherance of freedom as the possibility of a more active, creative life. According to Mendelssohn, the ruler could not, contrary to Hobbes's vision, dictate the forms of worship. Positive laws could never contradict or destroy natural law, nor the rights of man as defined and delimited by natural law. The laws derived from the contract are not sufficient to generate categories of rights and duties having no roots in the 'state of nature.' Mendelssohn responds negatively to the question he asks in *Jerusalem:* 'Can contracts and agreements create *perfect* rights and binding duties when there were previously, in the absence of any contract, no imperfect rights and duties, and no duties of conscience?' Natural law is mankind's protection against oppression. No reason of state can do violence to the natural ethical law.

That is, in Mendelssohn's view, the spiritual basis upon which the Jews are to enter the City – without their religion having to suffer or to stand in the way of that emancipation.

The memory of the totalitarianisms that still haunt today's humanity underscores the timeliness of the liberalist scruples that orient that entire portion of Mendelssohn's work. As for the Jews, the hardships and trials they underwent in the tortured twentieth century, in which the people of Israel almost disappeared, do oblige them to conceive of their future, their place in the family of nations and the future traits of their mode of being and of their religious physiognomy in new terms. But the so very demanding Mendelssohnian ideal of freedom and the rights of man, the splendor of which dazzled the Jews of the liberal world of the nineteenth century, who recognized in it something close to their own prophetic traditions – that ideal remains dear to their hearts, despite the course of events and the fragility of Europe's democratic institutions, which were unable to prevent two world wars, fascism and Auschwitz. In whatever form Israel's past, traditions and culture have impressed themselves upon Judaism in the aftermath of the *Shoah,* the acute sense of their *Dasein* is quite consciously made up of their freedom of religious conscience vis-à-vis any purely institutional outside authority. Mendelssohn, in his philosophy in which religion begins, in a sense, in free thinking itself, without any possibility of that freedom's being relinquished, bears witness to the irreversible modernity of today's Jew. It is from this that his claim to the dignity of citizenship is derived. It is the status of this kind of citizenship that is sought after still today in the state of Israel, which aspires, particularly in this respect, to resemble the democratic, free Western peoples, and be a member of their community. Still today it is this status that is cherished by the millions of Jews who have remained in their European or American homelands as full citizens, even though for this group also the age-old loyalty to Zion has become a quasi – liturgical duty to support the young Zionist state; but a state thought of and felt to be an extraordinary state – 'not like the others.' This is a duty that reinforces or replaces the traditional ritualism; a devotion that excludes from the outset any political antagonism that might cast doubts upon one's duty to the homeland. This is a new way of thinking and feeling, whatever our judgement, from the outside, may eventually be as to the coherence of such a way of thinking or the persistence of such a feeling.

But has not that freedom of religious conscience shown itself also to be alien to the Jewish soul? Does not the Old Testament testify to the extreme harshness of sanctions against religious transgressions, and thereby to Judaism's incompatibility with the inner freedom championed by Mendelssohn? It was precisely in order to respond to such objections or insinuations elicited by the Jewish philosopher's liberalism that the second part of *Jerusalem* deals with the essence of Judaism and of faith in general. I will attempt to summarize Mendelssohn's fundamental positions on this point in four theses.

The general thesis is the following. Religious beliefs (truths relating to the existence and goodness of a creator God concerned with the happiness of human beings) are not the consequence of an oral or written supernatural revelation – neither in the case of Judaism nor of any other religion. As truths necessary to the happiness of human beings, they are communicated to mankind by divine goodness in a more direct manner. They are inscribed (in neither letters nor hieroglyphics) in the conscience of every person, and are rational self-evidence itself, our natural light itself, good sense itself. They are prior to all metaphysics (and in this Mendelssohn differs from the letter of the school of Leibniz), prior to all rational theology! These truths, necessary to man's bliss, are in themselves necessary! Nor do they need to be confirmed by any miracle. This is the optimistic monotheism of an infinitely benevolent providence. It posits from the outset beliefs that are common to all mankind, which constitute a theological guarantee of universal agreement centered upon eternal truths.

The second thesis is this. These beliefs need expression – symbols and signs – in order to be retained and meditated upon, and it is at this point that, having been set in imagery and letters derived from hieroglyphics, they are betrayed. They lose their true meaning as they are congealed into idols and give rise to all the idolatry of the world, separating man from God and setting man against man. I will not discuss here this philosophy of religious history, to which many pages of Mendelssohn's essay are devoted.

Hence (and this would constitute Mendelssohn's third proposition) a revelation was received by the Jewish people, a supernatural revelation accredited by miracles, which teaches a body of laws in which monotheism finds a form of expression that saves it from history's mistakes. This revelation, again supernaturally, and guaranteed by miracles, also contains truths about the extraordinary or holy history of the Jewish people. This body of laws and these historical truths bear a wise pedagogy: permanent reminders of innate beliefs and repeated explanations occasioned by the ritualistic and ceremonial acts with which the revealed law fills the lives of the faithful. The constant intervention of the living voice and living reason counters the intellectual aberration of dead images and signs that have become immobilized within systems. The yoke of the law frees minds.

The preservation of the monotheism that is written in the heart, in the purity of its reasonableness: this is the sole supernatural privilege of the Jewish people, according to Mendelssohn. This becomes Judaism's mission among the Gentiles. Judaism is thus necessary to the innate monotheism in man: it is not a revealed faith, it is a revealed law.[2] But between faith and the law there is, to use Mendelssohn's own expression, the relation of soul to body.[3]

The fourth and final proposition: The religious law revealed to the Jewish people was, in ancient Israel, set into political law. This is not to say that politics intervened in the determination of beliefs and articles of faith, which is the underlying supposition of the objections that furnished a pretext for all the debate about the essence of Judaism. The severity of the sanctions prescribed for transgressions in the Pentateuch only involved, in Mendelssohn's view, the political order that was supposed to ensure the revealed law. The political order is not made up of beliefs and ideas, but of laws protecting the freedom of ideas that quickens beliefs. Repression, then, never was directed against sins of opinion, but against purely political wrongs. This situation was one of a high spiritual level, in which politics was not yet accepted as a principle distinct from the principle requiring the preservation of freedom of religious conscience. Such a situation is unstable, one in which it is difficult for men to live. According to Mendelssohn, it was already breaking up in the course of ancient Jewish history. After the destruction of the ancient Hebrew state, it belonged definitively to history. Henceforth, the distinction between religious and political law would be a radical one in Judaism. That period was definitively over, as already reflected in the New Testament saying: 'Render unto God that which is God's, and unto Caesar that which is Caesar's.' That era being closed, there was no longer any obstacle to the Jews' entering the modern states. And Mendelssohn's text, which appears to lament the failure of a noble ambition of the Human and the end of the ancient Jewish state, appears at the same time to rejoice in the new fraternity that will henceforth be possible, within the modern nation-states, between Jews and Gentiles.

What is left of Mendelssohn's philosophy of Judaism in the eyes of the Jews of our time? And first of all, how can a common denominator be found for the diversity of today's Jewish consciousness, be it religious, national, or merely cultural, made up of indistinct memories or reduced to a simple 'of Jewish origin,' with no memories attached to it? This difficulty becomes apparent by the very impossibility of reducing these various categories to a unity. But we must also consider whether events and ideas (unforeseeable ones, to be sure) have not carried us beyond Mendelssohn's philosophical analysis. The Jews of our time have known Zionism, have undergone genocide and are citizens or contemporaries of the state of Israel. Nothing would seem to be further from their thought than the certainty of harmonious perspectives foreseen by Mendelssohn. The equilibrium between their religious loyalties and their relations with the nations is not that unproblematic. The ordeals undergone during the Hitler years of Europe and their current fallout have made it impossible to assume the quasi-Messianic style of the emancipation announced by Mendelssohn and by a certain sort of anthropology that did not foresee the danger that the barbaric forces of history might overturn the order of priority, willed by reason, between the religious and the national being of mankind. As for the Jewish faith, which, in a democratic state respectful of the inner man, is no longer exposed to persecution – has it not, in twentieth-century Western Europe, begun an accelerated process of dejudaization, to the point of conversion to the surrounding religions, or of total religious indifference? Has assimilation not shown itself to be unlimited, whereas Mendelssohn's *Jerusalem* foresaw the permanence of a religious particularism? And is it not the other *Jerusalem*, that of the state of Israel, that, even for those not becoming citizens of that state, henceforth safeguards the persistence and solidity of Holy History more strongly than the official consistories of emancipated Judaism?

Of course, there is still, in present-day Judaism, the unchanging minority of strict observance in which (need I remind the reader?) the ceremonial and ritual law is not just conduct intended to maintain, undeformed, a few representations of rational theology. On the contrary, it is the very means by which the believer's thought is devoted to a God whose will that law expresses. The practice of that law, like the study of it, is not the simple expression of faith, but the ultimate intimacy with a God who revealed himself in history. Throughout all the adventures of dejudaization, it was in these groups, which were indifferent to the changing times and as if devoid of any relationship with history, that the energy of the tradition and its invisible irradiation has been preserved.

But the history of the emancipated Judaism of the nineteenth century, which opened itself to European history, was an assimilation in which obedience to ritual law was progressively forgotten, and in which participation in the spirit of the times also meant the loss of those beliefs Mendelssohn thought innate to all human souls without the intervention of any supernatural revelation. Religious ideas, which have lost much ground in Europe (at least statistically) in the last two centuries, have not been able to retain an unchanged status in the Jewish soul, henceforth attentive to the outer world. It is perhaps unnecessary to recall the philosophical difficulties that – from the end of the Enlightenment on – were encountered by the doctrines upon which the natural theology of religious beliefs, 'written in the human conscience,' were founded. Need I recall the void left in human thought by the crisis of conceptual metaphysics, Kantian ideas and all that was soon to justify Nietzsche's announcement of 'the death of God?' Need I mention, on the other hand, the whole renewal (but also all the new paradoxes) of philosophy, of theology, of faith, or of 'the experience of the divine' or of religious sensibilities that the world discovered in what is termed practical reason, in ethics, but also in the revolt against social injustice and sensitivity to the other man's suffering? And must we not insist, regarding the Jews, on all the unforeseeable and unforeseen dimensions that the very despera-tion brought about by National Socialist persecution opened up within Israel's ancient faith: the Passion of the *Shoah*, its meaning for the survivors who to this day feel they have been incomprehensibly, as it were unjustly, spared? Ordeals, abysmal depths conferring an unexpected meaning on very ancient texts – texts already bearing the trace of an extraordinary spiritual history, but that in the course of the nineteenth century, in the enlightened atmosphere of emancipation, were beginning to be seen as old scribblings of interest to no one except historians and doxographers. The state of Israel itself became the gatherer of the psychological dispersion of the Jews, beyond all the migrations of persons it brought about: the land of the prophets, the land of ethical hopes, the motivating force for the life termed ritualistic or ceremonial. Israel was a significant land, even for those who were no longer anything but 'Jews by origin'!

What is then the value of Mendelssohn's distinctions between faith and law, the premises for the normalizing of Judaism in nation-states of the West? Are we not now far removed from the distinguished portraits of the German, the Frenchman, or the Englishman of Mosaic confession, calmly issuing forth from the essay on the New Jerusalem?

But on second thought, all is not outdated for the Jews of our time in Moses Mendelssohn's vision of Judaism. The assimilation that did not occur in accordance with the philosopher's provisions was the product of an elevated mode of thought not yet exhausted.

I have already stressed the topicality of the lofty conception of human freedom in *Jerusalem*, as well as in Mendelssohn's entire work, and I have emphasized the significance that that difficult freedom still has for the Jews since Auschwitz. Let us also note that, despite the normalization of the Jewish question Mendelssohn heralded, he retained in his vision of Judaism that affirmation of the latter's extraordinary history, and of the unique role that devolved upon Israel among the nations. In his universalism he does not forget the singularity of the Jewish people and its universal significance, which stems from that very singularity: Israel is still necessary to humanity's monotheism. And Israel also attempted to carry out the superhuman adventure that consisted – though only for a time – in upholding a political law regulated by the religious law. This was exactly the opposite of a political conditioning of the spiritual! It was a unique attempt or temptation in history.

In the desire for emancipation as expressed by Mendelssohn, the vocation of Israel is never forgotten. To be with the nations is also to be for the nations. The consciousness of that universalist singularity is ancient, and proper to the Jewish religious mentality. It is the Hebrew genius itself; but Mendelssohn's work expresses a new dimension of it, that, not being tributary to the philosophical framework of the eighteenth century on all points, is relevant to and a vital element within today's Judaism. Mendelssohn's work heralds a new era in Jewish history. It bespeaks a Judaism that would enter into a symbiotic relationship with the non-Jewish human world, above and beyond the mystic universalism of being-for-the-others, which had always been a feature of Judaism. Such a symbiosis is presupposed by the state of Israel itself. It is a symbiosis whose structure or organization doubtless requires a philosophical elaboration more complex than the one made possible by the German or French Enlightenment: a less abstract theology and an eschatology less unproblematically optimistic.

But it was Mendelssohn who, in his idealist theory of religious revelation (integrally within the purview of our natural lights) and happiness granted by providence to all men, reached beyond ethical humanism and respect for the person in others. He placed particular emphasis on the intellectual unity of humanity centered on the same truths, or on conflicting but always reciprocally translatable truths – which indicates the profound unity of human civilization. And does not that possibility of conflicting truths constitute humanity's life in common, or the very definition, or at least the essential promise, of the West? Such a theology and eschatology was attempted, for example, with great loftiness of views and fruitful suggestions, scarcely 150 years after Mendelssohn's *Jerusalem*[4] (after the First World War and before the rise of Hitlerism) in Franz Rosenzweig's *The Star of Redemption*. That philosopher united Judaism and Christianity in one and the same destiny and perceived them as part of a common metaphysical drama, avoiding all syncretism. But Franz Rosenzweig was the child of that same assimilation of German Judaism that he lived through before coming back to himself – an assimilation he overcame by borrowing from his assimilation itself many resources necessary for his very independence in the bosom of a human community, forgetting neither his indebtedness nor the ties it established. It was an assimilation to be overcome at last, but an assimilation survived by its generous, innovative thought, to which Mendelssohn's *Jerusalem* bears witness. We must be thankful to Dominique Bourel for having translated this work with rigor, and for having presented it in the context of its time.

10
A Figure and a Period[1]

Mrs. Salomon Halperin, née Anna of Gunzburg, born in St Petersburg in 1892, died recently in Geneva, on the twenty-seventh of last June [1986].

She was the daughter, granddaughter, and great-granddaughter of the barons of Gunzburg. Social distinction and an entire period of Jewish history were sublimated, in Mrs. Salomon Halperin, into the perfect nobility of a human face, the harmonious blend of grace and authority, the consciousness of a permanent obligation to the other, the vigilance of a Jewish presence. Since 1917, the steps of her peregrinations in Europe with Salomon Halperin, her husband who died in 1955, were marked by her generous initiatives and her works. Her radiant personality shone forth both in her youthful manner with others and in the natural (or supernatural) elegance she gave, or received from, the ritual gestures of the ancient and subtle tradition of Israel – a tradition well known and precious to her. *Eshet hayil* (a woman of valor and a *grande dame*), her message and her ways were received lovingly by her descendants, down to the fourth generation. And how can I forbear to mention here her oldest son, Horace Halperin, who, as a member of the Central Committee of the Alliance Israélite Universelle, was involved in activity dedicated to defending human rights and to expanding, in schools, an ambitious, biblical and rabbinical Jewish culture, enlightened by France's universalist spirit. That activity or mission, in another form – as dictated by the conditions of the political regime of tzarist Russia – was carried out during the nineteenth century by the Gunzburg house in St Petersburg.

The Jews of the tzar's vast empire were left by and large without the protection of the essential rights of man and of the citizen. But the Russian Jews, in their vast numbers, were able, through study of the Torah, to elevate everydayness to the level of an authentic spiritual life, and keep the intellect on the alert. The study of the Torah comprised the Bible and the Talmudic dialectic, the daily repetition of their lessons at all ages of life. But these communities were subjected to the injustice, the whims and persecution of the powerful and of the crowd; they found compassion only in the opinion of the Russian liberal intelligentsia, and assistance only in the intervention that a small class of Jews who had achieved emancipation could afford, or dare, or risk undertaking on their behalf with the powerful. These Jews had privileged status based on various criteria: services rendered (whether of civil or military nature) and adjudged undeniable, professional excellence or competence, university degrees, exceptional abilities. And good luck, as well. But these Jews also desired, despite their favored status, to live as Jews, with and for the whole oppressed house of Israel. Their coexistence was organized in the form of a philanthropic order, but that was the only condition possible for social virtue under the authoritarian regime of the empire.

It was in this setting that the Gunzburg family played an exceptional, primordial, inspiring, organizing and directing role – but at the same time a role of pure devotion and sacrifice! Having obtained, through their success in business and their talents, a leading position at the international level, they were granted nobility by the principality of Hessen, and were authorized to bear their title of baron in Russia under Tzar Alexander II in 1871. They had contacts at the highest levels of the empire, and found themselves leading all the interventions in favor of the Jewish community, at a time when vexing and oppressive anti-Jewish measures had been on the increase since Alexander III. It may be of interest to consider, in the notes of Zalman Shazar (the future president of the future state of Israel), who was among the group of young men admitted to the *Cours des hautes études orientales* (Courses for Advanced Oriental Studies), founded in St Petersburg in 1908 by Baron David of Gunzburg, the uncle of Mrs. Anna Halperin, the following testimony on the Gunzburgs.

A Jewish family in Russia which, on the outside, enjoyed the consideration of the established powers and which was, on the inside, for the Jewish masses, the main family carrying the weight of the Jewish institutions of all Russia, from the Napoleonic War to the birth of a democratic society in tzarist Russia.

Approaches, interventions, the exercise of presidential offices in various philanthropic organizations, planification in which cultural concerns were always present. ... The high spiritual and religious level of Russian Judaism during that period could still be taken as an exotic particularism, and be lived as such, since although the Jews were not confined in ghettos in the strict sense of the term, they lived in social isolation, often without being able to speak good Russian, and without truly confronting European civilization. It is a well-known fact that since Peter the Great that civilization had awakened and transformed the particularism of Holy Russia herself, the land in which Pushkin and Tolstoy slumbered. Openness to the West, under the rubric *pro-sveshtchenye* (instruction, the contribution of the Enlightenment, or even illumination) and in its Russian guise, was a necessity that preoccupied the Gunzburg family.

There remains on these various points much historical research to be carried out. Let it suffice for us here – the better to understand, and the better to honor, the lady who has left us and the whole spiritual order she represented – to relate that order to the problematic that is still current in today's Jewry. The present-day Jewish collectivity is simultaneously (and perhaps paradoxically) more attached to Europe since Auschwitz than before, and summoned, on Russian soil, to a task in which the Jewry of Russian civilization was the pioneer: the task of overcoming the false opposition between the universal and the national. Let us briefly recall the last undertaking, already mentioned, of one of the Gunzburgs who, nearly on the eve of the First World War, was to crown the entire cultural action carried out during the nineteenth century by his family: the *Cours des hautes études orientales.* This was the official name under which, in 1908 in St Petersburg, an élite of Jewish professors was to be conceived, created and especially presented – an élite who had a Western cultural formation, prepared to teach young Jews, who came equipped with their own traditional culture, a modern Jewish culture! It is not certain, as one might be led to think, that the influence of that 'cohabitation' of the old with the new was necessarily supposed to flow in one direction!

Here, by way of conclusion, is another excerpt from Zalman Shazar's *Memoirs,* which I translate without commentary. It touches on the thought of Baron David of Gunzburg.

I remember a private conversation in which the baron tried to convince me that the concepts 'nationalism' and 'assimilation,' which I used in speaking to my comrades, were 'inadequate.' He explained to me how the use of those concepts dissatisfied him. Having gotten the sense that his arguments didn't really convince me, he produced the absolute, irrefutable argument: Maimonides! How could I define Maimonides, using those concepts I thought so solid? Would I say that Maimonides was a national thinker? But didn't he live on the summits of world thinking in his time, his mind filled with Greek wisdom, that master of all the treasures of the Western world, the friend of the princes of thought not from our land, writing his books in Arabic, criticizing all the 'achievements' that are considered sacred among us for generations and persecuted thereafter by the 'faithful keepers of the walls' among our people? But who among our people adored or sanctified Israel's thought more, in the rigor of all the concepts of philosophy and science? Who summarized and organized the *Halakhah* for his and all future generations? Who formulated the principles of the Jewish *credo,* the basis of all Judaism? And if the national versus assimilated distinction doesn't allow one to grasp what is essential and great in the nation, how could it be used to classify less important persons and events? It must therefore be recognized that the notions 'national' and 'assimilated,' so familiar to myself and my generation, do not express the complexity of the real, and are not suitable to their object. Supplementary or different concepts are needed!

Now here is the end of that note by Zalman Shazar, in which the anti-Maimonidean finds his inalienable part within the true complexity of living Judaism.

While the baron exalted and admired Maimonides as an exemplary figure in the thought of Israel, he considered the *Critical Notes of Rabad* (Rabbi Abraham David of Posquières) on Maimonides to be a permanent presence at the heart of the nation and took the quarrel between them (Maimonides and Rabad) as an ever current affair among us, until the time when, in the words of Isaiah, 'the earth shall be full of the knowledge of the Lord, as the waters cover the sea.'[2]

11

The Philosophy of Franz Rosenzweig
Preface to Système et Révélation *by Stéphane Mosès*[1]

Stéphane Mosès's book presents Franz Rosenzweig's philosophy such as it is expressed in that philosopher's main work, *The Star of Redemption (Der Stern der Erlösung),* first published in 1921. Everything in the person of that philosopher, in that book, in that philosophy, is remarkable. It has a very contemporary ring, despite the sixty years, despite the Holocaust, that separate us from its publication. It is eminently worthy of the enlightened attention Stéphane Mosès devotes to it, of the talent and intelligence his study manifests.

Franz Rosenzweig, born of a Jewish family profoundly assimilated by the culture and society of post-Bismarckian Germany, rediscovers, while on the brink of conversion to Christianity, the meaning and the sources of Judaism, and remains passionately faithful to them, though never forgetting his approach to Christianity. He wrote most of *The Star of Redemption* on postcards addressed to his mother while he was at the Balkan front during the close of the First World War. After the Armistice, he gave up a university career for which everything had destined him, founded an institute for advanced Judaic studies in Frankfurt, and died in 1929, at the age of forty-three, of a progressive paralysis. During the final stages of his illness, struggling with increasing physical problems, immobilized in his bed, he collaborated with Martin Buber on the translation of the Old Testament into German.

His book, written in six months, is extraordinary. Though created as if in a feverish trance of genius, it is admirably composed and balanced, reflecting an impressive universal culture, and contributing new philosophical insights. From these insights is derived in particular the astonishing idea of absolute truth splitting, by its very essence, into Christianity and Judaism – two adventures of the spirit that are both (and with equal claims) necessary to the veracity of the True. This philosophical and theological position, unprecedented in the history of thought, forecasts today's ecumenical tendencies, and is completely free of any syncretism. This philosophy does not, however, mean to confine itself to responding to confessional questions, nor to flaunt its own originality by formulating startlingly new theses. Its profound newness is derived from its rejection of the primordial nature of a certain type of rationality – namely the variety that inspired traditional philosophy 'from the Ionian Isles to Jena,' from the pre-Socratics to Hegel. It consisted in totalizing natural and social experience, in isolating and interrelating its categories to the point of building a system that included the religious order itself. The new philosophy attempts, on the contrary, to grasp religion – Creation, Revelation and Redemption, which orient religion's spirituality – as the primordial horizon of all meaning, including that of the experience of the world and history. But it is a philosophy probably deserving of the name, inasmuch as it was led toward that religious intrigue as the opening up of a primordial horizon of meaning, based on a rigorous reflection on the crisis of the intelligibility of the world, that is, on the crisis of the totality and of Hegel's system.

It is with this critique of traditional rationality that the first book of *The Star of Redemption,* which Mosès analyzes with strength and clarity, begins. Man, world and God – the objects of rational psychology, cosmology and theology in the metaphysical tradition, which in Hegel's speculation were brought together in the Idea – are shown by Rosenzweig in their originary irreducibility, resistant to the kind of synthetic thought that would combine them. Long before Heidegger, Rosenzweig reworked the Kierkegaardian themes of dread. In the dread of dying, which no system can dissipate by avoiding it or embracing it, the Hegelian totality breaks up into three absolutely separate elements. Man does not find peace – and thus finds no place – within the *all* that embraces him. He persists in not seeing himself as a part of it, and so God and the world also return to their isolation. They present themselves – they impose themselves – as being separate, thus thwarting the mode of thought that was considered all-encompassing in idealist speculation. This separation would constitute the 'truth' of paganism: the truth of a metaphysical mythical god, of a metalogical world of plastic forms, of a metaethical tragic man.

Stéphane Mosès, in the chapters of his book dedicated to book 2 of *The Star of Redemption*, describes the entering into relation of elements isolated by the breakup of Hegel's totality. They open up to one another, leave their imprisonment, go beyond themselves. But they are no longer united in a totality by I know not what synthesis of transcendental thought. God's coming out toward the world is a movement always already accomplished, always past; past to the point of bringing only to the intelligence the bare meaning of the past. But this coming out is accomplished precisely in the guise of Creation. This is God's coming out toward man closed up in his ipseity: Revelation that is presence ever renewed, i.e., love. And, in response to God's love, there is man's coming forth toward other men in the world, the tearing loose of the world from its *ipso facto* inertia, a calling forth as 'thou,' in their personhood, of the others, installed in the third person in the world as public personae, as third parties. Then also there are the hopes and anticipations of redemption – the dimension of the future. The 'elements,' not reintegrable into a totality, enter into relation, not to reconstitute the impossible totality, but to form time. Time that is no longer, as in Kant's schematization, a schema of categories. It is an order that, in itself, 'must be taken seriously,' and remain inseparable from Creation, Revelation and Redemption. This openness is thus the original temporality: Creation, pastness par excellence; Revelation, presentness of the present; Redemption, tension toward the future. This time is no more the form of sensibility, as the Critique of Pure Reason would have it; it receives its meaning from the horizon of religiosity. Temporality is conceived as the life of the 'elements,' of which language, in its essential transitivity, is the movement; but language that, henceforth, is not just the reflection of a prior thought, its subordinate function, but verb as the breaking out from imprisonment. The breaking out from imprisonment, a coming out from the self – from one to the other – the origin of which is not the passage from the 'subject' to the 'object,' but is in the religious event of the Revelation. To speak in Husserlian terms, the transitivity of language is the profound event of all intentionality. There is transcendence of intentionality because there was language of the Revelation. I shall return to this point. Revelation is central to *The Star of Redemption.*

Stéphane Mosès shows this with insistence, and this justifies the title of his meticulous work. Revelation is one of the three dimensions of temporality, and at the same time the dimension to which all openness refers – both that of Creation and of Redemption. Language, the movement of coming out, is also the event of existence. It is indeed possible to associate, to a certain extent, Rosenzweig's ontological 'experience' – which is language moving from one to the other, rather than a synthesis containing one and the other – with what today is still called the existential. Moses uses this term in his exposition, and returns to this association in his conclusion, particularly in reference to Karl Löwith's study on Rosenzweig and on Heidegger's *Being and Time*. It is interesting to note that, without having been influenced by Husserl's phenomenology, with which he appears to be unfamiliar,' Rosenzweig, setting out from the religious horizon of the Creation, the Revelation and the Redemption, and having read Nietzsche and Kierkegaard, heralds the philosophy of the literature of existence such as was to flower again in the prolongation of Heidegger, who rejected it.

The third book of *The Star of Redemption* is devoted to Redemption, described in its projection toward the future. The religious theme of Redemption is, according to this work, the very way in which the *futurition* of the future shows itself in it, just as Creation exposed the pastness of the past, and Revelation the presentness of the present. It is in this regard that *The Star of Redemption,* using religious notions, presents itself as a work of general philosophy rather than (or at least as much as) of religious philosophy. It describes a projection toward the future in the form of redemption: a future that thus reveals itself in the dual modality of Judaism and Christianity, and in an orientation toward eternity; and this thanks to a symbolism other than that of the signifying language in revelation. The ritualism of the religious communities, in its periodicity, is lived as a circularity of time. It breaks the linear 'temporalization' and delineates the image of a fixed eternity: an eternity that is at once signified and anticipated. The symbolism of the rite is not portrayed as being some deficiency in knowledge, but a surplus, halfway between the signifying of the signified and its accomplishment. Rosenzweig's concrete and multidimensional analyses border on sociology, aesthetics and theology. They are expressed in two modalities – both necessary and the only ones necessary: Judaism and Christianity. The modality of Judaism is inseparable from the structure of the 'eternal people,' outside history, already participating in eternity, but limited in its particularism; that of Christianity resides in its missionary universalism, in its being present to history and to the historical nations, but ever en route, yet assured of the two eternal termini of that same route: Incarnation and Parousia.

It is surely in this way that *The Star of Redemption,* beyond its speculative significance, introduces a new and profound concept to modern Jewish consciousness. That modernity consists, for Israel, in wishing and hoping for a concrete community with the surrounding Christian world that constitutes the West, after two millennia of segregation, lived, it is true, as sacrifice in the consciousness of its universal importance, but a purely spiritual or mystic universality. There is a need for concrete symbiosis! That need has survived Hitler's denial and reappears, in another form, in the state of Israel itself, which aspires – on all levels of human relationships – to be a member of the family of nations. It was in Moses Mendelssohn's *Jerusalem* of 1783 that that modernity found its expression and its doctrine. Had not the progressive dejudaization of the Jewish citizens of the nation-states of Europe already given evidence of the fragility of that first philosophy? Emancipation, which assured the Jews the continuation of a purely confessional Judaism, began to mean assimilation. To many Jews, that term had a pejorative ring. Is it possible, in Western civilization, which is 'informed' by Christianity, to preserve the Jewish religious essence? Is one not unwittingly, within that civilization, a Christian even if one refuses, in Simone Weil's words, 'every Christian dogma'? Here, *The Star of Redemption* innovates. According to it, there is between Christians and Jews very great closeness – a closeness centered around the truth. It is not the simple sharing of a few ideas, nor the continuity of a history in which some repeat or renew the opinions of others. Truth no longer means statements and affirmations, but the unfolding of an event, an eschatological drama. It is a truth that is all the more true because the partners in the drama are called to play different roles. The absolutely true splits in two, by its very truth – into Judaism and Christianity – and is played out in their dialogue. It is a life in common. But Judaism, thus brought back to its ontological dignity, henceforth requires of its faithful not just an occasional distracted attendance at service, but all the dimensions of the Torah that they were aware of during the time of their isolation.

Mosès's last chapter deals with the single truth to which Judaism and Christianity lead, a truth that cannot correspond to any experience and be presented as the vision of a visionary. *The Star of Redemption,* which is the six-pointed star, called the Star of David, schematizes, in that part of the book, the themes of the exposition itself which reaches its conclusion, and the human face, the sight of which is the ultimate apprehension of the truth in its absoluteness.

The pages Rosenzweig devotes to Redemption, very rich but at times dense, are admirably presented by Stéphane Mosès. His analysis is clear, subtle and suggestive. *The Star of Redemption,* a work written with a high lyricism, is often allusive and obscure. It is illuminated here by a sober, sure thought, which, without sacrificing any of the meaning, resists the temptation of imitation, speaking a precise but different language. It is a language ever attentive to the overall intent, its prolongation into the present, its indebtedness to Schelling's *Weltalter* (world-age), its German contexts of the nineteenth and twentieth centuries – including Hegel, who is, as Moses amply proves, a source, and not just the system to be destroyed. Moses consults the Jewish texts, as far back as the Kabbalah. German as well as Jewish texts are familiar to Stephane Mosès, who is both a Germanicist and a reader of Hebrew. Thanks to him, *The Star of Redemption,* whose entry into philosophical discussion was delayed by so many grave historical circumstances – but also by the unaccustomed novelty of its vision and the misunderstandings to which it gave rise – has been returned to Western thought.

The Star gives us full access to a thought possessing philosophical significance that reaches well beyond its more immediately obvious relevance to the theology and religious philosophy of our day, when there is incessant talk of the death of God – which is the death of the God of the Judeo-Christian tradition. Franz Rosenzweig's thought, which shared none of the presuppositions of phenomenology, nonetheless marks the end of a certain idealism. That end does not lead back to the facile solutions of naive realism, nor to the objectivism of mathematical structures. It ultimately leads to *the human,* to which the ideas relate, manifesting in that relativity a richer meaning than the one attaching to their *outward aspect* and their metaphysical *absolute.* But it leads to the human that is original on the basis of its presence to God, on the basis of the present of Revelation. And philosophy is not immediately held accountable for the verification of that presence and of that present, starting out from the transcendental subject or the man-in-the-world endowed with natural lights. The meanings of terms like natural lights, subject, and man-in-the-world, would, on the contrary, have their source in a certain constellation of meaning that appears in Revelation. It is this recourse to a new horizon of meaning and the acknowledgement of its intelligibility as having priority that doubtless constitutes the great originality of *The Star of Redemption.*

But I also think that that work, taken independently from the specific theses to which it leads in the end, bears several very characteristic general movements of thought that it is important to highlight, stressing the perspectives they open in their own right. Stéphane Mosès's book, so careful not to drop any of these perspectives, makes it possible to thematize them. Leaving aside the doctrinal content of *The Star of Redemption*, its references to cultural and historical data, the precise dogmatic terms of its teaching on God, the world and man, a few *speculative gestures* are new in Franz Rosenzweig's intellectual operations. Perhaps he, then, will offer a broader framework for what has been called, since Buber, a philosophy of dialogue.

First, there is the fact of Rosenzweig's having restricted himself to a totality that had burst apart: the idea that *all cannot be assembled*. God, the world, man (the three regions of *ontologia specialis*) cannot be reassembled into a whole. Clearly, this rupture of the totality is affirmed in opposition to Hegel. But it is also a more general speculative gesture, executed with a radicalism that casts doubts upon the most spontaneous, natural movement of philosophy: that of including, encompassing the thinkable, raising it to the universal in the unity of the genus, or integrating it within the moments of an ascending dialectic. All is not assemblable. The questioning of totality is carried out by beginning with the mortality of man, with a 'content,' an exceptional content, and not, as in Kant's transcendental dialectic, by setting out from the idea of totality itself, and its inadequation with experience. In a sense it is the shocking nature of death that breaks up the universal synthesis. Mortality is precisely the fact that everything cannot be handled – does not settle into place. This is an idea that Bergson, in the famous discussion in *Evolution créatrice*, seems to have missed, when he reduces disorder to a *different* order. The *social person* succeeds in *establishing himself* within the totality of a world. In *me*, the totality is shattered. Rosenzweig accustoms us to thinking the non-synthesizable – difference – contrary to a philosophical tradition in which the Same absorbs the Other into its interiority, and in which absolute thought is a thought thinking the identity of the Same and the Other.

The elements that have broken the totality become fixed in the separation in which absolute difference maintains them *on the hither side of formal totality*. Traditional thought dared, or had the ability, to group under the vacuous heading of 'something-in-general' (*etwas überhaupt*) the most disparate terms, resistant to the unity of genus. The irreducible diversity of genera still had the illumination of the Idea of the Good in common in Plato. In Aristotle, being *qua* being (be it only by the unity of analogy) united all the thinkable. In Rosenzweig, we glimpse the 'positivity' of an absolute pluralism. But the estrangement from all inclusive universality is not thought negatively. It becomes *mythical,* enclosing *in itself.* It is, in a sense, prelogical, and subjacent to our ontological culture that claims to have gone beyond it; or it is prereligious and subjacent to our culture of Revelation. Prelogic, prereligion – how so? Will the commonplaces on the unconscious suffice here? It is the entire first book of *The Star of Redemption* that, in its description of the mythical, develops the concreteness or the positivity of this abstract *pre-* and *sub-,* more formal than any form in the radical separation of the non-assemblable, remaining within the mythical secret of a pagan spell.

This description and this analysis only become possible after the fact: after the demythification of the myths, after the elements have left their elementariness. Revelation is the gesture (or the saga) of this coming forth, which is an original being-outside-of-self, and, *par excellence,* older, so to speak, than intentionality. It is a gesture that also tears the elements from the depths of the immemorial, where they are isolated in themselves. This *outside-of-self* is not the equivalent of some flowering of mythology into ontology, into understanding of being. Revelation is precisely an entering-into-relation completely different from the one that corresponds to a synthesis or that can be lodged within a category established between the elements. An *establishing* would only produce systems, whereas Revelation is life, language and temporality. The entering-into-relation by Revelation *establishes* nothing. It connects the non-additive; it connects it in a connection for which language or sociality or love is the original metaphor. *The Star of Redemption,* in its first two books, is none other than the story of that life that is neither mythical isolation nor gathering in being. It is, *before all else,* the transcendence of God coming out of his secret; its dimensions of past and future, *the semantics of which is here originary,* open out from two other modes of transcendence: Creation and Redemption. It is appropriate to stress the newness of this conception of life, that does not flow on as persistence or perseverance in being – does not equate with any sort of dynamism of that perseverance asserting itself in the form of a pure becoming – but as what Rosenzweig calls 'days of the Lord,' a crossing over toward the *Other*: beginning with transcendence (that of God in Creation, and of God-going-toward-man in Revelation), it is the transcendence of man-to-man in Redemption.

What seems remarkable in all these speculative developments is the deformalization of these conjunctions and prepositions. Their formalization, which seems to reflect the intelligibility ('taken for granted' and already universally understood) of the being of beings, and all that ontology in which they reside, are led back, to the hither side or beyond logical or ontological intelligibility, to a different dimension of the meaningful – denying ontology its rational primacy. There is no synthesis placing God and the world alongside one another like two beings coexisting *before* Creation, which is always already past, already prior to the conjunction that connects beings and is consequently concrete only in that Creation. There is no thematizable synthesis, such as 'God and man,' unless it is as Revelation in which man is addressed in all the acuity and actuality of the now (a 'frontal' relation, prior to any juxtaposition), a *now* in which the past itself is only affirmed as *represented* and thus as 'eternally present.' The conjunction 'and' in the phrase 'man and the world' is concrete only in the response of man to Revelation and God's love, in the openness on the world as world-to-come, in which this world is, in its way, 'eternally present.' This openness on the world is not the now famous 'being-in-the-world,' but an immediate relation to the future world, or better world, or world 'to be made better,' and especially relative to other men, 'social persons in the world,' 'they,' to whom we will learn to say 'thou.' Redemption, Rosenzweig says, is learning to say 'thou' to a 'he.'

Here we have, in the deformalization of the formal, a return toward the 'primordial events,' toward the 'ecstasies' of temporality. A curious signifying of eternity within the dimensions of time itself! We are far from relations as they signify intemporally in a system. Reciprocity of the relation does not obtain between the same terms: God's love for man has its reciprocal relation in the redemption of the world by man. Creation, Revelation and Redemption are involved in an intrigue in which the philosopher who names them is implicated, but it is an intrigue other than that of perseverance of a being in its being or its turning back upon itself, other than that of the *conatus essendi*, which is probably the primary ontological meaning. *The Star of Redemption*, which shatters totality in the anguish of nothingness, does not return human being to care for its own being; instead, it leads human being to a frontal relation with the other man. Is this not the concrete description of the *dia* of dialogue itself? It is a return to the source of what is called in our day philosophy of the dialogue, but all of whose partisans consider the principle to be almost empirically discoverable, insisting on the particular irreducibility of the

I-thou to objectification. It is restored, in *The Star of Redemption*, to all the concreteness of the 'day of the Lord,' to a horizon of meaning, an intrigue originally formed between God, the world and man – older, if one may say so, than the adventure of ontology.

This 'ancient' intrigue cannot be 'demystified,' in such a manner as to allow the *dia* of dialogue to be reduced to a mere juxtaposition of terms in the eyes of an absolute observer, placed 'higher' or 'behind the scenes,' who would have the last word, sum up the dialogue of transcendence and transform it into an ontology in which the Said (*le Diret*) rules the Saying (*le Dire*). There can be no speaker or observer behind the intrigue of *The Star of Redemption*. It is not in a philosopher's head or in the depths of transcendental consciousness that God, man and world are united, producing I know not what generic unity. It is, on the contrary, to the event produced by their coming out of mythical isolation into the light of the day of the Lord – it is to Revelation that the thinker owes his very ability to think. The *cogitatio-cogitatum, noesis-noema* correlation, submitted to idealist reflection, is no longer the ultimate structure of the spiritual. In that shattering of totality – within which pure inwardness does not succeed in getting out of the Myth and crossing the absolute interval that separates it from the Other, prior to the transcendence of Revelation – we can find the basis for the priority of language over 'pure thought.' And this is so, not because of the role played by rhetoric and metaphor in the intelligibility of the thinkable, nor because of the social and cultural treasures language contributes to the refinement of thought, nor because of its power to preserve thought's acquisitions. Rather this is so because the relation and movement in which thought becomes life is not originally intentionality, but Revelation, the crossing of an absolute interval; and because the ultimate bond of the psyche is not the one securing the unity of the subject, but the binding separation, so to speak, of society, the *dia* of the dialogue, of dia-chrony, of that time that Rosenzweig means to 'take seriously,' the binding separation known by the well-worn name of love.

12
Judaism and Christianity[1]

Emmanuel Levinas. – I would like, in all simplicity, to say how, through the years, my personal attitude toward Christianity has gone through a certain change, precisely thanks to reading Franz Rosenzweig. I shall speak frankly, with the intention of offending no one.

The first time I approached our theme was, as if by chance, in the corner of a drawing room, with a friend, the poet Claude Vigée. It was a kind of profession of faith toward him. A profession of faith that, by the way, engages no one but the speaker. Each one of us Jews retains his freedom of expression. We do not have, despite the rigor of the Law, any orientation dictated by the synagogue; neither obligatory nor even just official. So everyone is free, in a certain sense, to declare his 'inner events.' In that spirit I would like to tell you what I first expressed to a friend.

In my childhood (now three-quarters of a century ago) Christianity sounded to me like a completely closed world, from which, as a Jew, nothing good was to be expected. The first pages of the history of Christianity I was able to read told the story of the Inquisition. Already at eight or nine years old I was learning about the sufferings of the *Marranos* in Spain. A little later there was the crucial reading of the history of the Crusades. As a child, I lived in a country in which there was no social contact between Jews and Christians. I was born in Lithuania, a lovely country with beautiful forests and nice, very Catholic people – but a place where Jews and Christians did not socialize, unless it was in a purely economic context.

Later I came to read the Gospel. I believe that that reading, which no longer disagreed with me, marks an antithesis. The representation and the teaching of what is human, which I found there, always seemed close to me. I happened upon *Matthew 25*, where people are quite astonished to learn that they have abandoned or persecuted God, and are told that when they turned away the poor who knocked on their doors, it was really God in person they were shutting out. Having learned later the theological concepts of transubstantiation and the eucharist, I would tell myself that the true communion was in the meeting with the other, rather than in the bread and the wine, and that it was in that encounter that the personal presence of God resided; and that I had already read that, in the Old Testament, in chapter 58 of *Isaiah*. It had the same meaning: men already 'spiritually refined' who want to see the face of God and enjoy his proximity will only see his face once they have freed their slaves and fed the hungry. That was the antithesis. And, if I may be so bold, it was also the understanding of the person of Christ. What remained incomprehensible was not the person, but all the realist theology surrounding him. The whole drama of his theological mystery remained unintelligible. It is still so today, whereas concepts such as God's kenosis, the humility of his presence on earth, are very close to Jewish sensibility in all the vigor of their spiritual meaning.

That is not all. The worst was that those frightful things, from the Inquisition and the Crusades, were tied to the sign of Christ, the cross. That seemed incomprehensible and required explanation. In addition to that, there is the fact that, properly speaking, the world was not changed by the Christian sacrifice. That was even the essential thing. Being Christian, Europe could do nothing to put things right. Neither by what Christians did as Christians, nor by what, in Christianity, should have dissuaded people from performing certain acts. That is the first thing I have to say. I still feel that quite strongly. The reading of the Gospel was always compromised in my view – in our view – by history.

Then comes what you call the Holocaust and what we call the *Shoah.* At that time two things became very clear. First, the fact that all who participated in the *Shoah* had, in their childhood, received a Catholic or Protestant baptism; and they found no interdiction in that! And the second fact, very, very important: during that period, what you call charity or mercy appeared to me directly. Wherever the black robe was to be seen, there was refuge. There, discourse was still possible. A world without recourse is one of despair.

I am going to tell you a story. During 'the phoney war,' I had been drafted to serve in a department in the capital. A friend who worked in the same office lost a child. The father was Jewish and the mother Christian. The funeral service was held at the church of Saint-Augustin. It was before May 10, 1940, but our old world was already everywhere in jeopardy. During the religious service I happened to be near a picture – a painting or a fresco – depicting a scene from *I Samuel*: Hannah leading her son Samuel to the Temple. My world was still there. Especially in Hannah, that extraordinary figure of the Jewish woman. I thought of her silent prayer: 'Her lips moved, but her voice could not be heard.' I thought of the misunderstanding between her and Eli the high priest, and her answer: 'No, my lord, I am a woman of a sorrowful spirit; I have drunk neither wine nor strong drink, but I poured out my soul before the Lord.' That woman was truly praying from her heart: the pouring out of the soul. The authentic relation, concreteness of soul, the very personification of the relation. That is what I saw in the church. What closeness! That closeness remained within me.

I also think that I have a debt toward that charity. I owe the life of my little family to a monastery in which my wife and daughter were saved. Her mother had been deported, but my wife and little girl found refuge and protection among the nuns of St Vincent de Paul. What I owe exceeds gratitude – acknowledgement [*reconnaissance*] goes much further. The most important thing, in those times, was being able to talk to someone. But, after all, these are all feelings.

Already before the war I had read Rosenzweig, and I knew of his thesis on the philosophical possibility of thinking of truth as being accessible in two forms: Jewish and Christian. That was an extraordinary stance: thought does not move toward its goal by one sole path. Metaphysical truth was essentially possible in two forms of expression. That was stated for the first time. I do not always agree with all the links in Rosenzweig's system. I do not believe all the links, such as he presents them, are definitively valid. But the very possibility of thinking, without compromise or betrayal, in two forms – the Jewish and the Christian, that of Christian lovingkindness and that of the Jewish Torah – has allowed me to understand the relation between Judaism and Christianity in its *positivity*. I can formulate it in another way: in its possibility of dialogue and symbiosis.

I had a very positive reaction to *Nostra Aetate*, the decree of the Second Vatican Council. To me it is a logical consequence and proof of the fact that an attempt has been made to overcome certain things from the past. I am pleased to accept the parallelism in the theory of kenosis, and in the idea of an omni-human universality and a 'for all men.' I have understood Christianity in its 'to live and die for all men.' The authentically human is the being-Jewish in all men (may you not be shocked by this!) and its reflection in the singular and the particular. The Christians attach great importance to what they call faith, mystery, sacrament. Here is an anecdote on that subject. Hannah Arendt, not long before she died, told the following story on French radio. When she was a child in her native Königsberg, one day she said to the rabbi who was teaching her religion: 'You know, I have lost my faith.' And the rabbi responded: 'Who's asking you for it?' The response was typical. What matters is not 'faith,' but 'doing.' Doing, which means moral behavior, of course, but also the performance of ritual. Moreover, are believing and doing different things? What does believing mean? What is faith made of? Words, ideas? Convictions? What do we believe with? With the whole body! With all my bones (*Psalm 35:10*)! What the rabbi meant was: 'Doing good is the act of belief itself.' That is my conclusion.

Bishop Hemmerle. – It is difficult to respond to a testimony that moves the witness so deeply. And I have the impression that it would not be appropriate to say anything by advancing pure argument. Listening to you, I myself could not but be quite fearful. I, too, feel that everything that has happened in the name of Jesus and under his sign concerns me, even if I dare say, in all frankness, that I think I know him so well that I cannot do otherwise than believe in him, and believe in him precisely as a Christian. Otherwise, I would be unfaithful, for I have met him; and I would be as unfaithful as you would be if you abandoned your faith. But let me please try to give you two responses.

First, is that not the sign of the 'no defense' of God, of the 'no defense' of Jesus, which he too took upon himself, so that in the inmost depths of his mission he could encounter me without defense? The thing about him that, strictly speaking, compels me, is precisely the 'no defense' and the kenosis into which he entered. To me, the extreme point of the kenosis (and I am not bringing it up as some manner of dialectical excuse) resides in the fact that (*agape*, the love of God, charity, God's grace having taken on a body and become flesh for me) he was able to go so far as to ask me for nothing more than to love and follow him. It is up to him, if he wishes to send me the Spirit to guide my faith and my deeds; I have no assurance that I will not offend him by actions contrary to what he says and is, unless I open my heart and 'all my bones' to him. To me, the fact that it is possible to reach that point expresses the extreme degree of the divine kenosis.

I admit that, ever anew, I am frightened at so many things I must do as a bishop. I often wonder whether I am not betraying him, even when what I do seems right at the moment I am doing it. And I would not swear by putting my hand to the flame that I do not betray him each time anew. And perhaps it is for the best that I cannot put my hand to the flame. If I could, I would have a certainty that would no longer be like him – he who is a head, all blood and wounds.

My second point. I can do no better than to bear witness to what Franz Rosenzweig also signifies in this context to me, as a Christian. I have been able to open up the path of belief for many human beings who cannot believe, above all thanks to Franz Rosenzweig's theory of Messianic knowledge: I cannot recognize, otherwise than at the cost of the blood, things concerning the ultimate; I can only believe with 'all my bones' where the ultimate is involved. That insight moved me so deeply that it is really on that basis that I think I can open the path of faith to man – and even the path of Christian faith – when I feel that I am running the risk of vanishing in the aporias of thought. Remarkably, what leads Rosenzweig back to the path of Judaism is also what allows me, as a Christian, to understand the eucharist: the love that Jesus has for me is love with the heart, the blood and 'all the bones.' That is why ultimately I can believe only with all my bones. Rosenzweig freed me, in my encounter with the Gospel, from a purely metaphysical 'immobilization' in 'ready-made concepts.' Even in the mystery of the Trinity – which is far removed from Judaism – I have been able to deepen 'my possessions' because of what I discovered in Rosenzweig in the way of a 'universe of living relations,' in the way of temporality and the impossibility of substituting anything in the place of time and the relation to the other. Thus, I owe Rosenzweig a large part of my understanding and defense of Christianity. And I want to hope that on the basis of his thought a deep solidarity will be formed through the being-delivered-to-suffering that is common to us. Here a path of knowledge is opened, in which the horrible things that befall my neighbor call me toward sensibility and responsibility.

Hans-Hermann Henrix. – In the two accounts we have just heard, we learn what, in the language of Rosenzweig, can be referred to as the conjunction 'and,' placed between Judaism and Christianity. Professor Levinas was saying that the entirety of the theological theme of the kenosis as understood by Christianity remained closed to him. And the history of the relations between Jews and Christians was conveyed by Bishop Hemmerle precisely in such a way as to construe that history as the extreme manifestation of the divine kenosis. He used the words 'no defense.'

Emmanuel Levinas. – The 'no defense' in this case cost much human suffering. We are not engaged in a 'disputation' on the subject of divine compassion. You know, I don't understand that 'no defense' anymore today, after Auschwitz. Sometimes what happened at Auschwitz seems to mean to me that God requires a love that entails no promise on his part. Thought can stretch that far. The meaning of Auschwitz would be a suffering devoid of any promise, totally gratuitous. But even then I rebel, thinking it is too costly – not just to God, but to humanity. That is my criticism, or my lack of understanding, of the 'no defense': that kenosis of powerlessness costs man too much! Christ without defense on the cross eventually found himself leading the armies of the Crusades! And he did not come down from the cross to stop the murderers.

Bishop Hemmerle. – That was his 'no defense.'

Emmanuel Levinas. – A 'no defense' that was not only God's, but a 'no defense' of the victims!

Bishop Hemmerle. – I am not taking the 'no defense' as an excuse; I understand it to be that very costly, living requirement that wants to be reversal in actions.

Emmanuel Levinas. – But that sounds like theology.

Bishop Hemmerle. – As long as I am content with speaking, my words remain theological. I simply believe there is a concrete reversal in action behind my words, which only remain verbal, of course, as long as I do nothing but speak.

13
On Jewish Philosophy[1]

Françoise Armengaud. – Professor Levinas, on the theme of this special issue of *Revue de métaphysique et de morale,* you are among those who have contributed most – not only in framing the question, but also in demonstrating its fecundity, in a sense, by the momentum and the example you give. You have written on the subject explicitly in several instances:[2] in *Difficile liberté,* in your foreword to *Quatre lectures talmudiques,* in *Noms propres,* and in *De Dieu qui vient a l'idée,* and in your preface to Stéphane Mosès's study on Franz Rosenzweig's philosophy. You expressed yourself again on this recently in an interview, broadcast on France-Culture.[3] One might think, then, that all has been said, and that the reader need only read. But if you will allow me, I would like to ask you a few questions.

Emmanuel Levinas. – A dialogue generally includes questions. I expected to be questioned, and was attentive and curious in advance. Your first words appear to direct the conversation more particularly toward myself. Judaism and philosophy: I was thinking of their manifestation in history. But you seem to want to lead me to speak of myself.

Françoise Armengaud. – You are right. When you state, in the interview I just mentioned, that the tradition of biblical theology and that of philosophy were for you immediately in agreement, without your ever having explicitly undertaken to reconcile them, I'm a bit surprised. ...

Emmanuel Levinas. – I don't think we ever start out by explicitly setting ourselves a problem of reconciliation. Does the distinction between Judaism and philosophical reflection immediately emerge as a major conflict? We may start out (and this was the case with me, since you wish to speak of me) in a world in which Judaism was lived, and in a very natural way: not at all, or not only, in what is called piety or rigorous ritualism, but above all with the sense that belonging to humanity means belonging to an order of supreme responsibility. An order in which non-Jewish books also are perceived as being concerned with the meaning of life – which is contiguous with the meaning of human existence and already, perhaps, with the meaning of being. I am thinking of the Russian novels of my very youthful years, for example, or the 'To be or not to be' in *Hamlet*, or of *Macbeth*, or *King Lear*, or *L'Avare*, or *Le Misanthrope* and *Tartuffe*, which I experienced as dramas of the human condition. Philosophy speaks of it also, but in another language, that always strives to be explicit, adjusting its terms to one another and formulating problems where there are breaks in the coherence. But has the handing down of the Scriptures ever taken place without transmission through that language of interpretation, which is already disengaged from the verses that sustain it, always to be found in the gaps between utterances?

Françoise Armengaud. – I too was not thinking of contrasting two different theses, nor two theories about the world, but two languages. . . .

Emmanuel Levinas. – Perhaps Jewish texts have always been understood as constantly accompanied by a layer of symbolic meaning, apologues, new interpretations to be discovered: in short, always lined with *midrash*. And the language of philosophy does not mean that an intellectual wind has torn the reader loose from all literalness, all particularity, all features that are 'just so,' and as such reduced to insignificance. What may have been wished for as holiness of life, in the Judaism of my native Lithuania, was not separated from the holiness of the Scriptures themselves. That is why there was mistrust with respect to what remained obstinately mythological in a deciphered passage. There was a demythologizing of the text, but also the quest for a pretext for thought, down to the very letter of the text. That is, essentially, what that way of reading was. There was also a demythologizing of what was already demythologized, a quest for meaning to be renewed. It is as if the verses were saying over and over: 'Interpret me.' No doubt you know Rashi's expression: 'These verses cry out *darshenu*!' This is not yet a philosophical reading, but it is probably the acquisition of one of its virtues. Philosophical discourse will appear as a way of speaking addressed to completely open minds who require totally explicit ideas, a discourse in which all that is normally taken for granted is said. A discourse addressed to Greeks! A way of speaking that incorporates, and enlivens, that more confidential, closed and firm manner more closely linked to the *bearers of meaning* – bearers who will never be released from their duties by the signified. In this, too, the Scriptures are holy. Such are the biblical verses, and even the terms used in their first, ancient deciphering by the sages of the Talmud. Tireless signifiers! But one day it is discovered that philosophy is also multiple, and that its truth is hidden, has levels and goes progressively deeper, that its texts contradict one another and that the systems are fraught with internal contradictions. Thus, it seems to me essential to consider the fact that the Jewish reading of the Scriptures is carried out in the anxiety, but also the hopeful expectation, of *midrash.* The Pentateuch or *Hummash* never comes to light without Rashi.

Françoise Armengaud. – As you say in *Du sacré au saint*, the parchment is never approached 'empty-handed.'

Emmanuel Levinas. – So that is my answer to your first question, and I wonder whether the great reconcilers of civilizations experienced and lived out their undertaking any differently. I do not commit the error of denying the radical difference in spirit between the Scriptures and philosophy. But, having emphasized their agreement *in fact* at a certain moment in time – perhaps in the maturity or the modernity of Graeco-biblical civilization – I am now ready to speak (if your questions lead me in that direction) of their *essential* connection in human civilization altogether, which is measured or hoped for as peace among men.

Françoise Armengaud. – It just so happens I wanted to ask you – in connection with 'great reconcilers' – about the traditional contrast made between Maimonides and Judah Halevi. What do you think about it?

Emmanuel Levinas. – I do not know whether that division into two is definitive. I do not know whether all varieties of Jewish thought even during the brief medieval period enter into that dichotomy. It is an extremely important division, however. On one side there is the great philosophical tradition that finds intelligibility, rationality and meaning in knowledge. In Maimonides, spirituality is essentially knowledge: knowledge in which being is present to the mind, in which that *presence* of being to the mind is the truth of being, i.e., the exposure of being. It is as if *being* meant presence, even if designated as eternity: exposure of being to thought and exposition on the scale of thought, assimilation by thought and immanence, in which the transcendence of God can signify only negatively. This still leaves open the question of how that transcendence, *per se,* was ever able to let thought know of its very separation. The link between Maimonides (or that spiritual primacy of knowledge) and Greek thought is obvious; and the undeniable mastery of Maimonides in Jewish thought – despite all the attacks launched by certain medieval figures and a few young men of today – is a fact. This indicates that there is communication between faith and philosophy and not the notorious conflict. Communication in both directions.

Judah Halevi is considered a mystic, but he recognized philosophical knowledge to a great extent, and never developed the theme of pure and simple union with God – the disappearance of the thinker in the thought. What we can retain of his *Kuzari* is his description of the relationship with what he calls 'the order of God': *Inyan Elohi.* This relationship is not expressed in terms of an indeterminate coinciding with transcendence and the infinite, but in terms like 'association' (*hithabrut*) and 'proximity' (*hitqarvut*). It is as if these social meanings of 'the relation' did not indicate a deficiency in knowledge, some least bad approximations of knowledge, but were, rather, possessed of their own, sovereign positivity. What matters to me in that work, in which many significant traits are only hinted at (and many others which I find unacceptable), is that possibility of an original thinking and intelligibility other than the immanence of knowledge. (And there is no question, here, of dispensing with knowledge just for the sake of opposing Maimonides.) The proximity and sociality that the philosophers will seek in *knowledge* will appear in Judah Halevi as irreducible possibilities of the meaningful. Sociality together with transcendence!

It is, in fact, my opinion that the relation to God called faith does not primordially mean adhesion to certain statements that constitute a knowledge for which there is no demonstration – a knowledge that would from time to time be troubled by the anxiety of a certainty lacking proof. To me, religion means transcendence, which, as proximity of the absolutely other (i.e., of the one of its kind), is not a failed coinciding and would not have ended in some sublime projected goal, nor in the incomprehension of what should have been grasped and understood as an object, as 'my thing.' Religion is the excellence proper to sociality with the Absolute, or, if you will, in the positive sense of the expression, Peace with the other. But since proximity does not entail *knowledge,* can it not be reduced to the negative notion of distance – of separation from a *beyond* that would not concern the thought of any subject or would come down to a simple tolerant neutrality – a non-aggression, within the world? Unless it is that the positive way of being concerned with God (yet otherwise than by a representation, which would make him immanent) comes precisely from the alterity of man, i.e., from his being outside every genus, from his uniqueness, which I call face – unless proximity itself originally means responsibility for the neighbor. A face beyond the visible that offers itself to our gaze, or to the power of representation that already stares the other down, leaving us looking at the mere plasticity of form. The signifying of the face, defenseless nakedness, the very uprightness of exposure to death. Mortality, and at the same time the signifying of an order, a commandment: 'Thou shalt not kill!' The obligation of responding to the unique, and thus of *loving*. Love beyond all sensitivity, thought of the one and only. The love of God in the love of one's neighbor. This original ethical signifying of the face would thus signify – without any metaphor or figure of speech, in its rigorously proper meaning – the transcendence of a God not objectified in the face in which he speaks; a God who does not 'take on body,' but who approaches precisely through this relay to the neighbor – binding men among one another with obligation, each one answering for the lives of all the others.[4]

This seems to me fundamental to the Judaic faith, in which the relation to God is inseparable from the Torah; that is, inseparable from the recognition of the other person. The relation to God is already ethics; or, as *Isaiah 58* would have it, the proximity to God, devotion itself, is devotion to the other man.

The Jewish Bible I quote is not the originality of an ethnic particularism, no more so than is the Hellenic rationality of knowledge. The Bible *signifies* for all authentically human thought, for civilization *tout court*, whose authenticity can be recognized in peace, in *shalom*, and in the responsibility of one man for another. 'Peace, peace, to him that is far off and to him that is near' (*Isaiah 57:19*). This represents a spiritual event that transcends the anthropological: a questioning, through the human, of a certain *conatus essendi*, of being, which is preoccupied with itself and rests upon itself. Is the 'me' a substance, the subject of perception, and thus master of what is not itself, the one who originally knows, grasps and owns, and is hard and already cruel? Or is it, precisely as 'me,' already hateful to itself, that is, already called to owe itself to the neighbor, the first person to come along, the stranger? To the neighbor, who, somehow, is not merely of the world!

Françoise Armengaud. – To take up this word proximity in its everyday sense, may I ask if you feel a greater proximity to Maimonides or to Judah Halevi?

Emmanuel Levinas. – Who in their right mind would question the existence of Mont Blanc? Maimonides is one of the towering peaks of Judaism, and has left his mark on it in keeping with the way he understood it in the discussions of the Talmudic sages, and the way he understood its Reason, as a disciple of the Greeks. Maimonides is not an accident of Holy History. He has definitely disengaged the Scriptures and the Tradition from what the metaphors, taken literally, risked concealing, to the great delight of pious obscurantism. And in Maimonides himself, to whom rational knowledge of God, metaphysical knowledge, is the supreme good of the human person (and, precisely, an inalienable good, exalting the self in its own happiness, a good that 'profits yourself alone,' in such a way that 'no other shares the benefit with you' [*Guide of the Perplexed,* book II, chapter 54]), everything culminates in the formulation of the negative attributes. But the possibility of this knowledge is maintained as the ethical behavior of goodwill (*hesed*), judgement (*mishpat*) and fairness (*tsedeqah*), as 'for the other.' The imitation of God! The love of one's neighbor is at the summit of a life devoted to supreme knowledge. This is a remarkable reversal, unless we are to question the sincerity of this teacher, suggesting that he may have spoken otherwise than he thought, to avoid unsettling pious minds.

I will have occasion to return to the theme of how knowledge, its intelligibility and its judgement, are necessary to the signifying of transcendence as sociality or proximity to the other, which precede the discourse of knowledge. There is also the impressive fact that the signifying of transcendence and proximity is itself exposed in a discourse that communicates knowledge – is exposed in Greek and comes back clothed in the logical forms of knowledge; even though this communicating discourse presupposed the intelligibility of the interlocutor as other, and the forms of knowledge do not absorb the articulations of the dialogue they make it possible to relate.

Françoise Armengaud. – 'Being exposed in Greek.' This is an almost emblematic expression, a kind of motto you use often, it seems to me: to say Jewish things in Greek. How would you explain this?

Emmanuel Levinas. – We will speak of wisdom presently, and get back to the problem of the relationship between the two spiritual traditions. And be assured that there is not, in that formulation, the snobbism of a Hellenist that I am not. What I mean by 'saying in Greek' is the way of expressing ideas in accordance with our customary mode of presentation and interpretation in the universities. It owes much to the Greeks.

Françoise Armengaud. – We will return to the theme of wisdom in a moment, if you don't mind. First, I would like to ask you about something you said in 1975. You said: 'To me, philosophy is derived [*dérivé*] from religion. It is called forth by religion adrift [*en dérive*], and religion is probably always adrift. . . .'[5] This passage has an enigmatic ring to it. Is philosophy simply an offshoot or a debased version, a secularized product of religion, a purely human way of treating the same questions religion does? Or should your assertion be given a stronger meaning, bringing it closer, *mutatis mutandis,* to St Anselm's *fides quaerens intellectum,* faith seeking understanding?

Emmanuel Levinas. – The expression you are asking me to elucidate was probably inspired by the contemporary religious crisis and the remedies that have been suggested for it. And one might also wonder whether, despite the bedazzlement of Western science engendered by philosophy, philosophy's primordial curiosity for the hidden presuppositions of the various fields of knowledge was not a transposition of the cult of the sacred into which the proximity of the *absolutely other* precipitated thought before revealing itself in the face of the neighbor. But the remark in question has a less banal and less approximate meaning. Religion's recourse to philosophy need indicate no servility on the part of philosophy, nor any lack of understanding on the part of religion. It is rather a case of two distinct but linked moments in this unique spiritual process that constitutes the *approach* to transcendence: an approach, but not an objectification, which would deny transcendence. Objectification is necessary to the approach, but cannot take its place.

Indeed the intelligibility of knowledge, truth and objectivity are called to play their role in the ethical signifying of proximity, peace and God. 'Peace, peace, to him that is far off and to him that is near,' says the Eternal. Outside the one who is near, or before him, he who is far off compels recognition. Outside the other there is the third party. He is also an other, also a neighbor. But which is the closest proximity? Is it not always exclusive? Who then is the first one to whom I must respond, the first to be loved? There must be knowledge of such things! It is the moment of justice, inquiry and knowledge. It is the moment of objectivity motivated by justice. The unique incomparables must be compared. We must, out of respect for the categorical imperative or the other's right as expressed by his face, un-face [*dé-visager*] human beings, sternly reducing each one's uniqueness to his individuality in the unity of the genre, and let universality rule. Thus we need laws, and – yes – courts of law, institutions and the state, to render justice. And thus no doubt an entire political determinism becomes inevitable. But, faced with the 'violence' or rigors of the universal and of justice, when the rights of the unique are no more than a particular case of judgement, do responsibility, or concern for the other, or love without concupiscence answering to the word of God, abandon peace and remain without wisdom?

Françoise Armengaud. – We will get to wisdom in a moment. But I would like to know what you call 'the philosophical implications of the Jewish version of Scripture.'[6] In speaking of Rabbi Haim of Volozhin's book, *Nefesh Hahaim* (the 'Soul of Life'), you say you see it as an attempt to 'make the implicit philosophy of rabbinic study explicit.' Elsewhere, you also say that 'all philosophical thought rests upon prephilosophical experience.'[7]

One can well imagine that there is a difference between the prephilosophical and the philosophical implicit. Would you care to clarify that difference, and the philosophical role of these two orders, in your view?

Emmanuel Levinas. – I don't make a radical distinction between the philosophical implicit and prephilosophical experience. I believe that the implicit is enveloped in 'ways of being,' in 'behavior,' in 'mores' (which may clash with other 'mores'), and can thus bring about wars and persecution before declaring itself. We must also take into account the institutional life of philosophy in a university, and a language in which explication is pushed very far, and from which so-called prephilosophical experience that has not been rendered explicit may be quite remote. I am rather inclined to believe that in all meaningful thought transcendence is manifested or has been reduced.

Françoise Armengaud. – You have often expressed the reasons behind your mistrust of ontology; but your mistrust of knowledge and science in general may cause surprise. The former doubtless calls to mind Kierkegaard's protest against the System, as well as Rosenzweig's challenging of the totality. You have explained your views on that score. The latter had a Bergsonian, or even a Nietzschean ring to it – but it was to art, not ethics, that Nietzsche in his suspicion of the 'will to truth' appealed, in order to 'master knowledge.'

To what degree can a philosophy such as yours, which is not after all an irrationalism, relinquish taking the relation to science into account in a more positive manner?

Emmanuel Levinas. – I have mainly tried to place due emphasis on an 'intelligibility' or a signifying, differing from that of knowledge, and that tends to be construed as a simple lack. But in our exchange itself I have been sufficiently insistent upon the inevitable recourse of all meaningfulness to knowledge, and on the role incumbent upon knowledge in the ethically meaningful, to avoid the reproach of having underrated knowledge. Its derivative nature is not an indignity.

Françoise Armengaud. – Derivative, or dangerous?

Emmanuel Levinas. – Dangerous when it is taken to be the only kind of meaning. Dangerous when we forget, in speaking, that we are speaking to the other, that the rationality of discourse is already borne up by the previous signifying of dialogue or proximity. Dangerous when we think that the logical forms of knowledge – in which all philosophy is indeed expressed – are the ultimate structures of the meaningful.

Françoise Armengaud. – There is something that is not knowledge [*savoir*], and that is different from both religion and philosophy, though close to them. It is called wisdom. We have come to it at last. I have in mind your statement, in the preface to *Du sacré au saint:* 'We wished in these readings to bring out the catharsis or demythification of the religions that Jewish wisdom performs.'[8]

How is wisdom to be understood in this instance?

Emmanuel Levinas. – What I call wisdom (and I am glad that we have come to, or returned to, this question) implies precisely the whole culture of the knowledge (*connaissance*) of things and men. It is a thought guided by the care for objectivity and truth, but a thought in which, in this care, there is no loss of the memory of the justice that gave rise to them; justice that relates back to the infinite original right of the neighbor, and to responsibility for the other. Truth and objectivity do indeed limit this right of the other man, and the original *for-the-other* of the human, through respect for the rights of the one to whom I referred earlier as the third party. Thus I was able to write: 'Upon the extravagant generosity of the for-the-other, there is superimposed a reasonable, ancillary or angelic order, of justice through knowledge [*savoir*]; and philosophy, here, is a measure applied to the infinity of the being-for-the-other of peace and proximity, and as it were the wisdom of love.'[9] But it is still a question, in that wisdom, of preserving the face of the other man and his commandment amidst the harshness of justice based on a complete and sincere knowledge [*connaissance*], and behind the forms of knowledge [*savoir*] that, in Western thought, are taken to be ontologically ultimate. It is a question of preserving or revindicating within an order always to be created anew – a human order, ever to be created anew, in order to respond to the extraordinary of the for-the-other. It is a 'becoming,' visible to the naked eye, in the living duality between politics and religion, between science and philosophy, in the inevitable exteriority protected by the famous defense of the rights of man vis-à-vis the structure proper to the legitimacy of states. There, behind reason with its universal logic is the wisdom that is always listening to it, but also worrying it, and sometimes renewing it. Behind reason with its universal logic there is the wisdom that has neither method nor fixed categories. It is not serenity: the wise man is never wise enough. Wisdom as the freedom of reason, if not freed from reason. This wisdom is incumbent precisely upon the *uniqueness* of the one who thinks, as if, beyond all contingency, his identity as a monad, logically unjustifiable, indiscernible, were chosen. Wisdom as understanding of the unique and the chosen. This is in keeping with Israel's ancient belief in the positive function of the uniqueness of the 'I' in the infinite discovery of the truths of the Torah, to the point of thinking that one person less in the world means one less truth in the Torah, lost for all eternity. This is a belief expressed in the Jewish liturgy by the prayer: 'Give us our portion in Thy Torah.' The portion requested is the portion for which I, the unique, am the condition, by my uniqueness, and not just the portion that awaits me there. Wisdom as intelligence of the unique and the chosen, and yet wisdom that, without constituting the species in a genus, joins the wisdom of the others, according to this new type of unity that is the wisdom or the genius of a people.

Françoise Armengaud. – When you use the word 'wisdom' in this way, do you have the sense that you are precisely translating the word *hokhmah*?

Emmanuel Levinas. – *Hokhmah* certainly includes what I have attempted to describe as wisdom. A *hakham* of the Talmud is an erudite scholar, but one who remains within his personal uniqueness. When he is quoted, an effort is made to respect that uniqueness jealously. When he transmits the saying of someone else, it is meticulously noted, and often a few lines of the text are devoted to going back to the one who said it first, mentioning all the intermediaries.

Françoise Armengaud. – What you have just said also clarifies this passage from your preface to *Noms propres*: 'The proper names in the middle of all those common names and commonplaces – do they not help us speak?' But let us return, if you will, from wisdom to philosophy. Perhaps philosophy is not one sole entity. Its historical development, at any rate, justifies our hesitating between at least two different projects. There is one according to which, as you say, philosophy 'is not only knowledge [*connaissance*] of immanence but immanence itself.'[10] That is the philosophy that exhausts itself in the assimilating knowledge [*savoir*] of ontology: the philosophy of the System, or of Totality. And then there is a philosophy that is other; the one that is appropriately no doubt – called metaphysics. It is, to borrow an expression dear to you, a 'philosophizing otherwise.' This is an act of escape outside being, which you invoke, I believe, in speaking of Jeanne Delhomme and her unraveling the 'weave of the ontologies,' and attaining in the end 'an increasingly fertile multiplicity of meanings arising within meaning.'[11]

But do you not also say that 'all philosophy is Platonic'?[12]

Emmanuel Levinas. – That is a quote from an early text, I believe. I do not reject it, to the extent that the link between philosophy and transcendent alterity is affirmed in the Platonic theory of ideas, in which the problem or the anxiety of that radical alterity – even though there is an attempt to reduce it – seems to me to authenticate philosophy. I have already said that. I do not reject my attachment to Platonism, because to owe the daring formulation *beyond being* to Plato is good luck.

But, beyond being, it is not a matter of rejoicing in a world-behind-the-scenes in which it would be convenient to install the God of religion comfortably. My entire effort consists in separating myself, so to speak, from ontology, in which the meaning of the intelligible is attached to the event of being, because it would be *in itself* like *presence,* culminating in its repose and perseverance in itself, self-sufficient – a perfection that, in Spinoza's view, is its divinity. It is the human self, master and possessor of the world, all powerful in strength and knowledge, who would thus be divinized. To understand the for-the-other in a radical and original way as first philosophy – this involves asking oneself whether the intelligibility of the intelligible is not *prior* to the possession of the self by itself, prior to the 'hateful self,' and (without having previously evaluated what one is and has, before having made the assessment of oneself) caring for the other, whose being and death are more important than my own. It means asking oneself whether that responsibility for the other, which is, in a way, insane, is not the *human calling* in being, which (being) would thus be put in question – and whether the imperative of that obligation is not the very Word [*Parole*] of God, his very coming to mind, so to speak, where, as Descartes would have it, *He is thought beyond what that idea can contain.*

Françoise Armengaud. – Your text on Plato is from 1955. In 1967, in connection with Madame Delhomme, you bring up a different responsibility. ...

Emmanuel Levinas. – In the late lamented Jeanne Delhomme (to whom it is a pleasure for me to do homage, as she was one of the most subtle of speculative minds of the philosophers of my generation), there was no ethical problem underlying her attempt to free thought from allegiance to being.

This form of thought, which is qualified as modal or interrogative, was to be understood as the spontaneity of an intelligence that is not set in a ontology, and that, on the contrary, unravels the ontological fabric. Philosophy, or philosophies, as absolute freedom. Pyrotechnics of meaning. A linguistic modality like a poetic language, without my responsibility ensuing from that freedom assumed in relation to being. Intelligence as a difficult game. As a disontologizing of philosophy, that daring enterprise seemed to me suggestive (though absolutely opposed to responsibility-for-the-other) of the *otherwise than being* that constitutes the human as such, dispensing with the prior freedom that is invoked to justify obligation. There is also, in Madame Delhomme's mistrust of the *datum* – present, heavy and ready-made – a point in common with the phenomenology to which I am attached. You know that in Husserl's methodology there is at once a denouncing of the confusion between the object and the psyche intending it – which is the well-known critique of psychologism – and a return to the noetic concreteness of the noemata, as if the object looked at exclusively obstructed the gaze. ... But perhaps Jeanne Delhomme would not like my making her, if ever so slightly, a phenomenologist!

Françoise Armengaud. – Many of those who have written commentary on your work are aware of the highly paradoxical nature of your approach, and they emphasize it in their studies on you. Françoise Wybrands speaks of how 'Levinas's thought ... finds support in the philosophical tradition opened by Parmenides, a tradition from which it excludes itself.'[13] Catherine Chalier speaks of your 'daring intent of choosing the Greek *logos* only to surprise it utterly.'[14] And Jacques Rolland, just as strongly: 'It is by the resources of philosophy that it is appropriate to seek a way out of that with which philosophy is closely linked. ...'[15]

Is the paradox as described mandatory or optional for you?

Emmanuel Levinas. – I believe I have indicated, apropos of the idea of wisdom, both the exclusion and the inclusion of the paths 'opened by Parmenides' in what I call the 'opening [*percée*] by the human' in being, which latter would suffice unto itself in the *conatus essendi* – an opening that I take to be biblical. The paradox here is neither mandatory nor optional. It corresponds exactly to that advent of the human overturning 'the order of things,' that *for-that-other*, shattering the *in-itself*, that peace 'to him that is far off and to him that is near.' One might indeed wonder why it is that the one that is close is not the only one mentioned, in which case his uniqueness would correspond to pure love. And yet again, one might ask, Why does the far-off one – the third party – precede the other? One might thus invoke a structure that is given, a constraining fact. I think it would not be impossible to elucidate this fact, but I will not attempt to do so here. In any case, the three friends you quote saw clearly and accurately. And Jacques Rolland, in his study published in *Cahiers de la nuit surveillée*, which he edits, has posed the problem of this paradox correctly and forcefully.

Françoise Armengaud. – While some, like Jacques Colette, seem simply to note that you are relatively far away from phenomenology, without having given up the 'phrasing of phenomenological research,'[16] others wonder whether you have sufficiently 'escaped' the premises of Husserl's phenomenology. So Roland Blum, in his 1971 conference in Montreal.[17]

Emmanuel Levinas. – Colette, who is a scholar and a keen philosopher, does indeed show that my texts are not always in agreement with Husserl's phenomenological 'rules of method.' It is true that I do not begin with the transcendental reduction. But the search for the concrete status of the given [*la donnée*], setting out from the 'I think,' the search for concreteness in its 'phenomenon,' i.e., in the noetic-noematic correlation revealing itself to reflection upon the 'I think" – and in which the datum [*la donnée*], having become purely abstract, no longer obstructs the gaze, to which it thus gives itself – seems to me to constitute phenomenology's fundamental teaching. That privileged 'intelligibility of the concrete is developed as early as in *Logical Investigations,* 3, and the term 'concrete' keeps recurring in Husserl's phenomenological descriptions. I have even taken the liberty of characterizing these descriptions as the reconstitution, for any object or notion thematized in man's 'natural attitude,' of their *'mise en scène.'* From this perspective, my philosophy would consist in seeing that the identity of the *me* and of this 'I think' is not equal to the task of encompassing the 'other man,' precisely because of the alterity and irreducible transcendence of the other; and in realizing that that reduction to powerlessness is not negative, in the 'appresentation' in which representation fails, but that it is rather a thought that is *other*, in the conversion (or the return) of the egological 'for-oneself' into its original 'for-the-other.' It is a responsibility responding to a call from beyond being, signified through the face of the neighbor. A *me* of the *for-the-other*, infinitely obligated, who identifies himself as unique, chosen, in that calling. The framework of Husserlian phenomenology may have been broken open in the course of the transcendental analysis, but the 'destruction' of the dominant *me* in which it was anchored is not some step along the way to the insignificance of the person; it is his election to responsibilities, responding to the Word of God in the face of the other; God who never 'appears,' who is not a 'phenomenon,' who 'is never embodied' in any thematization or objectivation. That is probably the meaning of the indetermination held to by Judah Halevi's expression *Inyan Elohi*, in speaking of God. There is a subversion of my self that is not its extinction. I have in mind Pascal's 'Le moi est haïssable' (My self is hateful), which is not a lesson in good style or courtesy, but the rejection of him who would be master of the world, and who posits himself, sufficient, substance or subject. A 'usurpation of the world' that, according to another of Pascal's thoughts, already begins, even if it is the case of a *me* that posits itself in the name of that 'place in the sun' that is in appearance, or in worldly wisdom, so 'legitimate.'[18]

Françoise Armengaud. And that is the opposite of what you call 'dis-inter-estment'?

Emmanuel Levinas. – Yes. And I am very pleased that the abstract and negative notion of dis-inter-estment has received, at the heart of my phenomenology, all its concreteness and all its positivity in the intimate responsibility for others.

Françoise Armengaud. – To return to the point of view of methodology, Francis Jacques does, nevertheless, seem to me to ask a pertinent question when, in the course of the elaboration of his 'Anthropology from a relational point of view,' he says: 'Either Levinas's discovery of the person of the other as an irreducible datum subverts the phenomenological approach with incomparable depth, or the method marked by Husserl, and unquestionably associated by him with egological premises, does not fail to reintroduce a paradoxical primacy of the myself.'[19] How would you respond to the alternative formulated by Francis Jacques?

Emmanuel Levinas. – Yes, that is a constant in Francis Jacques's critique of me. I think I have already answered, above. The 'discovery' of others (not as a *datum* exactly, but as a face!) subverts the transcendental approach of the I, but retains the egological primacy of this I that remains unique and chosen in its incontestable responsibility.

In Francis Jacques, there remains a priority of knowing [*connaître*]. To me it is important for it to be recognized that all thought is not knowledge [*connaissance*], nor is it founded (directly or indirectly) on presence or representation; that the meaningful is not exhausted by the knowledge [*science*] or experience that takes place in consciousness, nor in the secrecy of the hiding – place or the modesty of the unconscious. The face [*visage*] of the other is not straightaway representation or the presence of a facial form [*figure*]; it is not a datum [*donnée*], not something to be taken. Before the countenance it assumes or expresses (and through which it enters the system of the world and is perceived, grasped and possessed, comprehended and apprehended within that system as an identity card), it is surprised as the nakedness, destitution and uprightness of a defenseless exposure to death. It signifies mortality, but, at the same time, a sanction against killing: the 'Thou shalt not kill.' It signifies mortality and ethical commandment before appearing. It appeals to responsibility before appearing to the eye. Thus, a falling of the 'I think' – of the knowledge [*savoir*] that includes and engulfs the world – back into that original obedience that is perhaps also the severe name of a love without concupiscence. There, uniqueness without genus, i.e., alterity itself, succeeds in signifying, in the occurrence of peace.

Françoise Armengaud. – Just as, a moment ago, in connection with Jeanne Delhomme, we touched on the possibility of a different way of philosophizing, similarly I could at this point bring up a conception of knowledge [*savoir*] no longer based on presence or representation, but on the interlocutionary relation and the alterity of relation.[20] We do not have time. As for that 'occurrence of peace' you mention, is it not also a real relation?

Emmanuel Levinas. – I avoid, at the level on which we are – before wisdom – the word 'relation,' which always indicates a simultaneity among its terms in a system, and that is the synchronic representation of the world, society and its institutions, its equality and justice; to which it is wise to return, if what I just said about wisdom had any meaning. But one cannot begin with that, if wisdom is the wisdom of love.

I avoid the synchrony of the relation and of the system, because the responsibility for the other that reaches the meaning of the other in his uniqueness does not have a 'synchronic' structure. In its devotion – in its devoutness – it is gratuitous or full of grace; it is not concerned with reciprocity. It is younger than the order of the world. Strange irreversibility! It brings to mind the dia-chrony of time, i.e., the ultimate secret of its very order. It is probably the very articulation, the very concreteness of the temporality of a time that signifies through the other.

But for today let us leave off further ascent toward temporality's ethical modes.

December 1984–January 1985

Notes

Author's Foreword

1   [The first two collections (*Quatre lectures talmudiques, Du sacré au saint*) are available in English, under the title *Nine Talmudic Readings*, trans. A. Aronowicz (Bloomington and Indianapolis: Indiana University Press, 1990). – Trans.]

1 For a Place in the Bible

1   Published in *Actes du xxiiᵉ colloque des intellectuels juifs de la langue française*, under the title *La Bible au présent* (Paris: Gallimard, coll. 'Idées,' 1982).

2   '*Les Juifs reconnurent et acceptèrent* pour eux, pour leurs descendants et pour tous ceux qui se rallieraient à eux, l'obligation immuable de fêter ces deux jours-là suivant la teneur des écrits et à la date fixée année par année.'

3   [I.e., the sanctity of the letters in which it is written. – Trans.]

2 The Translation of the Scripture

1   Published in *Actes du xxiiiᵉ colloque des intellectuels juifs de la langue française*, under the title *Israël, le judaïsme et l'Europe* (Paris: Gallimard, coll. 'Idées,' 1984).

2   Here I have used Miss Elkaïm-Sartre's excellent translation from her '*Ein-Yaacov*' *et* '*Haggadoth*' *du Talmud de Babylone*, (Lagrasse: Verdier, 1982), p. 502.

3   [In French the neologism '*sacralité*.' Levinas strongly opposes the notion in vogue among French sociologists that the 'sacred' is at the basis of all religion, and sees Judaism as the champion of 'holiness' instead. This important dichotomy runs through much of Levinas's writings. See

especially the section 'From the Sacred to the Holy' in Levinas's *Nine Talmudic Readings*, op. cit., esp. pp. 14Q–1. – Trans.]

4 See *L'au-delà du verset, lectures et discours talmudiques* (Paris: Minuit, 1982), p. 109, n. 4.

5 For the historical aspect of the situation out of which the Septuagint emerged, I have consulted the fundamental studies of Professor Dominique Barthélemy. Cf. esp. his study: 'Pourquoi la Thora a-t-elle été traduite en grec?' *Approaches to Semiotics 56* (1974), pp. 23–41, reprinted in *Dominique Barthélemy, Etudes d'histoire du texte de l'ancient testament*, Orbis Biblicus et Orientalis 21 (Fribourg: Editions Univ. Fribourg Suisse, 1978), pp. 322–40.

6 The *Mekhilta*, a very old collection of *midrash* connected to *Exodus*, in which our *midrash* on the Septuagint corrections reappears, gives only thirteen corrections.

7 [Model of the Western World] This piece is published in the collection *L'au-delà du verset*, op. cit., pp. 43–45.

8 [An allusion to Claude Lévi-Strauss's *Savage Mind*, of which Levinas was not an admirer. See, e.g., François Poirié's *Emmanuel Levinas, Qui êtes-vous?* (Lyon: La Manufacture, 1987), pp. 114, 131. – Trans.]

9 [An allusion to a well-known verse from Paul Verlaine's 'Art Poétique': 'Prends l'éloquence et tords-lui son cou.' ('Take eloquence and wring its neck.') – Trans.]

3 Contempt for the Torah as Idolatry

1 First published as *Mépris de la Thora comme idolatrie (Leçon talmudique)*, in the collection: J. Halperin and G. Levitte, eds., *Idoles: données et débats (Actes du xxive colloque des intellectuels juifs de la langue française)* (Paris: Editions Denoël, 1985), pp. 197–217.

2 [Oblique allusion to the opening line of Mallarmé's poem 'Brise Marine': 'Je suis triste, hélas! et j'ai lu tous les livres.' ('I am sad, alas! And I have read all the books.') – Trans.]

3 [David Kessler was one of the twelve presenters (including Mr. Claude Riveline, mentioned later in this chapter, and Levinas himself) at the 24th Colloquium of Jewish Intellectuals of French Expression, which was held in Paris on January 28–30. Levinas's Talmudic lesson, translated here, was the last presentation. Kessler's presentation, 'Idealogies and Idolatry,' attempted to establish a relationship between those two concepts by evoking a variety of ideologies which required an idolatrous commitment to a cause that led people to a 'renunciation of what defines them as human beings.' Kessler is the author of *Proche et lointain: l'impératif éthique du politique*, in *Les Nouveaux Cahiers*, 21 (1985), n. 82, pp. 18–24. For further information on these colloquia, see Annette Aronowicz's informative introduction to *Nine*

Talmudic Readings (Bloomington, IN: Indiana University Press, 1990), p. xxxiii; and *Idoles/Données et débats/Actes du xxive Colloque des intellectuels juifs de langue française*, ed. J. Halpérin and Georges Lévitte (Paris: Denoel, 1985). – Trans.]

4 ['Dis-interestment' ('le dés-interessement') is a Levinasian coinage that plays a key role in that philosopher's entire thought. It refers to the movement from being to 'otherwise than being.' – Trans.]

5 Cf. note 2, *supra*.

4 Beyond Memory

1 Published in the collection: J. Halpérin and G. Lévitte, eds., *Mémoire et histoire: données et débats (Actes du xxve colloque des intellectuels juifs de la langue française)* (Paris: Editions Denoël, 1986), pp. 159–75.

2 [I.e., the *Mishnah*. – Trans.]

3 [Hebrew word for memory. – Trans.]

4 [Levinas is assuming here that the final 'i' of Sarai is the Yod of the first person singular possessive, which would 'deform' the vowel of Sara by dipthongization. Others view this form as an archaic fem. ending: cf. *Gesenius' Heb. Gr.*, art. 801. – Trans.]

5 *Life and Fate*, trans. from Russian by Robert Chandler (New York: Harper & Row, 1987), pp. 27, 29, 405–10.

5 The Nations and the Presence of Israel

1 First published as *Les nations et la présence d'Israël. Leçon talmudique*, in the collection: J. Halpérin and G. Lévitte, eds., *Les soixante-dix nations. Données et débats (Actes du xxviie colloque des intellectuels juifs de langue française)*, Paris, Editions Denoël, 1987.

2 Translation [into French] by Israël Salzar: *Traité Pess'him* (Lagrasse: Verdier, 1986), pp. 369–72.

3 [Levinas is alluding to a group of Young Jews, ill-disposed toward philosophy, who set up a firm opposition between the Talmud and (especially) the Kabbala, on one hand, and philosophy on the other. My thanks to Catherine Chalier for providing this information. – Trans.]

4 [The *yeshiva* is a Talmudic college, but also Hebrew for sitting. – Trans.]

5 [Hebrew: place of accommodation. – Trans.]

6 [Hebrew: India. – Trans.]

7 [Hebrew: Rome the wicked. – Trans.]

8 'Fâche-toi contre la bête fauve des roseaux, communauté des vaillants avec les veaux des peuples – elle ouvre la main pour les dons volontaires en argent. Il a dispersé les peuples qui se plaisent aux batailles.'

9   'Gourmande la bête tapie dans les joncs, la troupe des puissants taureaux
    mêlés aux bouvillons des nations qui viennent s'humilier, munies de lingots
    d'argent. [Dieu] disperse les peuples qui aiment les batailles.'
10 ['ni leur sens ni leur portée originels.' – Trans.]
11 [In Hebrew, *qerav* is battle, and *qirvah* proximity. – Trans.]

6 From Ethics to Exegesis

1   [First published in *Les Nouveaux Cahiers* 82 (1985), but written as a preface to
    the Italian translation of Levinas's *L'au-delà du verset*, which appeared the
    following year. – Trans.]

7 Judaism and Kenosis

1   First published in *Archivo di filosofia* 53 (1985), pp. 13–28.
2   This commentary is also found in the *midrashic* texts *Mekhilta,* section *Jethro.*
3   [The Hebrew Bible is divided into three sections: the 'Torah' in the narrow
    sense (Pentateuch), the 'Prophets,' and the 'Writings.' – Trans.]
4   [The contrast here is between the *'esprit de finesse'* and the *'esprit
    de géométrie'* made by Pascal at the beginning (in most editions) of his *Pensées.*
    – Trans.]
5   Published in 1987 by Editions Verdier, in a French translation with
    commentary by Professor Benjamin Gross.
6   Can this still be said since the passion of Auschwitz? Perhaps still
    from oneself to oneself; without putting that maxim into a sermon.
7   [An allusion to Pascal's *'Le moi est haïssable'*; the self is hateful. – Trans.]

8 The Bible and the Greeks

1   First published in *Cosmopolitiques* 4 (February 1986).
2   [A play on the word *'chameau,'* which means camel, but one who is *'un peu
    chameau'* (a bit of a camel) is an old so-and-so. – Trans.]
3   [Vasily Grossman, *Life and Fate,* trans. from Russian by Robert Chandler
    (New York: Harper & Row, 1987). – Trans.]

9 Moses Mendelssohn's Thought

1   Published in Moses Mendelssohn, *Jérusalem – Pouvoir religieux et judaïsme,*
    trans. from German by Dominique Bourel (Paris: Les Presses d' Aujourd'hui,
    1982).
2   A suggestion of this thesis may be found in Maimonides, who presents the
    revelation of God to Abraham as the patriarch's own reflection on the givens
    of the world, and who makes the revelation to Moses responsible for the law

protecting the Jewish people from idols, to which they were still exposed by the idolatry surrounding them as they were leaving Egypt. See Maimonides' *Rabbinical Code* (*Mishneh Torah*), *Treatise on Idolatry*, chapter 1, paras. 2 and 3.

3 This metaphor itself says a great deal. It is as if rites were to belief what the movements of our own bodies are to the 'states of soul' they express, rendering them concrete by expressing them. These states become thereby ontologically inseparable from their expression. But is this the meaning of that metaphor in Mendelssohn, who elsewhere has attributed distinct sources to belief, which comes about through one's natural lights, and to the law, which springs from a supernatural revelation?

4 [In fact, the publication dates of Mendelssohn's *Jérusalem* (1783) and Rosenzweig's *Der Stern der Erlösung* (1921) are separated by 138 years. – Trans.]

10 A Figure and a Period

1 Published in *Les Nouveaux Cahiers*, 86 (Fall 1986).

2 *Isaiah 11:9*.

11 The Philosophy of Franz Rosenzweig

1 Published in Stéphane Mosès's *Système et Révélation* (Paris: Le Seuil, 1982). [In English, trans. by Catherine Tihanyi as *System and Revelation, The Philosophy of Franz Rosenzweig* (Detroit: Wayne State University Press, 1992.) – Trans.]

2 Which he seems in any event to disregard, judging from two references to Husserl in Rosenzweig's correspondence. See *Briefe und Tagebücher*, 619.

12 Judaism and Christianity

1 First published in *Zeitgewinn* (Frankfurt am Main: Joseph Knecht Verlag, 1987).

13 On Jewish Philosophy

1 First published in *Revue de métaphysique et morale* (July–September 1985).

2 [Emmanuel Levinas, *Difficile liberté* (Paris: Albin Michel, 1963 and 1976), trans. Seán Hand as *Difficult Freedom* (London: The Athlone Press, 1990); *Quatre lectures talmudiques* (Paris: Minuit, 1968), trans. Annette Aronowicz as 'Four Talmudic Readings,' in *Nine Talmudic Readings* (Bloomington: Indiana University Press, 1990), pp. 1–88; 'Philosophie et religion,' *Critique* 289 (June 1971), pp. 532–42, included in *Noms propres* (Montpellier: Fata Morgana, 1976), pp. 119–30, notes 191–2 (in 2nd edn., 1987, pp. 93–103,

171

notes 153–4), trans. Michael B. Smith as *Proper Names/On Maurice Blanchot,* forthcoming from The Athlone Press, London, in 1995; 'Dieu et la philosophie,' *Le Nouveau Commerce* 30–1 (Spring 1975), pp. 97–128, and *De Dieu qui vient à l'idée* (Paris: Vrin, 1982, 1986), pp. 93–127, translated as 'God and Philosophy' by Alphonso Lingis in *E. Levinas/Collected Philosophical Papers* (Dordrecht, Boston, Lancaster: Nijhoff, 1987), pp. 153–73. Stéphane Mosès, *Système et Révélation* (Paris: Le Seuil, 1982), pp. 7–16, trans. by Catherine Tihanyi as *System and Revelation* (Detroit: Wayne State University Press, 1992), pp. 13–22. Included as chapter 11 of the present volume. – Trans.]

3 Emmanuel Levinas and Philippe Némo, *Ethique et infini* (Paris: Fayard, 1982), trans. Richard A. Cohen as *Ethics and Infinity* (Pittsburg: Duquesne University Press, 1985).

4 This is in keeping with an admirable *midrash* in Rabbi Ishmael's *Mekhilta* (section *Yethro,* chapter 5) which does not hesitate to emphasize, in the format of the Ten Commandments in two columns of five, the prolongation of 'I am the Lord thy God' as 'Thou shalt not kill.'

5 *Nine Talmudic Readings,* op. cit., p. 182.

6 *L'au-delà du verset* (Paris: Minuit, 1981), p. 21.

7 *Ethics and Infinity,* op. cit., p. 24.

8 *Nine Talmudic Readings,* op. cit., p. 92.

9 'Paix et proximité,' in *Les Cahiers de la nuit surveillée,* Emmanuel Levinas, no. 3 (Paris: Verdier, 1984),346.

10 *E. Levinas/Collected Philosophical Papers,* op. cit., p. 158.

11 *Noms propres,* op. cit., 1st ed., p. 70, 2nd ed. (1987), pp. 57, 58.

12 *Noms propres,* op. cit., 1st ed., p. 169, 2nd ed. (1987), p. 135.

13 F. Wybrands, 'La voix de la pensée,' in *Les Cahiers de la nuit surveillée,* op. cit., p. 73.

14 C. Chalier, Figures du féminin, Lecture d'Emmanuel Levinas (Paris: *La nuit surveillée, 1982), p. 16.*

15 J. Rolland, 'Présentation,' in *Les Cahiers de la nuit surveillée,* op. cit., p. 12.

16 J. Colette, 'Levinas et la phénoménologie husserlienne,' in *Les Cahiers . . .,* op. cit., p. 33.

17 R. Blum, 'La Perception d'autrui,' in *La Communication (Actes du colloque de l'A.S.P.L.F.)* (Montreal: Presses universitaires de Montréal, 1971).

18 [The allusion is to another of Pascal's *Pensées,* one of Levinas's five luminary quotes at the beginning of *Otherwise than Being or Beyond Essence,* viz., ' "That is my place in the sun." That is how the usurpation of the whole world began.' – Trans.]

19 F. Jacques, *Différence et subjectivité* (Paris: Aubier, 1982), p. 165.

20 See F. Jacques, *L'Espace logique de l'interlocution* (Paris: Presses universitaires de France, 1985).

General Index

Index of Biblical Passages

New Testament and Talmudic passages are listed in the General Index